ZONES OF PEACE IN THE THIRD WORLD

D1568246

SUNY Series in Global Politics
James N. Rosenau, Editor

ZONES OF PEACE IN
THE THIRD WORLD

South America and West Africa in Comparative Perspective

Arie M. Kacowicz

State University
of New York Press

Published by
State University of New York Press

© 1998 State University of New York

For information, address the State University of New York Press,
State University Plaza, Albany, NY 12246

Production by Bernadine Dawes • Marketing by Dana Yanulavich

Library of Congress Cataloging-in-Publication Data

Kacowicz, Arie Marcelo.
    Zones of peace in the Third World : South America and West Africa
in comparative perspective / Arie M. Kacowicz.
        p.   cm. — (SUNY series in global politics)
    Includes bibliographical references and index.
    ISBN 0-7914-3957-7 (hc : alk. paper). — ISBN 0-7914-3958-5 (pbk.
: alk. paper)
    1. Zones of peace—South America. 2. Zones of peace—Africa,
West. I. Title. II. Series.
JZ5584.S63K33   1998
327.1'72'096609045—dc21   98-5620
                                                            CIP

1 2 3 4 5 6 7 8 9 10

To Itai
With the hope that he will be able to grow in a zone of peace

Contents

Tables and Figures

Preface

Several years ago, during my graduate studies at Princeton, I was puzzled by the subject of peaceful territorial change, trying to explain the conditions under which a process of change in the international status quo of territories could take place "peacefully," by means other than war. The focus of my inquiry was then dyadic (looking at pairs of states) and the starting point was dynamic—dealing with the problem of change in international relations.

In this book, I attempt to explain the maintenance of extensive periods of interstate peace in two regions of the Third World—South America, since 1883; and West Africa, since its independence in the early 1960s. While domestic conflicts, endemic violence, and even virulent civil wars did take place within their states, a common pattern between these two otherwise disparate regions emerged from my inquiry: a majority of the countries in South America and West Africa have supported actively their territorial status quo (which I have defined here as "being satisfied"). Thus, their complex political reality has been characterized by a juxtaposition of domestic violence with international peace, in contrast to the tenets of the diversionary theory of war.

Unlike my previous book, *Peaceful Territorial Change*, the focus of this volume is regional rather than dyadic, diachronic, and evolutionary, looking at the possible transitions among different levels or gradations of regional peace over extended periods of time. Interestingly enough, the practical question of how to maintain and deepen peace has been almost ignored by scholars of international relations, who have been concerned only with studying the transitions from war to peace, or from peace to war. Moreover, terms such as "long peace" and "zones of peace" have been usually associated with the absence of war in Europe during the Cold War period (1945–89) and/or with the separate peace among democracies progressively developed throughout the last two hundred years. In this book, by contrast, I consider the historical and theoretical relevance of "zones of peace" in the particular context of the Third World, beyond the original Eurocentric scope.

This project, which was originally conceived back in the summer of 1992, has benefited immensely from the intellectual input and encouragement of a large number of colleagues, friends, and graduate students. Several ideas, versions, papers, and drafts were presented at undergraduate and graduate seminars and colloquia at the Department of International Relations of the Hebrew University of Jerusalem, ISA and APSA Conferences, and at the Center for International Studies of Princeton University.

Many colleagues from North and South America, Europe, New Zealand, and Israel have suggested precious comments and advice for the general theme of the book. Among them I want to thank Yaacov Bar-Siman-Tov, Sammy Basu, Jacques Bertrand, Raymond Cohen, Michael Doyle, George Downs, Alan Dowty, Miriam F. Elman, Alexander George, Nils P. Gleditsch, Kal Holsti, Mathias Kaelberer, Korina Kagan, Jack Levy, Benjamin Miller, C. R. Mitchell, Bruce Russett, Avi Segal, Arik Shamir, Richard Ullman, Yaacov Vertzberger, and Bill Wolfhort. I especially appreciate the warm support and inspiration given by Emanuel Adler, Michael Barnett, and Jacob Bercovitch.

In addition, I was lucky enough to contact area specialists who read and commented on my two case studies. For the West African case, I am grateful to David Blaney, Henry Bienen, Jeffrey Herbst, Philip Huxtable, and especially to Crawford Young. For the South American case, I acknowledge the advice and comments of Rut Diamint, Yale Ferguson, Andrew Hurrell, Helio Jaguaribe, Carlos Moneta, Roberto Russell, and especially Michael Barletta.

Throughout these five years, I received generous support from the Research and Development Authority of the Hebrew University of Jerusalem, its Leonard Davis Institute for International Relations, and a special fund for postdoctoral research grants from the Israel Foundations Trustees.

Through the sponsorship of those institutions, I was fortunate to get research assistance from exceptional students such as Tzion Elam, Avigail Freizer, and Mirav Yaacovson. For their precious help, I want also to thank the staffs of the Harry Truman Institute Library, Social Sciences Library at the Hebrew University, and Firestone Library at Princeton University, as well as Meir for technical assistance at the photocopy center of the Faculty of Social Sciences at the Hebrew University. The production stages of this book benefited from the hospitality and research environment provided by the Helen Kellogg and Joan Kroc Institutes of the University of Notre Dame. I also want to express my appreciation for the superb assistance and cooperation from the State University of New York Press editorial staff, including Clay Morgan, Zina Lawrence, and Bernadine Dawes, in the transformation of the manuscript into a book.

Some sections of chapters 1, 4, and 5 were published in earlier versions in my articles "Explaining Zones of Peace: Democracies as Satisfied Powers?" *Journal of Peace Research* 33, no. 3 (August 1995); "Third World Zones of Peace," *Peace Review* 9, no. 2 (June 1997); and "'Negative' International Peace and Domestic Conflicts, West Africa, 1957–96," *Journal of Modern African Studies* 35, no. 3 (September 1997). I thank the publishers of those journals for allowing me to use that material.

Finally, three individuals have been generous enough to read most if not all of the manuscript: Moshe Abalo, a Ph.D. candidate and good friend whose insights and ideas contributed decisively to improve the overall quality of this book; Oded Levenheim, an incisive graduate student who finally got the opportunity to criticize my own work after I graded him several times in different courses; and my beloved wife Orly, who encouraged me to write about zones of peace even if the subject reads like a novel of "political fiction" in the local Middle Eastern context. The idea of this book has coincided with the birth of our son, Itai, and the hope that he might be able to grow up in a zone of peace, even if it will be an incipient "negative" peace, characterized only by the absence of international wars.

CHAPTER 1

ZONES OF PEACE IN THE INTERNATIONAL SYSTEM

International relations scholars have traditionally focused their efforts in explaining war rather than peace, both in dyadic and in systemic terms. As a result, different explanations for peace have been understudied or underemphasized, with the exception of normative approaches (see Rummel 1981; Rapoport 1992; Galtung 1964, 1975; Smoker 1981; Stephenson 1989; and Johnson 1976). Most of the research on security issues has focused upon the genesis of peace (i.e., war termination), or the termination of peace, escalation of international crises, and conflict eruption (i.e., the beginning of wars). By contrast, in this book I explain the maintenance of extensive periods of international "negative" peace—defined as the absence of international wars—in two regions of the Third World: South America and West Africa. Unlike other studies of peace and war, the unit of analysis moves here from the dyadic level to the subsystemic or regional level.

Terms such as "long peace" and "zones of peace" have been respectively associated with the absence of war in Europe during the Cold War period (1945–89), and with the separate peace among democracies progressively developed throughout the last two hundred years (see Gaddis, 1986; Doyle, 1986). As mentioned in the preface, in this study I consider the theoretical and historical relevance of these two terms in the context of the Third World, beyond the original, Eurocentric scope. More specifically, I argue that zones of peace, characterized by the absence of interstate war, have developed in South America since the 1880s and among the West African countries since their independence in the early 1960s. Instead of the usual focus upon Europe, North America, and the "zone of peace" among the advanced, industrialized democracies, therefore, this book devotes attention to the neglected fact that there have been long periods of regional peace in disparate regions of the Third World. This regional peace has persisted in spite of the fact that most of the countries in those regions, most of the time, have not been democracies.

In the last two decades there has been a lively academic and empirical debate around the lawlike association between democracies and peace. While democracy supports and enhances peace by increasing its quality, it is not a necessary condition for all types of peace. This book aims to explain why this is so. In the following chapters I suggest different, even competing explanations and conditions for different types of peace at the regional level. There are several types or gradations of peace, as there are several gradations of conflicts, crises, and wars. The conventional theories of international relations (i.e., realism, liberalism) do not provide a comprehensive explanation for the phenomenon of zones of peace, so that they should be complemented by a more complex, eclectic, and original explanation that links international and domestic politics. Around this explanation I design a theoretical framework that defines the maintenance of zones of peace in terms of necessary, sufficient, and favorable conditions, by differentiating among the three types or gradations of zones of peace: negative peace, stable peace, and pluralistic security communities. According to this framework, democracy is one (sufficient) explanation, among several others.

WHY STUDY ZONES OF PEACE
IN THE THIRD WORLD?

A study of zones of peace in the Third World can be justified on the following grounds:

   1. *As a revision and extension of the liberal explanation for a separate and exclusive peace among democracies.* Specifically, I suggest that if all the political regimes of a region are democratic, then it is a sufficient, though not a necessary, condition for the existence and maintenance of a zone of peace. In other words, they can include nondemocratic regimes as well. Hence, I offer both a critique and a refinement of the "democratic peace" theory in its theoretical and empirical formulations.

   The effects of democracy and democratization upon regional peace are rather complex. Non-democracies, as well as mixed groups of states, can establish and maintain peaceful relations among themselves, including possible zones of stable peace. Nonetheless, regional democratization seems to be crucial in defining the quality of the peace, and democratic dyads may enjoy a more stable peace. Thus, the democratic peace theory may help to explain how stable peace and pluralistic security communities evolve, while it may be less helpful in explaining other, previous gradations of peace, such as the emergence of a peace that is characterized simply by the absence of war. In short, whether democracy reduces international conflict depends not only on the way we define democracy and war, but also on the way we think about peace.

2. *As a test of major theories in international relations and comparative politics in the context of the Third World.* Zones of peace encompass a synthesis between international relations theories dealing with peace and war, and the need to focus upon the domestic structure of states and the state–society nexus, emphasized by the literature on comparative politics. In turn, this convergence allows an analysis of the possible links among different types of states and political regimes and international behavior in the Third World, an analysis that addresses the more general issues of conflict management and resolution. In this book, I combine both approaches to address the theoretical and empirical phenomenon of zones of peace.

3. *As a critique and update of Deutsch's (1957) seminal study of pluralistic security communities, by assessing its relevance in the context of the Third World.* The concept of pluralistic security communities remains a powerful analytical tool to explain and to understand the dynamics of regional peace. It is also a policy-relevant framework that transcends the narrowness of the national domain of sovereign states, without being entrapped in the irrelevant utopia of world government. In its original formulation, the empirical examples of these communities were confined mainly to the North Atlantic area, where historically the full-fledged democratic states have been geographically located. Thus, Deutsch and his associates did not refer to the possibility of forming security communities in the emerging Third World, which was characterized until recently by authoritarian and transitional regimes. In this book, I show a possible implementation of the concept of pluralistic security communities for the South American case and its current irrelevance for the West African case.

4. *As an empirical study of the intraregional international relations of South America and West Africa, focusing upon the phenomena of long periods of negative peace.* From the perspective of peace research, the study of the historical processes by which regional peace developed has been generally neglected by historians (Boulding 1991, 110). The empirical chapters of this book trace the diplomatic history of both regions as zones of negative peace.

The Phenomenon of Zones of Peace

The genesis of a zone of peace can be attributed to the last war and its aftermath, or to decolonization processes. Conversely, its decay and disruption is the product of a growing dissatisfaction with the status quo, due to nationalistic forces, including secessionist or irredentist claims, and/or changes in the distribution of power, or changes in the perception of that distribution. What remains to be explained and assessed, moreover, is why and how zones of peace persist over long periods of time.

In this book, my major intellectual concern is to link different types or gradations of peace to different regions of the world that have been characterized by the absence of international wars for extended periods of time ("zones of peace"). More specifically, I want to explain the phenomenon of "zones of peace" (negative peace) in the Third World by comparing South America and West Africa, and by developing a model that can be applied to other regions as well, such as ASEAN in Southeast Asia. I want to show the importance of the predisposition of states to accept their existing borders as a foundation for regional peace and as an explanation that transcends the conventional inventory of international relations theories.

The two main questions formulated in this book are: (1) How can we explain the preservation of peace at the regional level in general, and in South America and West Africa in particular? and (2) Can regional peace be maintained among states that do not sustain democratic regimes? In other words, is democracy a prerequisite for the existence of peace?

These two questions are relevant both in theoretical and empirical terms. From a theoretical point of view, it is important to emphasize the regional perspective, as opposed to a dyadic or a systemic one. Moreover, the second question directly addresses and criticizes the liberal explanation for a separate and exclusive zone of peace among democracies.

From a policy-oriented point of view, governments are concerned with transcending the mere absence of war, reaching stable peace, and consolidating and stabilizing it vis-à-vis their neighbors (Wolfers 1961, 138). Interestingly enough, these practical questions have been almost ignored by scholars of international relations. Through the empirical examination of long periods of peace in two disparate regions of the Third World, we can draw some interesting lessons about how to "upgrade" the degree of regional peace from the mere absence of war (negative peace) all the way up to the establishment of pluralistic security communities.

To answer these two questions I examine alternative explanations for the maintenance of regional peace in the Third World, and I assess the necessary, favorable, and sufficient conditions for its resilience. The first question is addressed in chapter 2 through a literature review of the conditions of peace and the causes of war, according to realist and liberal approaches. Since realists still consider international relations as the realm of international anarchy and as a state of war, the persistence of peace represents for them an anomaly or a puzzle. For realists, the paramount question remains how to prevent war, rather than how to expand and deepen peace. Conversely, from a liberal perspective, this question addresses a more "normal" situation by which many neighboring states have coexisted over long periods of time in peaceful relations, without any expectations that they might be involved in war (see Miller 1985, 85). While realists are mainly concerned with the origins of peace, liberals focus their analysis upon its expansion and "deepening." From this literature review nine hypotheses are distilled to explain the maintenance of regional peace, as follows:

1. A zone of peace is more likely to be maintained when a state within or outside the region assumes the role of regional hegemon and induces or imposes a peaceful regional order among the countries of the region;

2. A zone of peace is more likely to be maintained when the states of the region develop and maintain a regional balance of power;

3. A zone of peace is more likely to be maintained when the states of the region confront a common threat emanating from a third party;

4. A zone of peace is more likely to be maintained when the states of the region are isolated from each other by geographical and natural factors, and by technological means that favor defense over offense. Moreover, institutional and political/economic constraints create a condition of impotence that favor the maintenance of regional peace;

5. A zone of peace is more likely to be maintained when all the states in the region sustain liberal democratic regimes;

6. A zone of peace is more likely to be maintained when all the states of the region are prosperous and economically developed;

7. A zone of peace is more likely to be maintained when the states of the region establish relations of economic interdependence and integration at the interstate level, and transnational links among their peoples;

8. *A zone of peace is more likely to be maintained when the states of the region sustain a normative consensus regarding the rules of international law to be implemented in the management and resolution of their international conflicts. This normative consensus is sometimes facilitated by a common cultural framework;*

9. *A zone of peace is more likely to be maintained if most, if not all, of the states of the region are satisfied with the territorial status quo.*

Obviously, there is not a single explanation for the creation and persistence of zones of peace, contrary to some claims of the "democratic peace" argument, but rather a myriad of alternative explanations that are not mutually exclusive. In conceptual and empirical terms, these explanations somewhat overlap and reinforce each other. Logically, this leads to a problem of overdetermination: there seem to be several reasons why peace has been kept in different regions of the globe at different times. To overcome this problem, and based on these alternative hypotheses, I have built a model stating the necessary, sufficient, and favorable conditions for the different types of regional peace. Consequently, the second question can be answered in an affirmative way. Peace can be indeed preserved among nondemocratic states, though there is a direct relationship between the quality of their regional peace and their type of political regime.

Among the nine hypotheses presented in chapter 2, I particularly emphasize the last one—satisfaction with the territorial status quo. The vast majority of international wars appear to arise from territorial disputes (see Boulding 1978, 109–10; and Vasquez 1993, 7). This hypothesis implies that a zone of peace will be maintained when states are "conservative" in territorial terms. Thus, democracies and nondemocracies might be satisfied with the status quo, though for very different reasons.

DEFINING PEACE, ZONES OF PEACE, DEMOCRACIES, AND STRONG/WEAK STATES

To cope with the two questions formulated above, we should first clarify a series of concepts that are crucial for the understanding of the phenomenon under study. One of the pitfalls of the recent literature of democratic peace has been precisely its failure to define its core terms in clear and simple ways. The key concepts for this study are: "peace," "zones of peace," "democracies and well-established democracies," and "strong and weak states."

Peace

What is peace? Probably the most significant quarrel in the field of peace studies relates to a proper definition of this term. A major debate, carried out by Johan Galtung and Kenneth Boulding since the 1960s, has been whether to define peace simply as the absence of war ("negative peace" in my own terms), or as a more encompassing concept, which includes also social and economic justice, and some kind of world order that meets the needs and interests of the human population as a whole ("positive peace"). For instance, Johan Galtung juxtaposed negative and positive peace by relating them to his notions of personal (physical) versus structural (socioeconomic) violence. The absence of personal violence constitutes negative peace, while the absence of structural violence means the achievement of positive peace. Absence of violence should not be confused with absence of conflict; thus, the achievement of peace does not necessarily imply the elimination of conflict. Therefore, the concept of peace has both positive and negative connotations. On the positive side, it signifies good management and even resolution of conflict, harmony, gentleness, love, and the integration of human society. On the negative side, it is understood as the absence of "something"—the absence of turmoil, tension, and war (see Galtung 1975; Boulding 1977, 1978; Dedring 1976, 20; and Stephenson 1989, 10).

For the purposes of this study, I am interested mainly in the explanation of *negative peace*, conceived as the absence of systematic, large-scale collective violence between political communities. Furthermore, my research focuses mainly upon *international* negative peace; that is, the absence of war between independent states. This negative conception of peace as the absence of interstate war implies that peace is something to be "maintained" or "restored." This narrow definition of peace could be criticized on the grounds that it serves the interests of the status quo at the expense of social change and distributive justice (see Kelman 1981, 101; and Johnson 1976, 19). My normative assumption (or even prejudice) is, however, that a condition of negative peace is a prerequisite for achieving a better, positive peace. As Herbert Kelman (1981, 105) suggests, "granting that peace is not necessarily the *highest* value at all times, we are still right in insisting that the preservation of human life and the avoidance of violence and destruction are *extremely high* values."

Regions or Zones of Peace

An international region, zone, or subsystem can be broadly defined as a limited number of states linked by a geographical relationship and by a degree of mutual interdependence. Accordingly, for each state in the region, the activities of other members of the region (be they cooperative or antagonistic) are significant determinants of its foreign policy (Nye 1968, vii; and Cantori and Spiegel 1970, 1). Regional subsystems are characterized by clusters of states coexisting in geographical propinquity as interrelated units that sustain significant security, economic, and political relations (see Wriggins 1992, 4; Kaiser 1968, 86; and Buzan 1991, 188).

One of the difficulties in dealing with any region is the problem of delineating its exact spatial borders. Although many regions are denoted by obvious geographic or cultural boundaries, there is always some arbitrariness in their definition. The major criteria remain geographical contiguity, interaction, and subjective perception of belonging to a distinctive community and having a collective identity (see Russett 1967, 7; Michael Haas 1970, 101). In addition, several common characteristics can be suggested, such as: (1) a certain degree of social and cultural homogeneity; (2) similar political attitudes or behavior toward third parties; (3) common political institutions, as an expression of political interdependence; (4) a certain degree of economic interdependence; and (5) a common behavioral criterion, such as the identification of norms pertaining to conflict management and resolution (see Russett 1967, 11; Cantori and Spiegel 1970, 2; Michael Haas 1970, 101; and Modelski 1961, 149).

This focus on regions or subsystems suggests an intermediate level of analysis located between the dyadic (interactive) level and the entire international system as a unit of analysis. In this way, we reduce the number of units to be analyzed, as compared to the dyadic level, while we lessen the generality, abstractness, and complexity of our research, in contrast to the system level (see Berton 1969, 330). Thus, a regional analysis allows us to define several *zones* of peace instead of just one democratic zone, taking into consideration the geographical and historical contexts of different clusters of states at specific points of time. Moreover, it should be emphasized that many of the insights embedded in a regional perspective are particularly relevant for the post–Cold War world, in which regions are likely to have much more autonomy from the major powers as compared to the 1945–89 period. Hence, the indigenous or region-specific (intraregional) causes of war and peace have become especially significant.

I define then a *zone of peace* as a discrete geographical region of the world in which a group of states have maintained peaceful relations among themselves for a period of at least thirty years—a generation span—though civil wars, domestic unrest, and violence might still occur within their borders, as well as international conflicts and crises between them. This definition refers strictly to the international relations domain. Moreover, no particular type of political regime is a prerequisite for membership in a zone of peace.[1]

This minimalist definition should be distinguished from the broader concept of zone of peace as general disarmament and dismantling of military systems, as commitment to social justice and human rights (positive peace), and as the basis for a more radical social transformation on a global scale (Boulding 1992, 76). In terms of international security and international law, another current usage of zones of peace is associated with the Nuclear Weapon–Free Zone concept. There is some logical and empirical overlap between this usage and mine, although not all the zones of peace I have traced are nuclear weapon–free zones (NWFZs).[2]

It is my contention that zones of peace in the international system develop when states are conservative in their territorial claims—in other words, when they are usually satisfied with the territorial status quo of their international borders and of the region in general. Within these zones of peace we should expect no international wars among the state-members of the region, though domestic and international conflicts might still persist. We can differentiate among three different gradations or categories of zones of peace in an ascending order of quality and endurance, as follows:

1. A zone of *negative or precarious peace* (mere absence of war), in which peace is maintained only on an unstable basis by threats, deterrence, or a lack of will or capabilities to engage in violent conflict at a certain time. The possibility of war remains tangible and real. In a region of negative peace, most of the states are at least passively satisfied with the status quo, to the extent that they do not attempt to change the territorial status quo by force. In this zone, civil wars, domestic and international conflicts and crises, and even limited military interventions (below the level of international war) are still possible.[3]

2. A zone of *stable peace* (no expectations of violence), in which peace is maintained on a reciprocal and consensual basis. In this zone the probability of war is so small that it does not really enter into the calculations of any of the parties involved. The essential conditions for the development of a zone of stable peace include: (a) that territorial changes are removed from national agendas, except by mutual agreement and peaceful means; (b) that there is a minimum of nonmilitary intervention by each nation in other nation's internal affairs; and (c) in terms of perceptions, the countries of the region sustain an economic, rather than romantic or heroic, attitude toward their national states (Boulding 1991, 108). Unlike negative peace, stable peace requires a permanent condition of peace both in international relations and within the borders of the states involved. Thus, a zone of stable peace is a community or society of nation-states satisfied with the status quo, in which domestic and international conflicts might occur, though they are kept within nonviolent limits.[4]

3. A *pluralistic security community* of nation-states, with stable expectations of peaceful change, in which the member states share common norms, values, and political institutions, sustain an identifiable common identity, and are deeply interdependent.[5] The concept of a pluralistic security community is directly linked to the notion of integration. According to Ernst Haas (1971), the study of regional integration is concerned with explaining how and why states voluntarily mingle, merge, and mix with their neighbors so as to lose several factual attributes of sovereignty. A successful integration is reached when states in the region cease to prepare for war against one another. At a more subjective level, integration is achieved when there is a prevalence of mutually compatible self-images of the states participating in the process up to the point of developing a common identity and mutual expectations of shared economic gains.

Karl Deutsch and his associates (1957) draw an important distinction between integration and amalgamation. While the former has to do with the formation of communities, the latter refers to the establishment of formal organizations, associations, or political institutions. This distinction is crucial. In logical terms, we can envision a situation of amalgamation without integration (i.e., without a sense of community), as in a nation-state torn apart by civil war. Conversely, there exists the possibility of integration without amalgamation, which is the case with pluralistic security communities that keep both the regional peace and the political sovereignty of the integrated members of the community. The shared expectations of peaceful change are a function of shared values, mutual responsiveness and trust, and the abandonment of war as a policy option to resolve conflict. In this sense, pluralistic security communities represent the highest form of zones of peace.

According to this categorization, stable peace and pluralistic security communities greatly overlap with one another. The former is a broader category of zones of peace than the latter, since by definition while every pluralistic security community implies a zone of stable peace, not every zone of stable peace has to be a security community intersubjectively defined by the emergence of a common regional identity. Thus, the main distinction seems to be that a security community encompasses a higher sense of community and institutionalization through the sharing of a similar political system (such as democratic regimes), political institutions, and economic interdependence. Although these two types of zones of peace are logically linked, I would refer to pluralistic security communities as zones of institutionalized stable peace with a common regional identity.[6]

Although there is a serious problem of aggregating the relationships of a number of peaceful dyads within a specific geographical region into one single characterization of that zone of peace as negative, stable, or pluralistic security community, a regional pattern can be nevertheless traced that encompasses *more* than the sum of the dyads in a given region.[7] Moreover, the geographical characterization of zones of peace does not rule out the possibility that a member state in a given zone of peace might participate in an extraregional war beyond its immediate borders (i.e., the United States in Vietnam in 1965–75; the United Kingdom in the Falklands/Malvinas War of 1982). Thus, membership in a zone of peace does not necessarily imply a pacifist or even a peaceful attitude toward international relations in general.[8]

Democracies and Well-Established Democracies

Another key term essential to the understanding of zones of peace is "democracy." As Schmitter and Karl (1993, 39) point out, "we are 'stuck' with democracy as the catchword of contemporary political discourse." In fact, the manner in which democracy is defined and assessed partly determines the validity of the democratic peace explanation.

There are several problems related to the attempt to define democracy in a proper way. First, the concept is usually confused with related though different terms, such as "prosperity," "capitalism," "liberal regime," and "stability." Second, there is a tendency to see democracy in binary terms (states are either democratic or nondemocratic), rather than as a continuous concept (states are more or less democratic). Third, any operationalization of democracy implies several underlying assumptions about its measurement that are not spelled out in clear terms. Fourth, different scholars use different terms to identify a similar phenomenon—such as "democracy," "liberal regime," "libertarianism," and "polyarchy." Conversely, different authors use the same term to identify quite different phenomena. For instance, "democracy" might imply political liberties, economic equality, and social justice. For the purpose of this book, democracy will be examined essentially in political, rather than social or economic, terms.

Political democracy can be defined as "a system of government in which rulers are held accountable for their actions in the public realm by citizens, acting indirectly through the competition and cooperation of their elected representatives" (Schmitter and Karl 1993, 40). Three conditions are deemed essential for the existence of political democracy: (1) meaningful and extensive peaceful and recurrent competition among individuals and political parties for all effective positions of governmental power; (2) a highly inclusive level of political participation in the selection of leaders and policies, at least through regular and fair elections; and (3) a level of civil and political liberties sufficient to ensure the integrity of political competition and participation (Diamond 1989, 142-43).[9]

According to this definition, the concept of political democracy focuses upon the *procedural* aspects of the phenomenon rather than on the outcomes that it is supposed to bring about, such as stability, peace, prosperity, and efficiency (Ray 1993, 256). Furthermore, this concept of *political* democracy should be kept apart from "economic" or "social" democracy, so that the political system should be analytically distinguished from its economic and social milieu (Diamond et al. 1990, 6).

Political democracy should be examined in the context of several zones of peace, both among the developed countries and in the Third World. At this point, it is useful to distinguish between continuously democratic Third World democracies since independence and recently established Third World democracies (see Rothstein 1992, 35). In other words, we can compare the simple concept of "democracy" to that of a "well-established democracy." According to James Ray (1993, 256–59), a *well-established democracy* is a "constitutionally secure" regime in which at least one peaceful transfer of power has already taken place between contending political groups through fair and competitive elections. Similarly, one can classify a political regime as a well-established democracy if the regime in power has existed long enough (for at least three years), to demonstrate its stable and legitimate character.

Strong and Weak States

In addition to the definition of democracy we should also refer to the concept of "strong" and "weak" states (see Nordlinger 1981; Buzan 1983; Migdal 1988; and Holsti 1996). According to Samuel Huntington (1968, 1), the most important political distinction among states concerns not their form of government (such as democratic or autocratic), but rather their degree of political institutionalization. In this sense, the weak state/strong state continuum—measured by state autonomy, degree of legitimacy and institutionalization, and state capabilities vis-à-vis its own society—is essential to understand the resilience of zones of peace. Specifically, the strength or weakness of the member states in a region seems to affect their predisposition toward satisfaction with the status quo, and thus the quality of their regional peace.

A state's strength and weakness are associated with the institutional capacities of the state turned inwards, vis-à-vis its own society (Job 1991, 20; Migdal 1988, xiii). The strength of a state neither depends on nor necessarily correlates with its international power and status. In theoretical and empirical terms, we can find strong states that are weak international powers (such as the small democratic states of Western Europe) or, conversely, weak states that have been considerable regional powers (such as Argentina until the mid 1980s in South America, or Nigeria in West Africa).

When the state is strong vis-à-vis its society, the idea of the state, its political institutions, and its territory are all clearly defined and stable (Buzan 1983, 67). Hence, any threat to the state tends to come from its external environment rather than from within. Strong states are characterized by the recognition of their international borders, the assimilation of most social groups into their polities, and the civilian control of their militaries. In addition, many (but not all) of the strong states are ruled by democratic regimes and sustain liberal economic policies (see Holsti 1993, 13-14; Holsti 1996).

When the state is weak, the idea of the state does not coincide with that of the nation and/or the civil society. According to Barry Buzan (1983, 67), the main feature of the weak state is its high level of concern with domestically generated threats to the security of its political regime and government. Hence, weak states are characterized by multinational societies, the proliferation of primordial loyalties, the seizure of the government apparatus by an exclusive and restricted group at the expense of the rest of society, and the lack of legitimacy of its political regime, which relies on patrimonialism, violence, coercion, and intimidation.

In many parts of the Third World, the typical state has been a notoriously weak, rather artificial entity lacking both social cohesion and social capabilities (Job 1991, 12). The security dilemma confronted by the weak state in the Third World tends to be primarily internal: the sense of insecurity emanates in the first place from within its boundaries, rather than from without.

Several authors have distinguished between strong and weak states on the basis of different time trajectories available for them to complete the twin processes of state-making and nation-building. According to this argument, strong (usually First World) states have benefited from a gradual and long process of accommodation between the state and the nation, leading to the identification of the people with the state (legitimacy) and of the people with each other (integration). In contrast, weak (usually Third World) states have had to reach legitimacy and integration in decades rather than in centuries. This argument is plausible, but not entirely valid. We can find in Latin America a peculiar variant of semiweak (or semistrong) states that are relatively old in terms of years of independence in which states developed and consolidated into homogeneous nation-states, without reaching a sufficient level of legitimacy for their political regimes. Thus, as with the concept of democracy, we can then establish a gradual scale of weak and strong states ranging from "quasi states" (usually in Africa), to weak though established nation-states (as in Latin America), to strong states in East Asia and especially in Western Europe.[10] When one combines the type of political regime or government (democracies, autocracies) with the type of state (weak or strong), it becomes possible to understand why different states and regimes have been satisfied with the territorial status quo.

OVERVIEW OF ZONES OF PEACE IN THE INTERNATIONAL SYSTEM

According to the definitions elaborated above I have identified the follow-ing historical and geographical zones of peace since 1815: (1) Europe, 1815–48; (2) Europe, 1871–1914; (3) Western Europe, since 1945; (4) Eastern Europe, 1945–89; (5) North America, 1917 to the present; (6) South America, 1883 to the present; (7) West Africa, 1957 to the present; (8) East Asia, since 1953; (9) Australasia, since 1945; and (10) the ASEAN countries of Southeast Asia, since 1967. In the description of these zones, I ask the following questions: How many democracies and nondemocracies are in the zone? How many international conflicts and civil wars have taken place, if any? Is the region considered an area of negative peace, stable peace, or pluralistic security community?

Historical Zones of Peace

(1) Zones of Peace before 1815
The phenomenon of zones of peace in the international system historically predates the European Concert of 1815–48. Peaceful societies in which political entities coexisted in peace for more than a century have been traced by Matthew Melko (1973) back to the ancient times. These peaceful societies were characterized by the lack of physical conflict either with their neighbors or with their own people (Melko and Wiegel 1981, 2).

   Among the ancient peaceful societies at least two could be character-ized as international zones of peace: the Phoenician Peace (1150–722 B.C.) among five city-states (Aradus, Berytus, Byblos, Sidon, and Tyre); and the Roman Republic Peace (203–90 B.C.) among several members of the Latin Confederation, with the clear predominance of Rome.[11]

   Among the peaceful societies in the Western World prior to 1815, the Scandinavian states established among themselves a zone of peace for ex-tensive periods of time: Iceland has been at peace since 1262 without inter-ruptions; Norway, between 1371 and 1612 and 1814 to 1940; Denmark, between 1660 and 1801; and Sweden, since 1721 (Melko and Hord 1984, 66).[12] In most of these long periods of peace, Scandinavia remained geograph-ically marginalized from the main centers of European action. Small coun-tries such as Norway, Finland, and Iceland remained under the protection of larger powers and channeled their energies toward trade and shipping. The Scandinavian countries found ways of satisfying the demands for resources by their populations without turning to territorial acquisitions and military buildups (see Choucri and North 1972). Moreover, their relative isolation from the major power struggles was an important force for preserving their regional peace.

(2) Europe, 1815–48

After the Napoleonic Wars of 1803–15, a more refined and institutionalized balance of power emerged in the form of the European Concert (see Elrod 1976; Jervis 1985; Lauren 1983). The Concert of Europe marked a growth of cooperation and consensus among the European powers; it aimed at the maintenance of peace and the preservation of the status quo. The European Concert was a loose international institution that grouped together satisfied status quo powers. The rules of the Concert established that changes in the territorial status quo were deemed legitimate—and peacefully instrumented—only when Great Britain, France, Austria, Prussia, and Russia had assented to them, often by holding an international conference. An equilibrium was sought and found between the forces of change and the preservation of peace within the European system, through a sophisticated exercise of preventive diplomacy. The five great powers managed to establish a stable zone of peace that included both themselves and also Switzerland, Denmark, Portugal, Sardinia, Sweden and Norway, Belgium, the Netherlands (after the Belgian war of secession against the Netherlands in 1830–33), Spain, Piedmont, Naples, and Greece (after the successful revolt against the Ottoman Empire in 1821–28). Among the sixteen members of this European zone of peace only four were democracies: Switzerland, France between 1830 and 1849, Belgium (after 1830), and the United Kingdom (after 1832). The Netherlands, Piedmont, and Denmark became democracies after 1848. Greece was a constitutional monarchy after 1844 but became a democracy only after 1864.[13] All the members of this zone of peace had a vested interest in keeping the status quo both domestically and internationally.

In the earlier years of this period, there had been brief military expeditions sent by one or another of the great powers into Naples, Piedmont, Spain, and Greece to suppress or support liberal and nationalist revolutions. In addition, there were civil wars and domestic violence in Greece (1821–

28), Spain (1820–22), Poland (1830–31), and Portugal (1831–34). Yet, there were no major wars or even military crises of any kind between two or more of the great powers. This zone of stable peace, which was considered as a European community or society of satisfied nations, did not include the Ottoman Empire.

(3) Europe, 1871–1914

After the Crimean War of 1853–56 and the wars of national unification of Italy and Germany, a balance of power was reestablished. The five great powers, if not reunited into a homogeneous Europe concert as before, managed to reestablish a zone of peace among themselves that also included all the smaller European powers, with the exception of the Balkan states (Greece, Serbia, Bulgaria, Montenegro, and Romania) and the Ottoman Empire. Throughout this period, all the international wars occurred in the Balkans and the Ottoman Empire, which were on the periphery of this zone of peace, due to nationalist and revisionist forces opposed to the status quo of the multiethnic empires (Austria-Hungary and Turkey). Widespread domestic violence was restricted to Spain (the Carlist War of 1872–76). The territorial status quo was kept by the Bismarckian system of alliances (1871–90) and by the subsequent balance of power between the Triple Alliance and the Triple Entente during 1907–14.

Among the fifteen members of this region, ten were democracies (Switzerland, Great Britain, Belgium, Netherlands, Italy, Denmark, Sweden, France, Norway after 1905, and Luxembourg after 1890). Among these democracies, only France and Italy made revisionist claims. The French wanted to regain their territories of Alsace and Lorraine that were lost to Germany, though they sought territorial compensations through their colonial enterprises in Africa and Asia. Moreover, they were deterred from initiating a war against Germany because of their relative weakness. The Italians, for their part, initiated a war against Turkey in 1911 in pursuit of their colonialist claims in North Africa.

This second period of European peace in the late nineteenth century was a zone of negative peace only. The sense of a society of states deteriorated and was replaced by a balance of power between two hostile armed coalitions, which ultimately clashed in World War I (see Craig and George 1990, 35–47; Taylor 1971).

Contemporary Zones of Peace

The contemporary zones of peace in the international system include: (1) Western Europe, since 1945; (2) Eastern Europe, between 1945 and 1989; (3) North America, since 1917; (4) South America, since 1883; (5) West Africa, since 1957; (6) East Asia, since 1953; (7) Australasia/Oceania, since 1945; and (8) the ASEAN countries, since 1967.

(1) Western Europe, 1945 to the Present
After World War II the European continent became a zone of peace. During the Cold War, there was a precarious negative peace between the two blocs in Europe. Some realist writers attribute the peacefulness of the postwar era in Europe to the bipolarity of the distribution of power, the rough equality in military power between the United States and the Soviet Union and the presence of nuclear weapons with their deterrent effect (see Gaddis 1986; Mearsheimer 1990). We can identify in Europe *two* distinctive zones of peace: Western Europe and Eastern Europe.

   If we exclude Turkey and Cyprus from the membership in the Western European zone of peace, we can define this region as a zone of stable peace and as a pluralistic security community with stable expectations of peaceful change. The nineteen states of this region—Austria, Belgium, Denmark, Finland, France, Great Britain, Greece, Iceland, Ireland, Italy, Luxembourg, Malta, Netherlands, Norway, Portugal, Spain, Sweden, Switzerland, and West Germany/Germany—are all democratic (Portugal, Spain, and Greece having experienced successful democratic transitions in the late 1970s). Interestingly enough, with the exception of West Germany until the German reunification of 1990, Ireland vis-à-vis Northern Ireland, and Spain vis-à-vis Gibraltar, they have all sustained a common interest in maintaining the status quo both domestically and internationally. There have been no international wars and even no serious international crises in this region. A civil war took place in Greece between 1946 and 1949. In addition, domestic violence has been widespread in Northern Ireland since 1969, and to a lesser extent in the Basque region of Spain and in French Corsica. Overall, this region has become the most pristine example of a *democratic* zone of peace. Besides being democratic, all the nations of this region are economically developed and highly interdependent in economic and social terms. As Raymond Cohen (1994, 220–22) suggests, their democratic structures have also been nurtured by their continuous peace since 1945, a peace created by the bipolar structure after World War II and maintained by nuclear weapons and the presence of a third-party threat (the former Soviet Union) until recently.

(2) Eastern Europe, 1945-89

Between 1945 and 1989 the central and eastern half of Europe constituted another zone of peace, though qualitatively different from its Western counterpart. All the nine members of this zone—Albania, Bulgaria, Czechoslovakia, East Germany, Hungary, Poland, Romania, the Soviet Union, and Yugoslavia—were authoritarian or totalitarian (Communist) regimes until 1989. The Soviet Union, as the regional hegemon, was in charge of keeping the status quo among the Eastern European countries both within and across their borders. On two occasions—the invasions of Hungary in 1956 and Czechoslovakia in 1968—the Soviet Union intervened militarily in order to keep the domestic status quo. In addition, revisionist and irredentist claims by states like Poland, Hungary, and Romania and nationalist demands by subnational groups in Czechoslovakia, Yugoslavia, and different parts of the Soviet Union were repressed by the overarching political and military presence of the Soviet Union and its Communist ideology.

Since the revolutions in Eastern Europe and the collapse of the Soviet Union in the late 1980s and early 1990s, domestic violence and international wars are currently replacing the negative peace maintained by the Soviet hegemon. While territorial claims and changes were "frozen" during 1945–89, they are currently thriving in the former Soviet Union, ex-Czechoslovakia, and former Yugoslavia through both peaceful and violent means. Since 1989 Albania, the ex-Yugoslavian republics (Slovenia, Croatia, Serbia, and Bosnia-Herzegovina), Romania, Hungary, Poland, the Baltic States, the Czech Republic and Slovakia, Russia, and several other former Soviet republics, are all experiencing transitions toward democracy from a previous Socialist or Communist regime. It is unclear whether these new and fragile democracies will be able to maintain a new zone of peace to replace the old hegemonic negative peace, established and maintained by the Soviet Union since World War II up to the end of the Cold War.

(3) North America, 1917 to the Present

Since the Mexican-American war of 1846-48 there has been no international war in the North American region, which includes Canada, the United States, and Mexico. Moreover, since the aftermath of the Mexican Revolution in 1917 there has been no international crisis or serious dispute among the three countries of the region. Instances of domestic violence and civil wars have occurred in the period between 1848 and 1917—the Mexican civil war of 1858–61, the American civil war of 1861–65, and the Mexican revolution of 1911–17. While the United States and Canada are considered well-established democracies, Mexico can be classified at best as a new democracy, a "quasi democracy," or a "partly free" regime.[14] These three countries have been satisfied with the status quo in North America, despite (or perhaps because of) the lopsided power distribution in favor of the United States. This satisfaction with the territorial status quo on the part of the United States contradicts its revisionist ambitions in other parts of the Americas and the world, as expressed by the U.S. war against Spain in 1898 and by numerous U.S. interventions in Central America ever since. Overall, this area can also be considered as a zone of stable peace and even as a pluralistic security community, at least in terms of U.S.-Canadian relations.

(4) South America, 1883 to the Present

Since the end of the Pacific War between Bolivia, Chile, and Peru in 1883, the South American region has been another zone of peace, with the exception of two international wars: the 1932–35 Chaco War between Bolivia and Paraguay and the war between Ecuador and Peru in 1941.[15] There have been a number of long-standing territorial disputes that eventually escalated into international crises, such as the "tug of war" between Argentina and Chile over their Patagonian border in 1902 and again in 1978 over the Beagle Channel Islands. The vast majority of border disputes in South America have been resolved peacefully, however, leading to some cession or exchange of territories. The basis for a peaceful settlement of these disputes was established through the principle of *uti possidetis*, according to which the South American countries recognized the colonial borders as their postindependence international frontiers (see Child 1985; Ireland 1938).

   While South American armies have rarely been involved with one another, they have frequently intervened in the domestic affairs of their own countries. The peaceful relations among the South American countries starkly contrast with the violent relations within their borders, at least until the recent trend toward democratization. Among the twelve states that comprise South America, only six were democracies before 1979 (Chile between 1891 and 1973; Uruguay, between 1919 and 1973; Colombia, between 1910 and 1949 and since 1958; Venezuela, since 1959; Guyana, since 1966; and Suriname, since 1975). Domestic violence, civil wars, and numerous coups d'etat have been widespread in the region. Since the beginning of the 1980s, however, military regimes in Ecuador, Argentina, Uruguay, Brazil, Bolivia, Peru, Chile, and Paraguay have been replaced by democratic regimes.

Irrespective of the changing nature of their political regimes in the last two decades, the vast majority of South American countries have been more or less satisfied with the territorial status quo, with the exceptions of Bolivia and Ecuador. The peaceful international relations of the South American states have been a reflection of their traditional institutional weaknesses, their low levels of military preparedness, and their minor or subordinate position vis-à-vis external powers such as Great Britain in the nineteenth century and the United States in the twentieth century (see Shafter 1978, 369–70). Furthermore, this widespread satisfaction with the regional order has been associated with a long practice of diplomatic management and peaceful resolution of international disputes, linked to a common normative and cultural framework (Ebel et al. 1991, 49–86). Until the 1980s South America was a zone of negative peace only. However, with the spread of democracy in the last decade, the South American region might be moving in the direction of stable peace and even an incipient pluralistic security community in its Southern Cone (see Schmitter 1991).

(5) West Africa, 1957 to the Present
Among the several African regions, West Africa stands out as the only zone of peace in that continent since the beginning of the decolonization process after World War II. With the exception of the brief Mali–Burkina Faso war of 1985, there have been no international wars among the sixteen states that comprise this region.[16] But as in the South American case, this lack of interstate wars contrasts with widespread domestic violence, military coups, and even virulent civil wars, such as the Nigerian civil war of 1967–70 or the recent Liberian conflict.

Among the sixteen members of the region, only Sierra Leone and

Gambia, and to a lesser extent Senegal, were democracies before 1991. Nigeria experienced only short periods of democratic rule in 1961–64 and 1979–83; Ghana in 1969–71 and 1979–81; and Burkina Faso at some points. In the last six years, however, Benin, Cape Verde, Mali, and Niger have also experienced transitions toward democracy. Conversely, Sierra Leone withdrew into a military dictatorship marred with a virulent civil war, and The Gambia ceased to be a democracy in 1994. The rest of the countries in the region are still ruled by one-party or military regimes. Whatever the nature of their political regimes, however, most of the countries of the region, with the exceptions of Burkina Faso, Ghana, Mali, and Togo, have consistently adhered to the territorial status quo.

Although the boundaries of West Africa were determined by colonial administrators arbitrarily—with no regard to ethnic or even geographical realities—they have been thoroughly respected by most of the new independent West African states. Thus, a similar principle of *uti possidetis* has been adopted partly as a solution to the institutional weaknesses of the new countries, which, having to govern over multiethnic populations, were states but not "real" nation-states. Since the West African states had to define themselves according to the preexisting colonial boundaries, most of them realized that they had a reciprocal interest in keeping the territorial status quo (see Herbst 1989; Jackson and Rosberg 1982). Yet West Africa remains only a precarious zone of negative peace, due to the continuing domestic disarray within the borders of many states in the region.

(6) Northeast Asia, 1953 to the Present
Since the end of the Korean War in 1953, the countries of Northeast Asia have managed to keep a fragile negative peace among themselves, interrupted only once by the Sino-Soviet border fighting of 1969. Until 1990, the only democracy in the region was Japan, all the other states being ruled by authoritarian or Communist regimes. South Korea has moved in the direction of democracy since the late 1980s, while Mongolia, Russia, and Taiwan are currently experiencing transitions toward democracy.

In terms of political, economic, and military power, this region is clearly paramount in Asia and among the most important in the world. Domestic violence and civil wars have been absent since the Chinese civil war of 1946–49, pointing to the domestic strength of most of these states. Several long-standing hostilities *have not* escalated into war: the Japanese-Russian dispute over the Kurile Islands, the quarrel between the two Chinas, the antagonism between the two Koreas, and several other maritime disputes, such as those involving Japan and China and Japan and South Korea. Only the Sino-Soviet territorial dispute developed into a brief armed conflict in 1969. Unlike other zones of peace, however, this region is composed of pairs of status quo and revisionist states: Japan sustains revisionist claims against Russia over the Kurile Islands, North Korea seeks the reunification of the Korean peninsula even by forceful means while South Korea clings to the current status quo, and China has frequently adopted revisionist policies vis-à-vis Taiwan and Hong Kong. The prevalence of authoritarian and Communist regimes, in addition to the dissatisfaction with the territorial status quo among half of the members of this region, have made East Asia a precarious and volatile zone of negative peace. In this case, it is not the common satisfaction with the status quo that has kept the peace, but a rather delicate regional balance of power among the states of the region, bolstered by the U.S. military presence in the Pacific area (see Friedberg 1994).

(7) Australasia and Southwest Pacific, 1945 to the Present
The Southwest Pacific and Australasia is a vast region that covers one-sixth of the earth's surface. Since World War II the island-states of this region have formed a zone of stable peace, and even a pluralistic security community. Among the eleven members of this zone, eight states are democracies—Australia, New Zealand, Papua/New Guinea, Tuvalu, Vanuatu, Kiribati, Nauru, and the Solomon Islands. Only Fiji and Tonga have been ruled by authoritarian regimes. The major countries of the area are Australia, New Zealand, and Papua/New Guinea. These three states and the smaller island-states of Oceania are part of the South Pacific Forum set up in 1971. At their 1985 meeting in the Cook Islands, they decided to establish the South Pacific Nuclear Weapon-Free Zone Treaty, known as the Rarotonga Treaty. There have been no serious international conflicts or crises involving the countries of the region. Similarly, domestic violence has been very limited—a colonial rebellion in Nouvelle Caledonie against France, a coup d'etat in Fiji (1987), and the violent attempt of secession by Bougainville Island from Papua/New Guinea between 1988 and 1991. There is a shared interest in keeping the status quo, which might be a product not only of the democratic character of most of the states, but also of their geographical distance and isolation.

(8) The ASEAN Countries, 1967 to the Present

Following a change of government in Indonesia in 1965 that ended the hostilities between Indonesia and Malaysia, several countries in Southeast Asia—Indonesia, Malaysia, the Philippines, Singapore, and Thailand—established in August 1967 the Association of Southeast Asian Nations (ASEAN), later joined by Brunei in January 1984, Vietnam in 1995, and most recently by Myanmar and Laos in 1997.

In 1971, the ASEAN countries issued the Declaration of a Zone of Peace, Freedom and Neutrality in Southeast Asia, so that a nuclear-free zone has been also established to buttress this effort. In 1976, they signed the Treaty of Amity and Cooperation in Southeast Asia that effectively established peaceful relations among its members, despite their recurrent territorial and maritime disputes. The lack of war or even acute international conflicts between the ASEAN members stands in sharp contrast to the long Vietnam War, the Vietnamese occupation of Cambodia from 1979 to 1989, and the domestic violence widespread within some of these countries (e.g., the Indonesian repression of East Timor and the former struggle of the Philippines against its New People's Army).

With the setting of mechanisms for regional cooperation in all areas of policy, ranging from international refugees to trade liberalization, the ASEAN countries have moved from a zone of negative peace to the establishment of stable peace among themselves. The degree of economic, military, political, intellectual, and social interaction among the ASEAN countries has grown tremendously since the 1960s (Yuen Foong Khong 1994, 3). The states of ASEAN have managed to change their international environment, leading to a security regime of cooperation and collaboration and development toward a pluralistic security community. It should be pointed out that most of the ASEAN countries are not democratic, with the exceptions of the Philippines (since 1987) and Thailand (after the elections of 1992).

COMPARING SOUTH AMERICA AND WEST AFRICA

Among the eight contemporary zones of peace, four include the democratic and advanced industrialized countries (i.e., North America, Western Europe, Australasia, and East Asia with Japan); one the now defunct "Second World" (Eastern Europe); and the remaining three Third World or developing regions (South America, West Africa, and Southeast Asia). In this study, I do not discuss in depth the ASEAN countries, which are only a subregional group of recent origin (1967) within the larger Southeast Asian region. To discuss regional peace in the Third World, then, we should focus upon a comparison between South America and West Africa.

To complement the widespread analysis of the post–1945 long peace between the superpowers and the continuing fascination with the democratic zone of peace that includes all the democracies throughout the world, we need to pay more attention to regions such as South America and West Africa, where international negative peace has existed for long periods of time without democracy, in order to understand what such regions do and do not share with the fully democratic zones of peace of North America and Western Europe. Thus, I compare these two different regions of the Third World in order to assess the possibility of peace among nondemocratic states and how the democratization process has affected the quality of that regional peace. It should be noticed that the last wave of democratization dates from the late 1970s and early 1980s in the case of South America, and from the mid 1980s and early 1990s in the case of West Africa. Hence, in both regions the phenomenon of international negative peace has preceded by many years the current transitions towards democracy.

In terms of methodology, the research design follows the comparative method, similar to the method of "structured focused comparison," as proposed by Alexander George (1979). The two case studies selected are considered as an heuristic device, deliberately used to discern important general problems and possible theoretical solutions related to the maintenance of regional peace in the Third World.

These two regions of the Third World have both commonalities and differences. They are obviously very different in their political, economic, and social indicators. Although they share a common genesis—the breakdown of immense colonial empires into artificial new states that originally were not nations—their trajectory has been obviously distinctive, due to their disparate dates of decolonization (in South America 180 years ago, in West Africa only about 40 years ago). Thus, a better comparison might be between the states of West Africa today and the South American states in the nineteenth century, except for the fact that up to the 1880s South America was *not* a zone of peace.

Another major difference between these two regions is that the growth of national sentiment in South America, as opposed to West Africa, was impeded by neither ethnic nor religious cleavages. In the South American case, the relative similarity in ethnic and cultural background diminished the perils of irredentism and tribalism, in contrast to the West African case. Thus, although the South American states were generally weak vis-à-vis their own societies (as it was evident from the recurrent coups d'etat throughout the region until a decade or two ago), they became eventually full-fledged nation-states and not just "quasi states" as some of their West African counterparts.[17]

Despite these differences, the similarities between these two regions in terms of explaining their long peace are remarkable. As I argue in chapters 3 and 4 the satisfaction with the territorial status quo in both South America and West Africa has been linked to a normative consensus regarding *uti possidetis* and the peaceful management of international disputes, the presence of an aspiring or potential regional hegemon, and the development of institutional frameworks of economic integration and interdependence.

PREVIEW OF THE BOOK

In the next chapter, I review and criticize the relevant theoretical literature that deals with the conditions of peace and the causes of war at the dyadic, regional, and international levels of analysis. From this review I construct the relevant hypotheses that cope with the preservation of international peace at the regional level. Moreover, I formulate my own explanation based on the notion of "satisfaction" and devise a theoretical model that describes the necessary, sufficient, and favorable conditions for its maintenance.

Chapter 3 turns to the analysis of the South American zone of peace, in contrast to the Central American zone of conflict. First, it presents a narrative of South America's diplomatic history since 1883, emphasizing the different periods and the different gradations of peace through the present development of an incipient pluralistic security community in the Southern Cone. Second, there is an assessment of the alternative explanations for this long South American peace.

Chapter 4 examines the case of West Africa as a zone of negative peace. The first section includes the diplomatic history of the region since 1957 to the present. In an attempt to explain the dual reality of domestic conflict and international peace, the second half of the chapter examines the empirical evidence in terms of the hypotheses formulated above.

Finally, in chapter 5 I draw several comparisons and suggest some theoretical inferences and practical conclusions. I compare South America and West Africa, and both together with other regions of the world. Later, I establish several theoretical linkages between different types of political regimes and gradations of peace, and between types of state and conditions of regional peace.

CHAPTER 2

EXPLAINING ZONES OF PEACE
IN THE INTERNATIONAL SYSTEM

Explanations of long periods of peace have been limited to an examination of the systemic long peace of the Cold War period, or alternatively, to the dyadic peace between pairs of democracies that ultimately developed into a unique zone of democratic peace, such as that among the OECD countries. In the latter case, peace among these industrialized democracies is overdetermined. There have been many reasons, ranging from economic development and prosperity through sharing of democratic norms and institutions, why those countries have remained at peace (Jervis 1991, 47). These explanations of peace overlap, though they are not always identical with, those of regional peace in the Third World.

Any avid reader of the literature on war and peace will discover, to her or his surprise, that the question of how peace, once obtained, can be maintained has been barely addressed. In 1957 Karl Deutsch and his associates published a seminal work on the required and favorable conditions for the development of pluralistic security communities among states that had kept peaceful relations among themselves. More recently, Stephen Rock has explored the historical process by which great powers may make a transition in their mutual relations from a state of negative peace to a state of stable peace (Rock 1989, 4). But otherwise the literature is almost nonexistent. The paucity of important research on the conditions of peace might be related to the inherent difficulties of identifying the particular variables that are significant in building up and maintaining the peace strength of any international system or subsystem (see Boulding 1978, 63). Paradoxically, it seems much easier to study the causes and conditions of war than those of peace, although peace should be considered the normal situation (at least in statistical terms), since interstate wars have become an aberration or deviation from the norm, at least since 1945 (see Melko 1973; Gaddis 1992, 25; and Holsti 1996). As with the study of deterrence, however, most of the academic research has focused in explaining the causes of failure rather than success, the anomaly rather than the norm, war instead of peace.[1] When deterrence actually "works," we never know whether the reason has been deterrence or impotence, or both. Similarly, when peace is maintained, it is very difficult to discern the reasons why states have not had recourse to violence to settle their differences. Thus, we do not know whether peace has been an artifact or not.

Not only has the study of the conditions of peace been understudied, but the most recent empirical research on security and peace studies has been fixed upon the dyadic level, as if regional and systemic levels could be inferred from the analysis of any pair of states writ large. It is my contention that the regional level cannot be axiomatically deduced from either the dyadic or the systemic level. Thus, the question of peace maintenance can and should be examined in regional terms, since any zone represents more than the sum of isolated dyadic interactions of its member states, and obviously less than the configuration of the international system as a whole. This is particularly pertinent to the post–Cold War period, since intraregional international relations can be at last separated from the former systemic, East-West conflict.

In sum, the theoretical goal of this chapter will be to present a series of explanations for the maintenance of zones of peace by assessing several necessary, sufficient, and favorable conditions for the persistence of (and variations upon) different gradations of regional peace. In addition, I will offer a critique of the "democratic peace" theory by showing, in logical terms, that while regional democracy might be a sufficient condition for regional peace it is not a necessary one.

CAUSES OF WAR AND MAINTENANCE OF PEACE

It is usually thought that understanding the causes of war necessarily leads to an understanding of the causes of peace and vice versa. For instance, by defining negative peace as the mere absence of war we tend to refer to war and peace as the two sides of the same coin (see Schahzenski 1991, 295). The origins of peace can be traced to the results of the last war and its subsequent formalized status quo. In the same vein, if states can pursue and obtain their political goals without waging wars, then peace can be maintained insofar as it provides a functional equivalent to war (Vasquez 1994, 209). Yet, we have to differentiate between peace maintenance, on the one hand, and peace termination or origins, on the other. The focus of the book is upon peace maintenance. Moreover, to explain war (or peace) means confronting similar problems of underdetermination and overdetermination, due to a myriad of existing political, social, economic, and psychological conditions that tend to promote or inhibit the recourse to war (Deutsch and Senghaas 1971, 31).

To understand the causes of peace and how to maintain it, we have to be cognizant of the vast literature on the causes of war. In fact, most of the empirical research of peace studies has been associated with conflicts, crises, and wars. Conversely, there is a widespread argument, especially among realist writers, that "most theories about the causes of war are also theories about peace, and exploring ways to reduce the risk of war has been part of the field [of security studies] since its inception" (Walt 1991, 224).[2]

However, we should keep sight of the limitations and possible fallacies of this simplistic argument. In the first place, the symmetry between peace and war, or between peace and security, is at best limited. The concept of negative peace, for instance, is too narrow to encompass dimensions of security beyond the absence of war, such as economic, social, and ecological ones. Conversely, the concepts of stable peace and pluralistic security communities are too broad to be confined merely to war prevention. In logical terms, the parallelism between the causes of war and the causes of peace is far from being perfect. I argue in the course of this book that active satisfaction with the territorial status quo is a sufficient condition for the maintenance of regional negative peace. This active satisfaction derives from the predisposition of states to accept their existing borders as an important foundation for their regional peace. Yet the *absence* of active satisfaction (namely, revisionist grievances or enough motivation and will to change the territorial status quo by force), is at best a necessary, but not a sufficient, condition for waging war. In other words, negative peace can also be maintained without a widespread satisfaction with the territorial status quo; it can be maintained on the basis of deterrence, hegemony, or a balance of terror. Moreover, it should not be inferred from this statement that all interstate wars have been determined by territorial grievances. There have also been wars over ideology; commerce, navigation, and economic rights; succession and dynastic wars; government composition; colonial competition; and wars of national liberation/state creation (see Holsti 1991).

Any serious research on the causes of peace entails, or at least assumes, the possibility (if not acceptability) of conflict and war. The starting point of any inquiry into the conditions of peace involves a preliminary discussion of the causes of war. For instance, Nazli Choucri's work on "peace systems" depicts them as a variant of the basic model of "war-prone systems," in which two or more countries with high capabilities and unsatisfied demands extend their interests and borders outward, developing a feeling that such interests should be protected. The difference is that in peace systems competition and conflict are channeled through nonviolent, low-threat modes of action (Choucri and North 1972, 242).

Alternative Explanations of War and Peace

Whether the causes of war and peace can be collapsed and logically linked or not, it is clear that we should specify the different levels of analysis to which the alternative explanations refer, such as systemic, regional, dyadic, national, or individual actor. For instance, according to the realists, the underlying causes of war at the systemic level have been found in the anarchical structure of the international system, its distribution of power and changes in that distribution over time, and the collapse of balances of power, or alternatively, the decay of hegemonic powers (see Morgenthau and Thompson 1985; Waltz 1959, 1979; and Gilpin 1981). At the dyadic level, it has been posited that war is more likely to occur between pairs of states that are geographically contiguous, roughly equal in power, great powers, allied, undemocratic, economically underdeveloped, and militarized (Bremer 1992, 309, 338). Similarly, other scholars trace the roots of war to political, economic, social, and psychological factors located at the level of the nation-state, such as the type of political regime or economic organization (see Kant 1970; Lenin 1939), and the domestic political system in general (see Hagan 1994). Finally, war has also been explained by reference to the individual political leader, whether as a diversionary solution to his or her domestic problems (Levy 1989a, 1989b), or as a result of misperceptions, stress, or rational cost/benefit calculations (Jervis 1976; Lebow 1981; and Bueno de Mesquita 1981).

Explanations of peace should be arranged according to levels of analysis similar to those of the causes of war. At the systemic level, peace can be explained in terms of the evolving relationship between the great powers.

A "long peace" between the United States and the Soviet Union characterized the international system from 1945 until the end of the Cold War and the demise of the Soviet Union. It has been explained by alternative and complementary causes, including the presence of nuclear weapons, the replacement of a multipolar with a bipolar configuration of power, and a roughly equal distribution of military power between the two superpowers (see Gaddis 1991, 27; Mearsheimer 1990, 11).

At the regional level, commonplace explanations of peace have focused almost exclusively upon the region of advanced industrialized and democratic countries, the member states of the OECD. For example, Bruce Russett and Harvey Starr adduce five causes of peace among these states, as follows: (1) a response to a common threat by an external enemy; (2) the construction of supranational institutions, such as the European Union; (3) the development of strong economic ties and links of social communication; (4) the achievement and continued expectation of substantial economic benefits to all the members of the region; and (5) the acceptance of the values and institutions associated with liberal democracy (Russett and Starr 1989, 417–33).

At the dyadic level, peace has been associated with geographical distance, asymmetrical distribution of power between the parties, alliance links and third-party threats, economic development and prosperity, institutional and transnational links, lack of militarization, political stability, and democratic regimes (see Bremer 1993, 233–35; Ember et al. 1992, 574–75). Among these alternative explanations, the recent literature on international relations has emphasized the democratic dyad as a major theory of the causes of peace and war (Gleditsch 1993, 15). Although there is a growing consensus in the literature regarding the empirical validity of the proposition that democracies do not fight each other, there is still disagreement regarding the underlying causes of such phenomenon.

To sum up, most of the academic research addresses the classical questions on the causes of war and the conditions for peace. However, it does not cope with the related issue of how peace is preserved or even "deepened" once it is established. This issue is indirectly addressed in the study of security regimes, at least to the extent that negative peace is maintained and enhanced by decreasing the uncertainty and distrust that characterize international relations.[3] Yet, the establishment of security regimes is only a facilitating institutional framework to maintain peace at the dyadic or regional level; in itself, it is neither a necessary nor a sufficient condition for reaching and keeping it.

EXPLAINING THE MAINTENANCE OF REGIONAL PEACE

In contrast to the vast body of research on the causes of war (termination of peace), and the causes of peace (termination of wars), this book is concerned with the maintenance and deepening of peace at the regional level. Two research questions derive from this important issue: First, how can we explain the maintenance of international peace at the regional level? In other words, what are the necessary, sufficient, and favorable conditions for the longevity of different types of zones of peace? Second, can peace be kept among states in a given region that do not sustain democratic regimes? Is democracy a prerequisite, or a necessary condition, for the maintenance of peace at the regional level?

In practical terms, these two questions have also a direct policy relevance for the articulation of foreign policy. As Arnold Wolfers argues (1961, 138), "[B]ecause governments concerned with peace are interested in going beyond the mere prevention of open hostilities, much of their foreign policy or peace strategy is aimed at consolidating and stabilizing the peace."

To answer these questions I will examine alternative explanations for the maintenance of regional peace in the international system, and I will assess the necessary, favorable, and sufficient conditions for its resilience. I present three clusters of explanations for the maintenance of regional peace that are not mutually exclusive. The first cluster includes four realist and geopolitical conditions: (1) regional hegemony; (2) regional balance of power; (3) common threat by a third party; and (4) isolation, irrelevance, and impotence. The second cluster includes four liberal conditions: (1) regional democracy; (2) economic development and prosperity; (3) economic interdependence, integration, and transnational links; and (4) a normative consensus facilitated by a common cultural framework. Finally, the third cluster suggests a causal link between satisfaction with the territorial status quo and regional peace. This satisfaction is evidenced by the upholding of the international borders of states in a given region. This last explanation will be examined through consideration of the domestic and international sources of territorial satisfaction.

Realist and Geopolitical Explanations for the Maintenance of Regional Peace

From a realist perspective, the state of war is inherent to the anarchical international system. Although armed conflicts do not occur constantly, the possibility of war always persists. Thus, the maintenance of zones of peace in the international system is considered as an anomaly or puzzle to be explained through mechanisms and configurations of power that successfully prevent war. Four distinctive conditions seem to explain the persistence of zones of negative peace: (1) the presence of a regional hegemon; (2) a regional balance of power; (3) an external threat to the countries of the region; and (4) geographical isolation, irrelevance, and impotence to wage wars.

These four conditions combined respond to the logic of realism. Regional hegemons and balances of power (BOPs) are the two configurations of powers that explain the dynamics of peace and war at the systemic or subsystemic (regional) level. Both BOPs and hegemonic struggles are linked to the concept of external threats and alliance formation, both in intraregional and interregional (systemic) terms. In addition, when hegemons and BOPs are ineffective or irrelevant, peace can still be explained in pure power relational and geopolitical terms by the absence of material means to fight wars, impotence, geographical isolation, and irrelevance.

(1) The Presence of a Regional Hegemon
Like the logic of hegemonic stability at the systemic level (see Gilpin 1981; Bremer 1992, 10), the preservation of regional negative peace can be a function of the strong presence of a regional or extraregional actor, which performs the role of regional hegemon. According to Raymond Aron (1966, 152–53), hegemony can create and maintain peace by awing potential rivals. It is superiority of power, rather than equality or balance of power, that stabilizes and deepens the peace at the regional level; it does so by inducing and sometimes coercing the other surrounding countries to keep the existing international (regional) order. Through its paramount presence, the regional hegemon "relieves" the other neighboring countries from their inherent security dilemmas. My first hypothesis can be formulated as follows:

Hypothesis # 1: A zone of peace is more likely to be maintained when a state within or outside the region assumes the role of regional hegemon and induces or imposes a peaceful regional order among the countries of the region.

A regional hegemon is defined as a state that possesses sufficient power to dominate a regional subsystem. Three dimensions of power appear especially relevant to the exercise of its regional hegemony: the material or economic, the military, and the motivational (Myers 1991a, 5). Because of their size and self-conscious status, regional hegemons develop a vested interest in keeping a state of international peace in their regions, thus perpetuating a situation that underlines their paramount position and status.

The regional hegemon fulfills the role of peacekeeper, wherein peacekeeping is identified with the preservation of existing hierarchical relations among the countries of the region. Regional peace is then maintained through strength and the preponderance of power. It should be emphasized, however, that the exercise of regional hegemony does not always imply sheer coercion or use of military force, but rather the more subtle exercise of power through persuasion and socialization (see Ikenberry and Kupchan 1990).

(2) A Regional Balance of Power

A different realist explanation suggests that the maintenance of regional peace is not a function of preponderance of power, but rather of equilibrium and balance among a group of states in a given region. The major goal of the balance of power is to preserve stability, rather than peace (Bull 1977, 107). Hence, the most we can get through a balance-of-power system is regional peace based on prudent diplomacy as a by-product of power considerations within a permanent state of war (see Doyle 1983a, 220–24). Although the relationship between balance of power and peace is controversial, in principle both stability and peace can be achieved in multiactor systems, provided that unilateral attempts to use force are expected to be opposed by superior coalitions in favor of the status quo. Thus, a second hypothesis can be formulated as follows:

Hypothesis # 2: A zone of peace is more likely to be maintained when the states of the region develop and maintain a regional balance of power.

In ontological terms, it seems as if balance of power and maintenance of peace are contradictory terms. After all, a mechanism of balance of power is based upon the premise that states should be prepared to use force in a system of self-preservation. At the same time, the expected results of regional equilibrium tend to prevent war or, in other words, to promote negative peace. According to the logic of *Realpolitik*, the fabric of peace hangs everywhere on the thread of an equilibrium of power (Nelson 1994, 29). If balances of power work as expected, then there should be no wars. In sum, regional peace becomes the unexpected result of a quest for stability and equilibrium among the states of the region.[4]

The argument that peace is guaranteed by a balance of power implies a logic of deterrence. The stability of that peace is probably greater in bipolar rather than multipolar situations. In a regional multipolar context, a peace of equilibrium remains precarious, as there is always the possibility of shifting alliances. Nevertheless, when systems of regional balances of power have existed for long periods of time they are likely to create conditions propitious for the perpetuation of peace. They acquire a value of their own, so that states act to preserve them, leading incidentally to the maintenance of regional negative peace (see Melko 1973, 82, 183). The peace may be fragile, but it will persist as long as states respond to regional imperatives by forming alliances and counteralliances.

(3) An External Threat to the Countries of the Region

A third and related realist explanation suggests that the maintenance of regional peace is the result of common security interests, and even the establishment of a formal alliance among the states of the region against an external threat. Thus, the maintenance of peace is a consequence of nations coming together in response to a common threat by an external enemy (Deutsch 1957, 175). My third hypothesis reads as follows:

> *Hypothesis # 3: A zone of peace is more likely to be maintained when the states of the region confront a common threat emanating from a third party.*

According to this hypothesis, the countries of the region prefer to keep the peace among themselves because of the danger of war *between* regions. Thus, zones of peace can be regarded as by-products of polarization between different regions, as during the Cold War (see Russett 1967, 204; and Rapoport 1992, 166).

The assessment of threats from an extraregional third party is a slippery task, since the logic of alliance formations is governed by subjective perceptions of threat rather than by the objective conditions of the interregional or systemic balances of power (see Walt 1987, 17–22). Moreover, the analysis of the conditions under which an external threat promotes intraregional cohesion and cooperation, and thus helps to maintain the regional peace, entails knowing the prior diplomatic history of the region and its common perception of an external threat.

(4) Geographical Isolation, Irrelevance, and Impotence to Wage Wars
In contrast to the three realist explanations developed so far—a "peace of hegemony," a "peace of equilibrium," and a "peace of fear"—there is a fourth type of explanation, which can be labeled as a "peace of irrelevance" or "peace of impotence." This explanation is associated with geopolitical, technological, and institutional constraints that affect the power calculus of states and help to maintain regional peace. They include: geographical distance; natural and topographical barriers; technological advantages to defensive strategies and weapons, including the presence of nuclear weapons; and lack of political and economic means to wage war. The relevant hypothesis can be formulated as follows:

> *Hypothesis # 4: A zone of peace is more likely to be maintained when the states of the region are isolated from each other by geographical and natural factors, and by technological means that favor defense over offense. Moreover, institutional and political/economic constraints create a condition of impotence that favors the maintenance of regional peace.*

According to this hypothesis, there is a series of "environmental" factors that condition states in a given region to prefer peace. In the first place, countries in a region that are isolated from each other because of geographical, topographical, or other natural barriers will "enjoy" a dissociative type of peace, characterized by isolation and/or irrelevance (see Gleditsch 1993, 2–4). This peace of isolation and irrelevance approximates the ideal of autarky depicted by Jean-Jacques Rousseau more than two hundred years ago (see Rousseau 1953; Hoffmann 1987, 41–43). Moreover, this argument can be also formulated from a systemic, interregional perspective. According to this logic, regions that have been relatively isolated from great-power struggles have been more peaceful, such as in the cases of Scandinavia, South America, West Africa, and obviously Oceania/Australasia.

Second, technological factors might affect the value of maintaining regional peace. Such factors include technical military conditions and the likelihood or inevitability of wars (Rosecrance 1989, 54). In this regard, an offense-defense balance that favors defensive strategies and techniques over offensive ones tends to maintain peace (see Jervis 1978; Melko 1973, 183). Similarly, the presence of nuclear weapons among the countries of the region might provide a further incentive to preserve a "peace by terror," a minimal or negative peace maintained by nuclear deterrence (Aron 1966, 159). This nuclear peace can also be labeled as a "peace of impotence," given the futile prospects of any war.

Finally, institutional/political and economic constraints within the countries of a region might create the conditions for another version of the "peace of impotence." In this case the plain inability of states to initiate and wage international wars is due to lack of required means, both political (legitimacy) and economic (material wherewithal).

Liberal Explanations for the Maintenance of Regional Peace

From a liberal perspective peace at the dyadic or regional level is deemed possible and even normal, notwithstanding the anarchic structure of international relations. Hence, zones of peace are part and parcel of a complex and heterogeneous picture of an international society characterized by both zones of peace and zones of conflict. Zones of peace have been maintained and preserved due to four distinct and sometimes overlapping conditions: (1) the presence of liberal democratic regimes in a given region; (2) a high level of economic development and prosperity; (3) economic interdependence, integration, and transnational links; and (4) a normative consensus about conflict management and resolution, sometimes facilitated by a common cultural framework.

These four conditions together respond to the logic of liberalism, and they can be also linked to a neo-Grotian perspective. The *political* aspects of liberalism are evidenced in the pointed association between democracies and peace. In turn, the *economic* aspects of liberalism are emphasized by two overlapping, though distinctive, conditions: a certain level of economic development (prosperity), and a degree of interdependence and economic integration. Finally, the political and economic aspects of liberalism are complemented by cultural and normative arguments.

Although these four conditions might overlap and coexist, they appear in isolation and act independently from each other. For instance, cultural and normative arguments indicate a Grotian, but not necessarily a liberal political approach (e.g., a normative consensus among nondemocratic regimes, as in ASEAN). Moreover, political liberalism is possible without its economic components; there are democracies with low levels of economic development, as in South Asia or in Africa. Conversely, it is possible to have economic liberalism separated from political liberties; examples are the East Asian authoritarian regimes that are prosperous and interdependent. In sum, these four conditions might overlap and reinforce each other, but they are far from being identical.

(1) The Presence of Liberal Democratic Regimes

A general consensus has emerged in the literature of international relations that liberal democratic regimes do not fight each other. As Jack Levy (1989a, 88) emphasizes, "[T]his absence of war between democracies comes as close as anything we have to an empirical law in international relations." This agreement, however, is restricted to the description of the empirical phenomenon, not to its causal explanation. The effort to understand the democratic peace has yielded numerous attempts to revise or refute the Kantian "original" formulation, leading to sophisticated statistical analyses, including cross-cultural tests.[5]

Logically, we can posit that if the peaceful relations between democracies at the dyadic level is perfect, then a region composed of only democratic regimes will be by definition a zone of peace. Thus, we can deductively formulate a hypothesis that links the presence of liberal democratic regimes and the preservation of peace in any given region:

> *Hypothesis # 5: A zone of peace is more likely to be maintained when all the states in the region sustain liberal democratic regimes.*

According to this hypothesis, the political relations among the democratic countries in their zones of peace will not be influenced by their relative military power. In other words, the maintenance of peace becomes a direct result of the political regimes of the region being democratic (Singer and Wildavsky 1993, 3).

Why will democracies maintain peace in their regions? Given the fact that liberal democratic regimes are not more peaceful, in general, than their nondemocratic counterparts, a myriad of alternative explanations have been offered for this intriguing phenomenon. The Kantian explanations focus upon the normative consensus, political culture, and internal organization of states as the key to understanding war and peace (see Kant 1970). Nonliberal explanations stress the role of balances of power, hegemonic stability, and third-party threats as possible causes of this democratic peace. The democratic peace can also be explained with reference to the widespread satisfaction of democratic nations with the territorial status quo, high degree of domestic legitimacy, and their political stability and institutionalization.

In his essay on *Perpetual Peace*, Immanuel Kant (1970, 99–108) stated three "definitive articles" or conditions for the consolidation of a state of perpetual peace among sovereign nations: (1) "the civil constitution of every state shall be republican"; (2) "the right of nations shall be based on a federation of free states"; and (3) "cosmopolitan rights shall be limited to conditions of universal hospitality." Each of these three conditions—representative republicanism (liberal democracies in contemporary terms); respect for other liberal governments in the form of international law and normative consensus; and the cosmopolitan law expressed through the rules of hospitality, the "spirit of commerce" and transnational links—constitutes a necessary condition for reaching and maintaining peace. Together, these three "articles" make for a composite sufficient condition for the separate liberal zone of peace developed and maintained among democracies in the last two hundred years (see Doyle, 1983a, 1983b).

Following a global trend toward democratization in the late 1970s and 1980s, recently accelerated by the demise of the Soviet Union and the democratic transitions in Eastern Europe, international relations scholars have developed a booming industry of statistical analyses and "new theories" based on the insights originated by Kant. Nowadays, it is common to refer to "normative" and "structural" (or "institutional") explanations of this democratic peace. The normative explanation focuses upon the consensus developed by a common democratic political culture and a set of norms and rules that have allowed democracies to build a separate peace among them. Thus, democracy creates normative dispositions against war, derived from domestic norms of respect, autonomy, and "enlightened self-interest" that are externalized and extrapolated in relation to other fellow democratic regimes (see Starr 1992, 46; Russett 1993). By contrast, the structural argument maintains that domestic political institutions, with their emphasis upon accountability, constrain the choices confronting democratic decision-makers by reducing the possibilities of escalation and war with other democracies. These two explanations are logically related, overlap, and do not exclude each other.[6]

The normative and structural arguments assume that international outcomes (e.g., regional peace) are the result of internal factors (e.g., a similar democratic political system adopted by the countries of the region). If these explanations are correct, three implications follow. First, the persistence, deepening, and further expansion of regional peace are a function of domestic factors (such as the type of political regime), rather than of the international or regional distribution of power. Second, the presence of democratic regimes in a given region has a direct impact upon the quality of that regional peace. Third, the link between democracies and peace tends to create a self-perpetuating mechanism, by which democratization processes in a given region increase regional peace, which in turn stabilizes the new democratic regimes. Hence, there is a synergic effect involving democracies and regional peace.

In principle, one can accept the empirical validity of the correlation between democratic regimes and regional peace, while rejecting any causal link. Thus, the maintenance of peace among democracies in a given region could be epiphenomenal; it could be due to factors other than democratic norms and institutional restraints. In that case, the supposed causal relationship could be spurious, or at best irrelevant.[7] Moreover, if the phenomenon to be explained is peace at the regional level, and not only peace among the OECD countries, one must be aware that the democratic peace explanations are too limited and restrictive to "grasp" different types of peace in different regions of the world at different time periods.

(2) Economic Development and Prosperity
An alternative liberal explanation that proves the limits of the democratic peace argument is the one that focuses upon the level of economic growth and development and the indexes of economic prosperity. According to economic liberalism, the dominant feature of the contemporary zones of peace in the international system is the fact that their countries are prosperous and economically developed (see Singer and Wildavsky 1993, 12). The

assumption is that all the countries involved are interested in economic development and prosperity. In other words, the cost/benefit ratio of any war between economically developed countries seems extremely unpromising, or even "unthinkable" (Mueller 1989, 219). As a consequence, countries that have already reached a certain (high) degree of economic development and prosperity have a vested interest, or bias, in favor of keeping their peace. To sum up, the creation of a liberal economic order makes states more prosperous. In turn, this bolsters peace, since prosperous states are more economically satisfied, and satisfied states tend to be more peaceful. Accordingly, we can derive a sixth hypothesis, as follows:

> *Hypothesis # 6: A zone of peace is more likely to be maintained when all the states of the region are prosperous and economically developed.*

Wealth and prosperity become the key for the maintenance of regional peace, rather than liberal norms and democratic institutions. Hence, *economic*, not political, liberalism explains stability and peace. To maintain peace it becomes crucial to establish an international economic system (i.e., capitalism) that fosters prosperity and economic development for all the states in the system or subsystem (see Schumpeter 1950). Moreover, prosperity, economic development, and peace tend to reinforce one another. Since one of the first requirements for economic development is to have internal and external peace, regional peace is not only a consequence, but it is also a cause of further growth and prosperity. For instance, long periods of peace create conditions propitious to prosperity and economic development (Melko 1973, 181). Conversely, there is a clear evidence that many outbreaks of violent international conflict have been a result of a loss of prosperity and sustained economic failure (see Russett 1983, 381).

Whereas the democratic peace and the economic argument can be formulated as alternative explanations, in reality they are juxtaposed, as democracy and capitalism become inextricably linked. After all, most wealthy countries are democratic, while most democratic countries are wealthy. Thus, it is very difficult to discern which of the two is of primary importance in the maintenance of regional peace (see Parker 1994, 28–29). On the one hand, it can be argued that economic development is the driving force behind decisions made by *any* political regime, not just democracies, regarding peace and war (Merritt and Zines 1991, 229). On the other hand, if it is the case that higher levels of economic development have led to democracy, rather than to peace, then wealth is only indirectly related to the absence of war among industrialized countries since 1945 (Ray 1991, 5).

(3) Economic Interdependence, Integration, and Transnational Links
Economic development and prosperity are usually achieved through economic interactions between states in a given geographical region or across the international economic system as a whole. The prosperity-maintains-peace argument is closely related to a third liberal explanation, which links economic interdependence and trade, integration, and transnational transactions with the maintenance of regional peace.

According to the economic liberal doctrine, international economic interactions, through trade and other forms of interdependence, tend to create greater opportunities for mutual benefit through cooperation rather than confrontation. Thus, international economic relations and transnational links tend to reduce the likelihood of war. At the regional level, we can formulate the following hypothesis:

> *Hypothesis # 7: A zone of peace is more likely to be maintained when the states of the region establish relations of economic interdependence and integration at the interstate level, and transnational links among their peoples.*

This hypothesis underlines three dimensions of economic and social activity: economic interdependence, transnational links, and schemes of regional integration. All three are embedded within a neoliberal, functionalist approach to peace, according to which state sovereignty and political problems can be by-passed through economic and social constructions geared toward the establishment and flourishing of "peace in parts" (see Mitrany 1966; Clark 1989, 212; Dedring 1976, 92; and Thompson 1991, 340).

Relations of economic interdependence are usually established through the intensification of mutual financial and trade links. Trade is considered as a force for peace, either indirectly by promoting prosperity, which in turn brings and maintains peace, or directly, by enhancing the positive interdependence among nations in terms of frequency, volume, and scope of mutual beneficial transactions. As the functional web of interdependence further expands, it "raises the price" of violent conflict and thus bolsters the vested interest of the states involved to maintain their regional peace (see Nye 1971, 109–10).

Economic interdependence can also develop as a consequence of transnational transactions, beyond the interstate level of economic relations (see Keohane and Nye 1971, xix). The emergence of transnational linkages among individuals, private groups, and governmental agencies enlarge the interdependence among nations in a given region apart from the interstate (international) level. Moreover, transnational links of social communication can also enhance and maintain the regional peace, as it is postulated in the case of pluralistic security communities. According to this argument, ideas and people, as well as goods and services, penetrate and transcend national borders, helping to keep and to deepen the regional peace among peoples, and not only among states.

Moreover, transnational links and economic interdependence at the regional level might facilitate the creation of institutional schemes of regional integration. Regional integration is concerned with explaining how and why states voluntarily mingle, merge, and mix with their neighbors so as to lose several factual attributes of sovereignty (Haas 1971). A successful integration is reached when states in the region cease to prepare for war against one another and express a mutual commitment to preserve their regional peace. At a more intersubjective level, integration is achieved when there is a prevalence of mutually compatible self-images of the states participating in the process, up to the point of developing a common identity and mutual expectations of shared economic gains through their interdependence (see Deutsch 1957; Adler and Barnett 1996; Adler and Barnett, forthcoming).

Like the two previous liberal explanations, the interdependence-integration-transnational argument illustrates the point that there is not a single cause that can completely resolve the puzzle of regional peace. Moreover, the three explanations developed so far are logically concatenated through the liberal credo that liberal/democratic regimes, economic prosperity, and free trade by themselves and together promote and maintain peace in the international system (see Oneal et al. 1996).

(4) A Common Cultural Framework and Normative Consensus on Conflict Management

According to the political and economic liberal arguments presented so far, the maintenance of regional peace is associated with a series of common values related to the proper form of political regimes (i.e., democratic norms), economic standards (i.e., prosperity and economic development), and international and transnational links (i.e., interdependence, integration, and social and economic transactions beyond the realm of the sovereign state). These common values assume the existence of an international society with common norms, rules, and institutions that regulates the interactions among some of the member states of the international community, if not all (Bull 1977). This Grotian logic of an international society will suffice to explain the development of a common normative consensus on conflict management on a regional basis, even without necessarily endorsing all the liberal values emphasized above. We can formulate our eighth hypothesis as follows:

> *Hypothesis # 8: A zone of peace is more likely to be maintained when the states of the region sustain a normative consensus regarding the rules of international law to be implemented in the management and resolution of their international conflicts. This normative consensus is sometimes facilitated by a common cultural framework.*

The rationale of this hypothesis is composed of three different, though related dimensions: a cultural framework, a normative consensus, and its implementation through conflict management and resolution. In the first place, it is assumed that a "common universe of customs and beliefs" is the "true basis for international peace" (Levy 1989a, 84). A common culture or civilization on a regional basis implies a high degree of homology in terms of language and customs, which facilitates understanding and therefore the maintenance of regional peace (Galtung 1975, 35–36). Such common culture includes unifying elements like language, cosmic epistemology, religion, ethical code, and even aesthetic or artistic traditions (Bull 1977, 16). Furthermore, this leads to the development of a regional identity, or sense of "we-feeling" (see Deutsch 1957, 56–57; and Adler and Barnett, forthcoming), which is not necessarily restricted to the common political culture of democratic regimes.

A regional cultural framework is sometimes linked to a normative consensus among the countries of a region regarding certain "rules of behavior" among themselves and toward third parties. International norms usually reflect the value priorities and relationships of a particular cultural tradition within a region. This implies that the validity and effectiveness of such norms should be expected to break down at the boundaries between cultures and regions (see Johnson, 1991: 302). At the same time, a normative consensus can be established and institutionalized in spite of the lack of a preexisting regional culture or civilization. Likewise, there might be serious normative dissensus within the same culture or civilization.[8]

Turning to the normative dimension, I am specially interested in the rules of behavior dealing with conflict management, war, and peace. Charles Kegley and Gregory Raymond (1986) have shown persuasively that when states accept international norms such as *pacta sunt servanda* and alliance commitments, then the incidence of war is reduced. Hence, the maintenance of peace is associated with periods in which the dominant tradition in international law considers alliance norms binding and the unilateral abrogation of international commitments and treaties as illegitimate (see Vasquez 1994, 213). In the same vein, Peter Wallensteen (1984) refers to "norms of universalism" by which the major powers of a region or the system as a whole have tried to stabilize the territorial status quo by enhancing their normative consensus regarding conflict management and resolution. At the regional level, therefore, if a mechanism of normative consensus to cope with international conflict is well-established and entrenched, then international norms that enable political decisions to take place might fulfill a function equivalent to that of war (see Vasquez 1992, 1993, 1994).

The Missing Link: Satisfaction with the Territorial Status Quo and the Maintenance of Regional Peace

The liberal arguments asserted the existence, persistence, and deepening of the regional peace in terms of cooperation and even harmony, based upon democratic regimes, prosperity, interdependence and integration, and common culture and norms. By contrast, the realist explanations depicted regional peace as either a peace of power (preponderance or equilibrium), or as a peace of impotence and irrelevance. Although each of these alternative explanations and all of them pooled together seem plausible, they do not exhaust the range of possible causes for the maintenance of regional peace. On the conceptual level, we can envision a missing link between the realist and the liberal explanations, and between a "peace by power" and a "peace by impotence": a "peace by satisfaction." A world in which *all* the states were satisfied with the territorial status quo would be a world at peace (see Aron 1966, 160). In such a world states would seek neither territory external to that under their sovereignty, nor alien populations. However, since peace by satisfaction implies a general condition that is unattainable under the current international system, satisfaction is not coterminous with global peace; therefore, peace cannot be explained solely in terms of satisfaction with the territorial status quo.

At the regional level, however, the link between satisfaction and maintenance of regional peace can be posited as follows:

> *Hypothesis # 9: A zone of peace is more likely to be maintained if most, if not all, of the states of the region are satisfied with the territorial status quo.*

At first glance, this causal relationship between satisfaction with the territorial status quo and peace seems either meaningless or tautological. But a very large proportion of international wars, though by no means all of them, have been a product of dissatisfaction with existing boundaries, and attempts to forcefully change them (Boulding 1978, 109; Rummel 1981, 34; Maoz 1994, 7). Therefore, it makes sense to argue that satisfaction with the territorial status quo acts as a force for peace and its subsequent preservation. The main task remains, however, to explain *why* states in a given region are or become satisfied with the territorial status quo.

Satisfaction with the status quo refers basically to the territorial dimension, although it is not exhausted by it. "Status quo" refers in general to the economic, military, and diplomatic rules that govern a system or a subsystem at a certain point of time. According to Abraham Organski, the international or regional status quo is an "order" of stabilized relations. Disparate evaluations of the status quo—satisfaction versus dissatisfaction—are then potential sources of international conflict and war (Lemke and Werner 1996, 239). In Organski's own words,

> [For satisfied states] Everyone comes to know what kind of behavior to expect from the others, habits and patterns are established, and certain rules as how these relations ought to be carried on grow to be accepted. . . . Trade is conducted along recognized channels. . . . Diplomatic relations also fall into recognized patterns. Certain nations are expected to support other nations. . . . There are rules of diplomacy, there are even rules of war. (Organski 1968, 315–16)

Although intuitively one can understand the concept of satisfaction with the status quo in terms of volition and disposition to accept the existing regional order as such, it is not easy to measure it empirically. For instance, according to Zeev Maoz and Ben Mor (1995, 14–15), when an actor is satisfied with the status quo, she or he is likely to prefer it to any situation that may involve change. In terms of game-theory ranking, this means putting "CC" at the top of this actor's preference ordering. Moreover, this means that political motivations—satisfaction or dissatisfaction— are deemed more important than the mere assessment of the objective capabilities of the actors involved. Satisfaction and dissatisfaction with the territorial status quo can then be measured along a continuum of three ideal-type postures: (1) *active satisfaction with the status quo*, which implies a disposition not only to accept the existing order but also to uphold and defend it; (2) *passive satisfaction with the status quo*, which implies a passive or tacit acceptance of the given order, following a realization that there are no available means to change it violently; and (3) *dissatisfaction with the status quo*, which implies challenging the existing order verbally or through actual behavior, including military buildups, war preparations, and a general predisposition to use force to change the status quo (see Lemke and Werner, 1996).

An active satisfaction with the territorial status quo implies a normative acceptance of the existing borders and lack of territorial ambitions toward neighboring states. Thus, any change of borders is either inadmissible or subject to the prior peaceful, voluntary, and mutual approval of the states involved (see Kacowicz 1994a). Actively satisfied states have a vested interest in preserving the established regional and international orders. The more satisfied nations are with the established order, the more they are willing to make sacrifices to preserve the peace (Wolfers 1961, 134). Therefore, if all the countries of the region are satisfied states, it is expected that their regional peace will be maintained and even deepened.[9]

In logical terms, there seems to be a significant link between satisfaction with the territorial status quo and the maintenance of regional peace. But does this mean that satisfaction causes regional peace? After all, regional peace can occur because the dog does not bark (see Stein 1993, 12), or even because the dog *cannot* bark. To equate satisfaction with no open move to challenge the territorial status quo by forceful means is logically and empirically insufficient. For instance, we can think of a situation in which there is no challenge to the status quo because of lack of a material basis for that challenge, though ideologically there is a normative dissatisfaction with the status quo. In this case, we are back to the "peace of impotence" and to a state of passive satisfaction only. By contrast, states that are voluntarily committed to keep the territorial status quo, accept their international borders, and do not sustain territorial or irredentist ambitions toward their neighbors are actively (or "positively") satisfied.

The extent to which satisfied states are committed to keep the territorial status quo and, therefore, to maintain their regional order and peace, has to be measured both domestically and internationally in terms of norms of behavior and actual policy. Domestically, satisfaction is measured through the declaratory and actual policies of the ruling political elites and interest groups within their societies, including the configuration of a conservative political culture geared toward the preservation of the territorial status quo. Internationally, satisfaction is expressed through the development of international norms that support the territorial status quo across borders and generally in the region, as formulated by political elites, international law, and international public opinion. Moreover, at the underlying level of intelligence assessment, satisfaction is operationalized through the lack of revisionist intentions and territorial claims toward neighboring states.

As a consequence, and to avoid claims of circular reasoning, we should address the question *why* states are or become satisfied with the territorial status quo. I argue that satisfaction stems from two parallel and related sources: domestic and international. The domestic sources of satisfaction derive from the type of state, from the type of political regime, and especially from the link between the two. Conversely, the international sources of satisfaction are based upon the position states occupy in the regional and international hierarchies of power and prestige.

(1) The Domestic Sources of Satisfaction
To understand why states are satisfied with the territorial status quo in a given region we should look carefully not only at their type of political regime, but also at their type of state and degree of institutionalization, political stability, and domestic legitimacy (see Hagan 1994, 197).[10] Satisfaction can be explained in domestic terms as a result of the combination between two variables: the distinction between strong and weak states (vis-à-vis their societies), and the differentiation between democratic and non-democratic regimes. Accordingly, we can obtain a taxonomy of four possible ideal types, as follows:

(a) Strong states with democratic regimes. They are the typical satisfied (status quo) powers in their regions, and they enjoy a high degree of both domestic and international peace. The rationale for why strong and democratic states are satisfied has been eloquently expressed by Michael Walzer as follows:

> [W]ithin the world of liberal states, the ground of complaints and tumults on account of nationality has been largely eliminated. The pacific union is a union of satisfied nations. That satisfaction may have something to do with their liberalism; it also has something to do with the peace that marks their coexistence. (Walzer 1986, 231)

Thus, as full-fledged nation-states, well-established democratic countries have become satisfied with the territorial status quo and conservative in relation to the existing regional order. Since their nationalism has been completed, they usually do not sustain irredentist claims against fellow democratic nation-states. Thus, a "completed" nation—usually a strong state—tends to advocate a conservative policy both within and across the borders of its state, if and when it has a democratic regime. The national society is generally supportive of its state. Democratic nations also tend to have strong states in relation to their own societies: the idea of the state, its institutions, and its territory are all clearly defined and stable (Buzan 1983, 67; Holsti 1996).

In addition, strong and democratic states tend to have a stable and durable political system that discourages the "export" of domestic discontent into external conflict (Maoz and Russett 1992, 248; and Russett 1993, 29). There is a clear link between internal stability and legitimacy, domestic peace, and satisfaction with the status quo. Furthermore, those states enjoy a high degree of political institutionalization, which acts as a restraining or conservative force toward forceful attempts by societal forces to change the status quo both at home and across the borders.[11]

To sum up, strong and democratic states are usually satisfied with the territorial status quo because of the following reasons: (1) they are generally full-fledged nation-states, without irredentist claims, and they occupy a paramount position vis-à-vis their own societies; (2) in terms of international relations, they are usually strong powers, both from a military and a socioeconomic point of view; (3) as democracies, they share a normative consensus of international law and a common institutional framework, which reflect their inherent bias toward the status quo; (4) as democracies they are affected by domestic institutional constraints, which also favor the status quo; and (5) their high levels of economic growth, development, interdependence, and integration create a vested interest in keeping the existing regional and international orders.

At the same time, democracies have not been always satisfied with the status quo, especially beyond their zones of peace. Sometimes they have initiated wars out of dissatisfaction or misperceptions. For instance, Melvin Small and J. David Singer (1976, 66) recorded eleven wars between 1816 and 1976 in which democracies were on the side of the initiators. Moreover, democracies (whether strong or weak) can be dissatisfied with the status quo in relation to nondemocratic regimes (see Doyle 1983a, 1983b). Despite being active participants in the promotion of their exclusive zones of peace, democracies have intervened and fought wars beyond them (e.g., the United States in Korea and Vietnam; the United Kingdom in Egypt [1956] and in the Falklands/Malvinas [1982]).

(b) Strong states with nondemocratic regimes. These are usually the typical nonsatisfied (revisionist) powers in their regions. Although domestic conflict is absent, or at most latent or repressed, these states tend to be more involved in international armed conflicts than democratic regimes.

The combination of a strong state and a nondemocratic regime implies the absolute control of society by state institutions, which is the main characteristic of totalitarian regimes. In regional terms, these states usually tend to sustain revisionist claims toward the territorial status quo, unless they occupy an hegemonic position vis-à-vis the regional order or adopt an autarkic (self-enclosed) orientation in international relations. If they are not hegemons or self-enclosed, then they act as disruptive forces toward the maintenance of possible zones of peace. It is the combination of state strength and nondemocratic regimes that explains their proclivity for aggressive foreign behavior.

(c) Weak states with democratic regimes. Few of these states are consolidated nation-states. By definition, they enjoy some degree of domestic peace and a relatively high degree of international peace related to their status quo bias, which derives mainly from their democratic character.

The combination of weak states and democratic regimes creates a situation of contention and conflict within the domestic scene between the state and societal forces. Due to the democratic character of the regime, however, domestic conflicts are peacefully resolved or managed, so they are not usually "exported" or extrapolated into the international scene. Hence, weak and democratic states tend also to be satisfied with the territorial status quo for reasons similar to those of other (strong) democratic regimes, including a normative consensus of international law and domestic institutional constraints in favor of the status quo. Moreover, in contrast to them, it is also their institutional weakness that bolsters their conservative attitudes in international relations, in juxtaposition to their domestic turmoil.

Weak states with democratic regimes can be strong or weak powers in international relations. The former are consolidated nation-states and developed countries with a dominant liberal ethos, like the United States, in which the state is considered to be relatively weak vis-à-vis the societal forces.[12] The latter are new or weak democracies in the Third World, in which the state has not acquired the same degree of political institutionalization, legitimacy, and stability as of the most developed countries (see Rothstein 1992).

(d) Weak states with nondemocratic regimes. These are usually not consolidated nation-states. These states are immersed in serious domestic conflicts, which contrasts with the maintenance of the territorial status quo along their borders. While some of them are positively satisfied with the territorial status quo, others merely lack the means to change it (they are only "passively" satisfied). As Kalevi Holsti (1996) demonstrates, weak and nondemocratic states have been the loci of civil wars since 1945.

This category of states can be found mostly in the postcolonial Third World, including post-Communist central Asia. It parallels a weak position in international relations in terms of power and status. The main feature of the weak and nondemocratic states is the presence of domestic threats to the security (and even physical survival) of their nondemocratic political regimes and governments. These states have low levels of political institutionalization, legitimacy, and stability, as opposed to a high level of domestic conflict, which sometimes escalates into civil wars. Yet in contrast to what one might expect according to the diversionary theory of war, weak and nondemocratic states tend to be satisfied with the territorial status quo.

It is precisely their institutional weakness and sense of insecurity at home that explains the predisposition of weak and nondemocratic states toward the maintenance and promotion of their regional orders, a goal congruent with a strong status quo or conservative orientation (Ayoob 1989, 71; see also Job 1991, 12–13). This orientation translates into a positive (active) satisfaction with the territorial status quo and reciprocal respect for the inherited colonial boundaries, as in the case of most of the African states (Touval 1972, 33; Jackson and Rosberg 1982). According to this argument, the weakness of these states creates an explicit resolution to respect the territorial status quo in order to preempt possible secessionist claims from within; this focuses the efforts of the state in resolving domestic conflicts and building up its legitimacy. Moreover, even if these states want to change the status quo, they usually do not have the means to change it; hence, they are stuck at worst in a situation of "passive" satisfaction. Hence, dissatisfaction with the territorial status quo is very unusual and only appears in relation to other weak states (and weak powers).

This argument can be illustrated in the case of authoritarian regimes ruled by the military ("militocracies"), in several regions of the Third World. As Stanislav Andreski eloquently argues, there is little connection between military dictatorships and the preparation or waging of an international war. Thus, there seems to be an intrinsic "incompatibility between the internal and external uses of the armed forces, which makes them less apt for one if they are being employed for the other" (Andreski 1992, 104).

In sum, we can postulate that many countries in the Third World prefer the territorial status quo out of their institutional weakness at home, which is also reflected in their relatively weak position in the international hierarchy of power and prestige. As with strong states with democratic regimes, the reasons are various and not mutually exclusive: (1) Third World states support the territorial status quo when they are weak states vis-à-vis their own societies and anxious to gain international legitimacy of their ex-colonial borders; (2) nondemocratic Third World states are usually weak states and weak powers in international relations, both from a military and economic point of view; (3) weak Third World states have developed a normative consensus of their own in the form of a reciprocal respect for the international norms of territorial integrity and *uti possidetis;*[13] (4) frequent military coups act as a peculiar institutional constraint upon nondemocratic weak states by diverting attention from possible international to actual domestic conflicts; and (5), in general, weak states sustain a common interest in keeping the territorial status quo to focus their efforts in economic and social development and to enhance the legitimacy of their nondemocratic regimes.

From these four possible combinations we learn that strong states with well-established democracies are at peace with one another, in part because of their domestic characteristics, *but so are other, nondemocratic (weak) states*, although for very different reasons. In the short term, the impact of democratization in many countries of the Third World does not seem to affect the logic of this argument. While well-established democracies are usually strong states and status quo powers, new democracies among the developing countries might remain weak (both domestically and internationally), until they consolidate themselves in their emergent zones of peace. By contrast, the most volatile zones of the globe are those confronting strong and nondemocratic states, which still sustain irredentist and other revisionist claims vis-à-vis their weaker neighbors. To comprehend the extent of this logic, we should examine the *international* sources of satisfaction.

(2) The International Sources of Satisfaction

While the domestic sources of satisfaction focus upon the type of state and the political regime, its international sources refer to the position states occupy in the hierarchy of regional power and status and their degree of acceptance of the territorial status quo. The regional and international orders, like any other order, are ultimately based on power. On the international dimension, strong and democratic states are satisfied with the status quo since they have tended to be at the top of the hierarchy of prestige within their regions and in the international system as a whole. They are either the most powerful states in their regions or they are allied with them. Weak and nondemocratic states are also satisfied with the territorial status quo, but for the opposite reasons. Their weakness in international relations impedes them from changing the territorial status quo by forceful means, so they adopt an active or passive posture of satisfaction toward their borders and the regional order as a whole.[14]

According to Hans Morgenthau and Kenneth Thompson (1985, 53–56) and to Abraham Organski (1968, 365–71), the foreign policy of a satisfied nation aims at the maintenance of a given distribution of power at a particular moment in time, whereas the status quo is defined mainly but not solely in territorial terms. In international relations, the policy of the status quo (satisfied) state fulfills the same function as a conservative polity performs in domestic affairs. There is an intimate relation between satisfaction and power distribution, though the two are not identical. Moreover, the distribution of satisfaction may shape the effects of power distribution upon the conflict-proneness of the international system or subsystem (Stoll and Champion 1985, 76). In other words, the maintenance of peace in several regions of the world and in the international system as a whole seems to be directly related to a combination of both strength and satisfaction.

In international terms, the main variables that explain satisfaction with the status quo are the degree of power and the relative status states enjoy in their region and the international system as a whole. When there is a positive correspondence between degree of power and degree of status (position in the hierarchy of the system), then the expected result is satisfaction. By contrast, status discrepancy leads to attempts to change the status quo by forceful means in order to find a positive correspondence between power and status (see Gilpin, 1981). Accordingly, we can trace four possible logical outcomes, as follows:

(a) *The Powerful and High Status States.* They stand at the top of the pyramid of international relations in terms of power and status. These powers are usually strong and democratic states, with an inherent bias in favor of keeping the status quo both at home and in their immediate regional vicinity. By definition, these are satisfied states. Moreover, in regional terms, we can also envision the possibility of nondemocratic states that are also powerful and with high status sustaining a hegemonic position vis-à-vis subordinated neighboring states.[15]

In historical terms, the major modern democracies (i.e., the United States, France, and Great Britain) have been usually satisfied with the status quo in their immediate international vicinity, since they have been the dominant powers in their regions and in the international system as a whole. As Edward H. Carr points cogently,

> Just as the ruling class in a community prays for domestic peace, which guarantees its own security and predominance, and denounces class war, which might threaten them, so international peace becomes a special vested interest of predominant Powers. . . . Today, when no single Power is strong enough to dominate the world, and supremacy is vested in a group of nations, slogans like "collective security" and "resistance to aggression"

serve the same purpose of proclaiming an identity of interest between the dominant group and the world as a whole in the maintenance of peace. (Carr 1964, 82)

These sentences, which were written in 1939, are still relevant in the context of the post–Cold War era. In the interwar period, Britain and France were democracies and status quo powers that confronted rising revisionist powers, which happened to be also nondemocratic (Italy and Germany). A similar interest of Great Britain in the nineteenth century and of the United States in the second half of the twentieth century to preserve the peace and the international order was related to the fact that these two nations were both democracies and the dominant powers in the international system. This inherent bias toward the preservation of the international status quo might help to explain not only why democracies do not fight each other, but also why they tend to form alliances among themselves: their common interest in maintaining the status quo leads to a community of interests among them (Stoll and Champion 1985, 77; see also Lake 1992).

(b) The Powerful and Low Status States. This category of states includes strong powers that do not enjoy the status they think they deserve; therefore, they tend to be dissatisfied with the status quo. As Abraham Organski suggests, "[W]hen nations are dissatisfied and at the same time powerful enough to possess the means of doing something about their dissatisfaction, trouble can be expected" (Organski 1968, 366). Thus, the powerful and dissatisfied states fulfill the role of "challengers" or "wreckers" of the regional and international orders, disrupting the maintenance of possible zones of peace in their quest for hegemony. In domestic terms, these are usually strong states with nondemocratic regimes.

(c) Weak Powers with High Status. These weak powers tend to be satisfied with the territorial status quo, so that they accept the regional and international orders in positive terms. They enjoy a relatively high status in their regions and derive from the status quo certain benefits in terms of domestic stability and legitimacy. In spite of the fact that these weak powers do not dictate the rules of behavior and norms of the international system or region, they enjoy a privileged position at the regional level. Thus, they develop a vested interest in preserving the regional peace. This category of states can be found among the so-called second-rank powers, both among the

developed countries and the developing ones. In domestic terms, they include strong and weak states, with democratic and nondemocratic regimes.

(d) Weak Powers with Low Status. This category of powers is mostly restricted to states in the developing world, which usually lack the material power to change the territorial status quo. The majority of these powers are weak states with nondemocratic regimes. Three alternative outcomes may take place. First, there are weak powers that are conscious of their low status in the regional and international hierarchy and accept it because of domestic considerations such as institutional weakness (active satisfaction). Second, there are weak powers that perceive a discrepancy between their (low) power and (low) status. In this case, they resent the status quo and aim at changing it. Yet they do not have the means to challenge it, so they are compelled to accept the status quo as it is (passive satisfaction). Third, there are weak powers that are dissatisfied and ready to change the status quo vis-à-vis other weak powers by violent means.

It becomes clear now that satisfaction with the territorial status quo is an intervening variable for which we might look for deeper and perhaps multiple causes.[16] Linking the domestic and international sources of satisfaction leads to the following preliminary conclusions:

1. Notwithstanding the type of state, degree of power, and relative status, most of the democratic regimes tend to be conservative in relation to the territorial status quo in their regions, especially vis-à-vis fellow democratic regimes;

2. Dissatisfied powers vis-à-vis their regions are usually strong and nondemocratic states, which might be strong or weak powers in international relations. If they are strong powers (such as Germany up to 1945), they suffer from a status discrepancy that leads to their dissatisfaction. Conversely, if they are weak powers, their status discrepancy is a result of misperceptions and/or miscalculations.

3. Weak states tend to be also weak powers, with the possible exception of the United States. In general, most of the weak states tend to be actively satisfied with the territorial status quo, notwithstanding the configuration of their international power and status. Thus, the weaker the state, the greater its tendency to respect the territorial status quo in order to cope with its domestic threats. The result is a fragile international peace and the persistent of virulent domestic conflicts, including civil wars.

4. Weak and nondemocratic states and powers that enjoy a relatively high status in their regions tend to be actively satisfied with the status quo. Conversely, weak and nondemocratic states and powers with a poor status might be satisfied with the status quo because of either "positive" reasons (i.e., the willingness to focus their efforts at home), or "negative" reasons (i.e., they lack the material power to change the undesired status quo).

A THEORETICAL FRAMEWORK TO EXPLAIN ZONES OF PEACE

Once we have examined the different explanations, it is necessary to group them together in a framework that attempts to define the maintenance of zones of peace in terms of necessary, sufficient, and favorable conditions. At this point, it is important to differentiate among the three types or gradations of zones of peace; namely, negative peace, stable peace, and pluralistic security communities.[17] They are ordered in a logical and gradual sequence, according to which each "superior" stage assumes the existence and persistence of its inferior predecessor. In other words, pluralistic security communities assume the existence of stable and negative peace, while stable peace presumes a previous condition of negative peace. This framework is summarized in table 2.1.

Conditions for the Maintenance of Negative Peace

Since negative peace has been defined strictly as the absence of war, there are no necessary conditions for its maintenance. Peace can be maintained on a precarious basis by a series of causes, including threats, balance of power and deterrence, hegemony and preponderance, a lack of will or capabilities to engage in violent conflict at a certain time, or even plain luck and serendipity.

In a zone of negative peace, it will be enough for the member states to be satisfied with the territorial status quo in order to keep their regional peace. This satisfaction might be only passive. Moreover, the maintenance of zones of negative peace does not require the presence of democratic regimes. Hence, authoritarian and autocratic regimes can be members of that zone of peace, especially if they are part of weak states and weak powers.

Furthermore, there are several favorable conditions that might facilitate

Table 2.1. A Framework for Explaining the
Maintenance of Zones of Peace

Negative Peace

Favorable Conditions	*Necessary*	*Sufficient*
Some democracies	None	Satisfaction with the
Economic prosperity		territorial status quo
Interdependence		
Economic integration		
Normative consensus		
Regional hegemony		
Balance of power		
Third-party threats		
Geographical irrelevance		
Impotence		
Deterrence		
Plain luck, serendipity		

Stable Peace

Favorable Conditions	*Necessary*	*Sufficient*
Economic Prosperity	Normative consensus	Democracies
Interdependence	Satisfaction with the	
	territorial status quo	

Pluralistic Security Communities

Favorable Conditions	*Necessary*	*Sufficient*
Economic prosperity	Interdependence	Interdependence
Regional hegemony	Economic integration	economic integration
Third-party threats	Normative consensus	normative consensus
Democratic regimes	Satisfaction with the	Satisfaction with the
	territorial status quo	territorial status quo
		Democratic regimes

the maintenance of regional negative peace. They include: (1) the presence of at least some democracies in the region; (2) a relatively high degree of economic prosperity and growth; (3) a relatively high degree of interdependence and economic integration; (4) a common cultural framework, which sometimes translates into a normative consensus; (5) the overarching presence of a regional hegemon; (6) a stable regional balance of power; (7) a common third-party threat; and (8) geographical irrelevance and institutional impotence.

Conditions for the Maintenance of Stable Peace

A zone of stable peace is characterized by the fact that the states of the region take their national boundaries off their agendas, except by mutual agreement. International war becomes implausible, if not impossible (see Boulding 1990, 7). Moreover, by a gradual learning process, the parties develop a common normative framework about how to manage and resolve their international conflicts by peaceful means. Thus, two conditions seem necessary for reaching stable peace: an active satisfaction with the territorial status quo, and a common normative framework, sometimes enhanced by a common culture.

We can postulate that the presence of well-developed democratic regimes within all the countries of the region will guarantee by definition the maintenance and even expansion of a zone of stable peace. Thus, notwithstanding the character of the state (e.g., weak or strong) and its position in the hierarchy of the region (i.e., high or low), democracies constitute a sufficient, albeit not a necessary, condition for stable regional peace.

In addition to these conditions, according to the liberal logic, economic prosperity, interdependence, and integration facilitate the stabilization of regional peace. By contrast, realist and geopolitical factors, which had a positive impact upon negative peace, become quite irrelevant.

Conditions for the Development and Maintenance of Pluralistic Security Communities

The highest level of regional peace that can be reached is the formation and maintenance of pluralistic security communities. There is a great overlap between stable peace and pluralistic security communities, the difference being that the latter implies an even higher sense of community and insti-tutionalization through the emergence of a regional identity, the sharing of similar political systems (such as democratic regimes), political institutions, and economic interdependence. In the case of these security communities, the questions of development and maintenance of peace seem to converge; after all, these communities grow out of a condition of stable peace, so that the factors that explain their peaceful trajectory also help to understand their subsequent evolution.

According to the original formulation of Deutsch and his associates, two conditions seem essential for the attainment of pluralistic security com-munities: (1) compatibility of political values associated with common po-litical institutions, such as common democratic norms; and (2) links of social communication that reflect a sense of community and shared identity (an intersubjective "we-feeling") among the members of the region, in-cluding mutual empathy and loyalties. Thus, Deutsch et al. hypothesized that if a population in a given region shares values, common memories, self-images, interests, identifications, and goals, its members communicate and transact on a wide range of issue areas. These communication links reflect a dynamic process of mutual attention, perception of needs, and responsiveness in the decision-making process.

In terms of the conditions elaborated in my theoretical framework, three seem to be necessary for the development and maintenance of plural-istic security communities: (1) a continuing satisfaction with the status quo, which is compatible with dependable expectations of peaceful change; (2) a common normative framework, which incorporates the two essential Deutschian conditions indicated above; and (3) a high degree of interde-pendence, integration, and transnational links.

While the first two conditions are identical to those of a region of stable peace, the third emphasizes the institutional and transnational aspects of pluralistic security communities. In this context, we should ask what role democratic regimes play in the development and persistence of these communities.[18] Although the presence of democratic regimes is not a nec-essary condition for the formation of these communities, in the long run it becomes the main guarantee for their preservation. Moreover, in empirical terms, it can be demonstrated that democratic regimes (especially within strong states and powers) tend to cluster within these security communities.

By contrast, we can clearly stipulate the *sufficient* conditions for the maintenance of pluralistic security communities. Each of the necessary conditions described above is not sufficient in itself; it is only the aggregation of active satisfaction with the status quo, common normative framework, high degree of interdependence, integration, transnational links, *and* the presence of democratic regimes in the region that *together* guarantee their maintenance. In addition, economic prosperity, regional hegemony, and common third-party threats favor or facilitate their emergence and preservation.

CONCLUSIONS

Throughout this chapter I have briefly reviewed the literature that addresses the causes of war and the conditions of peace at the dyadic, regional, and systemic levels. From this review, I concluded that in logical and empirical terms there is an intrinsic link between causes of war and the maintenance of peace at the systemic, regional, and dyadic levels.

War and peace are obviously overdetermined; that is, there are a myriad of alternative explanations to account for these complex phenomena. Among them, I have formulated nine explanations for the maintenance of regional peace, grouped in three different clusters. The first cluster comprises four realist and geopolitical explanations, as follows: (1) the presence of a regional hegemon; (2) a regional balance of power; (3) an external threat to the countries of the region; and (4) geographical isolation, irrelevance, and impotence to wage wars. The second cluster includes four liberal explanations: (1) the presence of liberal democratic regimes in a given region; (2) a high level of economic development and prosperity; (3) economic interdependence, integration, and transnational links; and (4) a common normative consensus about international conflict management and resolution. The last cluster refers to satisfaction with the territorial status quo as a complementary explanation for the maintenance of zones of peace. I have traced the domestic and international sources of satisfaction, including the type of state and political regime and the degree of power and status in the region.

At first glance, it seems quite obvious that states will maintain peaceful relations among themselves if they are satisfied with the territorial status quo, though absence of war is not always a precise indicator of satisfaction. A better indicator would be a domestic and international declaratory policy committed to keep the territorial status quo, which is translated into a conservative foreign policy regarding territorial claims. Even more intriguing, however, is the fact that different states and regimes are satisfied with the territorial status quo for different reasons, linked to their domestic characteristics and to their international position in their region.

After presenting nine alternative explanations, I have designed a framework stating the necessary, sufficient, and favorable conditions for the maintenance of negative peace, stable peace, and pluralistic security communities. Territorial satisfaction is considered a sufficient (but not necessary) condition for negative peace, but a necessary (though not sufficient) condition for stable peace and for pluralistic security communities. Conversely, the presence of democratic regimes is a sufficient (but not necessary) condition for the maintenance of regional stable peace. As far as pluralistic security communities are concerned, the presence of democratic regimes, together with interdependence and economic integration, a common normative framework, and territorial satisfaction constitute a composite sufficient, though not necessary, condition for their emergence and subsequent evolution.

Through this deductive exercise I have indirectly entered the ongoing debate on explaining the causes of democratic peace by suggesting that democracies keep the peace among themselves since they are conservative powers, usually satisfied with the territorial status quo within and across their borders. In this way, I have expanded the Kantian argument by including elements from a more realist perspective in both domestic and international dimensions. I would agree with the liberals that the picture depicted here is heterogeneous, being a function of different political regimes. But I would also concur with the realists that any explanation of the peace among democracies has to take into consideration their power position in the hierarchy of prestige of their region and even in the international system as a whole.

In logical terms it is indeed possible to argue that nondemocracies will establish and maintain peaceful relations among themselves, and with democracies as well. Hence, it is better to refer to distinctive historical and geographical *zones* of peace rather than to an exclusive democratic zone of peace. The liberal approach might explain the quality of that peace and the transition from negative to stable peace and to pluralistic security communities. It seems that democratic states are the most capable of maintaining a pluralistic security community among themselves in the long run. Here lies the strength of the liberal explanation. Its weakness derives from the attempt to depict the liberal arguments as the only causes for the absence of wars among democracies. Ironically, liberals have been too much absorbed in drawing distinctions between war and peace and between democracies and nondemocracies, instead of emphasizing the special quality of their liberal peace.[19]

If the formation and maintenance of zones of peace is not the solely prerogative of strong and democratic states, then we should look at case studies in the developing world in which long periods of international peace have persisted at the regional level, despite the absence of democratic regimes and before the last wave of democratization that has also swept the Third World. In the next two chapters, I turn to an empirical analysis of South America and West Africa as a way to test these different explanations of zones of peace.

CHAPTER 3

THE SOUTH AMERICAN ZONE
OF PEACE, 1883–1996

In this chapter I analyze the South American zone of peace. First, I present a narrative of its international relations since 1883, emphasizing different gradations of regional peace from negative peace through the development of an incipient pluralistic security community in its Southern Cone. Second, I assess the alternative explanations for the maintenance of this long South American peace. Finally, I summarize the conditions for its maintenance.

Within Latin America we can clearly distinguish between two regions or subsystems: Middle America (Mexico, Panama, Central America, the Caribbean islands and rimlands) and South America, composed of the Northern Tier countries (Colombia, Venezuela, Suriname, Guyana, and the French colony of Guiana) and the Southern Cone countries (Argentina, Brazil, Chile, Peru, Bolivia, Paraguay, Uruguay, and Ecuador).[1] The South American region is defined by three clearly established criteria: geographic proximity within a common physical boundary; the extent of an intersubjective regional perception of collective identity, including the views of the external actors about the region; and a high level of interactions among the countries involved, especially since the 1960s (see Atkins 1989, 24–29; Van Klaveren 1984, 5; Kaufman 1976, 68–77; Astiz 1969, 13–14; and Agor and Suarez 1972, 153–54). Some authors exclude from South America the Northern Tier countries because of their links to the Caribbean area, Mexico, and the United States. Although I include them in my analysis, my inquiry will focus upon the Southern Cone.[2]

In general, the South American nations are larger, more stable, and stronger as states than their counterparts in Central America. In terms of international relations, they have been less dependent upon the United States, more open to economic, cultural, and political relations with Europe, and much more concerned with their own intraregional rivalries (Pastor 1992, 24). Furthermore, in contrast to Central America, the South American countries have been characterized by their relative isolation from the mainstream of international politics; they have been relatively beyond the global security agenda of the former East-West confrontation. As a consequence, ideological and superpower elements were much less significant within its regional dynamics. Paradoxically, despite the eminent Pax Americana since the turn of the century, more interstate armed conflicts and military interventions have occurred in Central America and in the Caribbean region than farther south in the Americas.

Unlike other areas of the developing world, South America has been one of the most harmonious regions in terms of absence of international wars. Despite the frequency and intensity of several territorial conflicts,[3] there have been only two wars in the twentieth century between South American states: the Chaco War between Bolivia and Paraguay in 1932–1935; and the Ecuadorean-Peruvian brief war of 1941 (followed by a sequel of iterated armed skirmishes in 1981 and 1995). The region has been beset by internal conflict, military coups, and virulent civil wars.[4] Moreover, military threats and other uses of military force, short of war, have been a consistent means of communication in the foreign policies of several countries. However, war has been the exception rather than the rule since 1883. The puzzle, then, is the following: Why have there been so many territorial conflicts but so few international wars? How can we explain this South American long negative peace? A multitude of answers can be offered, including many of the hypotheses presented in the last chapter. Among the explanations are: (1) the common historical, cultural and normative background of the South American countries, and their predilection for peaceful settlement of international disputes; (2) their concern with economic development and growth; (3) the pacifying effects of several cycles of democratization in the region; (4) the preponderant role of the hemispheric hegemon, the United States (Pax Americana); (5) the positive role played by Brazil, a potential regional hegemon; (6) the low level of economic, political, and military interactions among the South American countries, at least until the 1960s; (7) their sparsity of population and concern with domestic threats of security; (8) their dependence and subordinate position in the international economy vis-à-vis the great powers; (9) the persistence of an informal balance of power among Argentina, Brazil, Chile, and Peru; (10) the impact of geographic and geopolitical factors, leading to a peace of irrelevance characterized by defense dominance; (11) the lack of ethnic conflicts and irredentist claims, or of disputes whose resolution seems essential; (12) the relative strength of some key states in South America, such as Brazil and Chile; and (13) the satisfaction of most of the South

American countries with the territorial status quo, associated with the lack of significant territorial claims, with the exceptions of Bolivia and Ecuador.

This notable absence of international wars and relative isolation from the Cold War confrontation has led South Americans themselves to recognize and promote a juridical *zone of peace*, meaning by that a comprehensive concept of stable peace, disarmament, and more recently, a democratic perspective of regional security (Somavía 1992, 20). For instance, Argentina and Brazil cosponsored a proposal to create a zone of peace and cooperation in the South Atlantic, which was adopted as a resolution by the United Nations in November 1986. This proposal included several objectives, such as

> the promotion of the pacific resolution of interstate conflicts, the enhancement of the mutual trust and cooperation among the member-states, the respect of the principle of non-intervention in the domestic conflicts, prohibition of nuclear weapons, of extra-continental military bases, and the development of common policies to avoid the involvement of the region in the military conflict between the superpowers.[5]

Similarly, in the words of the former Argentine president, Raúl Alfonsín, this South American zone of peace "should become an expression of international law, realize regional integration, defend world peace and multilateralism, and search for global justice" (Alfonsín 1992, 30–37).

This South American concept of zone of peace can be criticized as being too comprehensive and diffuse in its attempt to link political, military, and socioeconomic dimensions. By contrast, my own use of the term is simpler and its scope more humble; the rest of the chapter deals with the absence of international wars, assessing why in South America there has been an inclination to *deal* with international disputes rather than to fight over them, and examining how this one-hundred-year zone of peace was upgraded from the mere absence of war (negative peace) to stable peace and the impossibility of war, at least in the Southern Cone since the early 1980s, and finally inched in the direction of a pluralistic security community in the 1990s. In this sense, the South American region in general and its Southern Cone in particular are an appropriate empirical laboratory to examine the changing quality of intraregional relations in the absence of war. Moreover, with the cyclical changes of political regimes and the last (third) wave of democratization since the late 1970s, South America offers an excellent case to test the effects of democratization upon this long peace.[6]

To what extent is the remarkable longevity of this South American peace an anomaly? South America has been the most peaceful area in the developing world in the twentieth century, and was so even before its political regimes became democracies (Holsti 1996). "Peaceful," however, refers *only* to the absence of international wars, not to domestic conflict. Hence, the anomaly is restricted to the dimension of international relations, not to the lack of political violence in general. With the advent of democratization since the late 1970s, international peace has been extended also to the domestic sphere, the result being a movement toward stable peace. We should turn now to examine the historical record of these transformations, before and especially after 1883.

The Historical Record: A Narrative of South America's International Relations

Because of their subordinate position vis-à-vis the United States and some European powers, the history of the relations among the South American nations has been usually neglected in favor of the study of U.S.–Latin American relations. Yet, the key for regional war and peace in South America has always resided in its intraregional international relations, rather than in any external influence, be it that of the United Kingdom in the nineteenth century or of the United States in the twentieth century.

The historical record of South America can be divided into the following periods: (1) a *formative* period, from 1810 to the 1870s, characterized by international and civil wars and widespread anarchy; (2) a period of *consolidation* between 1883 and 1919, with the emergence of more stable and stronger nation-states, a continental balance of power, and the triumph of liberalism (after the Pacific War [1879–83], this second period initiated the long negative peace); (3) the *interwar years*, from 1920 to 1945, which witnessed the Great Depression and its concomitant economic crisis and two serious armed conflicts in the region; (4) the *postwar* period, characterized by the U.S. hegemony from 1945 to the end of the 1960s, and a subsequent decade of "national security" doctrines typified by renewed tensions and militarized disputes among the countries of the region in the 1970s, but without escalating into wars; and (5) the *advent of democratization* in the 1980s, leading to the upgrading of peaceful relations into stable peace and the emergence of an incipient pluralistic security community in the Southern Cone in the 1990s.

The Formative Period: South America as a Zone of Conflict, 1810–1870s

In contrast to other areas of the developing world, the new South American states were already independent in 1810. Yet the wars of independence and the process of state formation were long and bloody—fifteen years of independence wars against Spain (1810–24), followed by another fifty years of intraregional and civil wars. Six postcolonial wars took place between 1825 and 1883: (1) the First Argentine-Brazilian War of 1825–28, which led to the independence of Uruguay as a buffer state; (2) the Peru-Gran Colombia War of 1828–29; (3) the War of the Peruvian-Bolivian Confederation (1836–39), involving Chile and Argentina against Peru and Bolivia; (4) the "Great War" (La Guerra Grande) of 1836–52, consisting of different factions of Argentina and Uruguay, Brazil, and short interventions by France and the United Kingdom; (5) the War of the Triple Alliance (1865–70), pitting Argentina, Uruguay, and Brazil against Paraguay; and (6) the War of the Pacific (1879–83), confronting Chile with Peru and Bolivia. Furthermore, in undeclared engagements Peru attacked Bolivia at Ingavi in 1841; Peruvian troops landed in Ecuador in 1859; and Ecuador and Colombia invaded each other's territory in 1862 (see Burr 1965, 1–2). All these wars took place in connection with the legal ambiguities of the inherited colonial borders after independence and subsequent local rivalries, so they could be considered as postcolonial wars. Furthermore, given the political instability and domestic anarchy that characterized most of the new states in South America, with the exceptions of Brazil and Chile, some of these wars overlapped with civil wars and domestic conflicts. In sum, unclear national boundaries, chaotic public finances, and internal political strife created the conditions conducive to conflictual intraregional relations, as well as to the sporadic intervention by European states (see Ray 1991, 220–21; and Davis 1977, 16).

During these formative years, boundary disputes held high priority in the foreign relations of the South American states, leading to wars and consequent problems of irredenta, revanchism, and nationalism that extended well into the twentieth century. At the same time, all of the South American states accepted by the mid 1830s the principle of *uti possidetis* of

1810, whereby the boundaries of the new states should coincide with those of the former Spanish administrative colonial divisions, sustaining their juridical basis (Clissold and Hennesy 1968, 403; Lyon 1973, 32–33). Moreover, throughout this entire period the new states entertained a lingering spirit of solidarity, keeping the idea of Hispanoamerican cooperation alive in a series of congresses designed to implement some form of political integration, such as at Panama, 1826; Lima, 1847–48; Santiago and Washington, 1856; and Lima, 1864–65.

Because of the disrupting legacy of the interminable wars of independence and the physical difficulties in implementing the norm of *uti possidetis*, the escalation of territorial conflicts into international wars remained commonplace until the later part of the nineteenth century. With the prominent exceptions of Brazil and Chile, all the states in the region were immersed in long periods of civil war and political instability that obstructed the process of state-building and consolidation, further contributing to a widespread climate of political violence.

In sum, in its formative period South America was a typical zone of conflict, characterized by both international and civil wars, military interventions, political instability, changing alliances, struggles for subparamountcy in the Atlantic and River Plate basin that involved two wars and the creation of Uruguay, and a parallel struggle in the South Pacific area among Chile, Bolivia, and Peru, leading to the Chilean hegemony there following the Pacific War of 1879–83.

The Period of Consolidation: Balance of Power, Liberalism, and Negative Peace, 1883–1919

This second period was characterized by six simultaneous and related phenomena: (1) the domestic consolidation, material progress, and economic development of the most important states of the region—Argentina, Brazil, and Chile, the so-called ABC powers; (2) the formation of a continental system of power politics, consisting of a balance of power that became institutionalized into a concert or condominium among the ABC powers until 1923; (3) the peaceful territorial expansion of Brazil; (4) the integration of the region into the world economy, under the aegis of the United Kingdom until the end of the nineteenth century, to be replaced after that by the U.S. economic paramountcy; (5) the triumph of the liberal ideology, expressed both domestically and internationally through the establishment of oligarchic democracies, the institution of free trade, and the emphasis upon economic development in a peaceful atmosphere; and (6) the absence of international wars.

Following a long and painful formative period, the major South American states finally stabilized their national structures and developed more or less stable political regimes and relatively strong political institutions. The process of consolidation included the centralization of the national government and the emergence of a state bureaucracy and national armies; the development of infrastructure, national institutions, roads, and education plans; the absorption of European immigration, linked to external investments that contributed to shape the national center; and the diversification and intensification of external relations with European powers, especially through the economic paramountcy of Great Britain and the cultural impact of France. Brazil, which was already a stable and relatively strong state, continued its vigorous growth under Pedro II and subsequently under the republic after 1889. Chile, after a brief civil war in 1891, established a parliamentary republic that lasted until 1925. Argentina, after fifty years of anarchy and civil war, emerged as a federal republic and gradually became an oligarchic democracy and the most developed country in the entire region by the turn of the century. Peru, after a long military-civilian conflict that lasted until 1895, established civilian rule until 1919. Similar, though more difficult, processes took place in Ecuador and Bolivia. Colombia, immersed in persistent domestic violence, lagged well behind.

A continental balance of power emerged in the region in the 1870s, after the war against Spain (1864–66) and the defeat of Paraguay in the War of the Triple Alliance (1865–70). Before that, Brazil, Peru, and Chile had been concerned with the power politics of their respective sub-regions. It was the emergence of a fourth South American power, Argentina, that helped the Atlantic and Pacific subsystems be integrated in a general balance of power. Moreover, it was only after the Chilean victory in the War of the Pacific (1879–83) that this balance of power involved a large number of South American states (see Burr 1955, 1965). In 1898 and again in 1901, Argentina and Chile were on the verge of war over their unresolved boundary dispute along the Andes; then, in May 1902 they reached a comprehensive understanding in their famous Pacts of May. They explicitly recognized each other's sphere of influence and stopped an exhausting arms race through a naval disarmament agreement.[7] After the rapprochement with Argentina, Chile managed to sign a final treaty of peace with Bolivia in 1904, according to which Bolivia recognized the absolute and perpetual ownership of Chile throughout the coastal zone. In addition, Chile improved its relations with Ecuador and Colombia, which sustained territorial disputes with Peru, and with Brazil and Paraguay, against Argentina. As for its relations with Peru, it took until 1929 to resolve the Tacna-Arica issue, a focus of irredentism and Peruvian revanchism. Conversely, to restore the equilibrium caused by the growth of Chilean power following the Pacific War, Argentina collaborated with Bolivia and Peru and reached an entente with Brazil.

The period from 1883 to 1919 can be regarded as an institutionalized balance of power among Argentina, Brazil, and Chile, a kind of "ABC Concert." Chile maintained its short-lived hegemony in the South Pacific, while Brazil and Argentina disputed their long-term paramountcy in the South Atlantic/River Plate area. Not only conflict, but also regional cooperation characterized the relationship among the ABC powers; the cooperation was formalized in their Tripartite Treaty of 1915, mediation and good offices in the Mexican-U.S. dispute, the Leticia conflict, and agreements on naval limitations (see Bailey 1967, 58; Ruiz Moreno 1961, 87). The ABC concert ended in the early 1920s when, in terms of power, Chile was left behind both Argentina and Brazil.

Between 1895 and 1909 Brazil managed to expand its territory and settle peacefully its border disputes with its neighbors. Under the leadership of the Brazilian foreign minister, the baron of Rio Branco, Brazil won approximately 342,000 square miles of territory at the expenses of all of its neighbors, with the exception of Peru. These brilliant Brazilian diplomatic achievements were accompanied by a policy of equilibrium and balance of power with Argentina in the River Plate area and a shift of Brazil's diplomatic axis from London to Washington, initiating a long unwritten alliance with the United States and against Argentina (see Burns 1969, 177–80; Roett 1984, 189).

As mentioned above, this period of consolidation coincided with the firm integration of the South American countries into the world economy. The economic relationship between the region and Europe after the 1870s could be described as "neocolonial." The advance of a primary export economy in most of Latin America signified the maturity of its neocolonial order in the final quarter of the nineteenth century, leading to the growing economic interest of the United States in the region and its several Pan-American initiatives since 1889 (see Halperín Dongui 1993, 118, 158, 161). As development and growth progressed in South America, investment flowed from the industrial countries, especially the United Kingdom. Between 1870 and 1913 the value of Britain's investments in Latin America went from 85 million pounds to 757 million pounds in 1913 (Skidmore and Smith 1992, 44). To attract foreign investment, political stability both within and across borders was considered essential. Thus, both the liberal doctrine and the structural conditions of dependency created strong incentives to keep peace domestically and internationally.

This era of consolidation embodied above all the triumph of liberalism. Republicanism, the supremacy of the secular state, pragmatism and positivism, or, as the Brazilian called in their national flag's motto, "order and progress," political stability, and the formation of semidemocratic, oligarchic regimes, characterized most of the South American states in the first two decades of the twentieth century (see Bushnell and Macaulay 1994, 286–90; Bethel 1989, 225–38). In international relations, the export economies of South America were closely tied to the international trading system, there were no wars in the region, and the United States emerged as the paramount power after 1904, following the withdrawal of the British presence in the Western Hemisphere.

The Interwar Period: Economic Crises, Political Changes, and Regional Wars, 1920–45

The third period in the history of South America's international relations was less harmonious and more violent than the former one; it was characterized by both continuities and momentous changes. In their relationships with each other, the South American states continued to be involved in boundary disputes and power politics. Chile's expansionism came to an end with its agreements with Argentina, Bolivia, and Peru, and its South Pacific hegemony gradually subsided. Brazil and Argentina continued their traditional rivalry in the River Plate area, this time disputing their quest for subparamountcy in the entire region (see Roett 1984, 190–91). The United States became more prominent in the region through economic and diplomatic activities. Above all, the long regional negative peace since 1883 was interrupted by two interstate wars (the Chaco War of 1932–35 and the Ecuador-Peru War of 1941), in addition to a severe militarized crisis that did not escalate into war (Leticia 1932–34). Finally, the Great Depression of 1929 reverberated into economic and political crises throughout the region.

The international relations of the 1920–45 period were dominated by the Argentine-Brazilian rivalry in the Southern Cone and by the U.S. diplomatic presence in the entire region. Following the Good Neighbor Policy of President Franklin D. Roosevelt, the United States increased its political involvement, which coincided with a regional climate of diplomatic initiatives. For instance, in 1923 and again in 1933 the Latin American foreign ministers agreed on a declaration to prevent armed conflicts among their nations (Varas 1983, 71). But these rhetorical commitments to peace did not prevent the eruption of two serious wars—the Chaco War and the Peruvian-Ecuadorean War.

The territorial dispute between Bolivia and Paraguay over the Chaco Boreal led to a long and bloody war in 1932–35 (about one hundred thousand casualties, according to Goldstein 1992, 200). In the colonial period the disputed area had been administered at various times as part of either Paraguay or Bolivia. After independence, neither state had been very much concerned with this inhospitable area. Bolivia and Paraguay were both the big losers of the two major wars of the nineteenth century —Paraguay lost territory to Brazil and Argentina in 1865–70; Bolivia lost its seacoast to Chile in the War of the Pacific in 1879–83. Since 1906, Bolivia was looking for a port on the Pilcomayo River in the Chaco to get access to the River Plate system and the Atlantic Ocean. Conversely, Paraguay was searching a way to recover its lost national honor, so it referred to the Chaco Boreal dispute as a matter of national survival. Both nations were revisionist and frustrated states, landlocked countries dependent on others for their trade route with the outside world. For them, the issues leading to the war were far from trivial. The Chaco War was a major event in the international relations of the 1930s, damaging the reputation of the League of Nations and eroding South American solidarity. By 1935, Paraguayan forces had established full control of the Chaco region and a truce was negotiated through the good offices of the United States and Argentina, leading to an international peace conference and the 1938 treaty that gave Paraguay most of the contested area.[8]

The second war that took place in South America during this period involved Peru and Ecuador in July 1941. They have had an old territorial dispute from their time of independence, claiming an area of about eighty thousand square miles lying to the north of the Marañón River, not far from the Amazon River. Their boundary conflict over the "Oriente" resulted from a confusion in border definition of the former colonial units and the emergence of wild rubber as a potential resource in the area. Despite occasional efforts at mediation (such as in 1936–38), no solution was found, and border skirmishes became frequent. They escalated in July 1941 into a short but intensive undeclared war, culminating with a Peruvian blitzkrieg into Ecuadorean territory. On 29 January 1942, Ecuador was compelled to accept the Protocol of Rio de Janeiro, negotiated between the parties through the mediation of the United States and the ABC powers. Its terms were stern. Ecuador recognized the Peruvian sovereignty over the disputed territory and surrendered another five thousand square miles. The new boundary line not only caused Ecuador to lose two-thirds of the Oriente Province, which she considered her own, but also deprived her of an outlet to the Amazon River. Ecuador subsequently became a revisionist state, declaring the protocol null and void in 1960. The conflict had not been resolved by the war of 1941, and was reignited in 1981 and most recently in January 1995.[9]

The territorial dispute between Peru and Colombia was initially resolved by negotiations in Lima in 1932. However, in September of 1932 Peru illegally occupied a strip of Colombian territory next to the Amazon River called the "Leticia Trapezium." Threats of war and skirmishes between the two countries took place in 1933; yet the crisis was peacefully managed through the Council of the League of Nations and the good offices and mediation of the United States and Brazil. An agreement was reached in May 1934, leading to the Colombian reoccupation of the disputed area.[10]

In the long term, this breakout of interstate violence in the 1930s and early 1940s was less consequential for the political future of South America than the effects of the worldwide economic crisis that erupted in 1929. International peace returned to the region after 1941. But the world depression of the 1930s put an end to the liberal era in Latin America until the early 1980s. In political terms, many democratic regimes crumbled under military coups, leading to unstable cycles of authoritarianism, such as in

Argentina, or to authoritarian and populist regimes, such as the dictatorship of Getulio Vargas in Brazil. In economic terms, between the late 1930s and the 1960s the major South American states adopted an economic policy of ISI (import-substitution-industrialization), designed to accelerate the growth of a manufacturing sector intended to serve national markets at the expense of traditional exports. Liberalism was buried, and an uncertain period of change and political anomie followed.

The Postwar Period: Pax Americana, Geopolitics, and the Persistence of Negative Peace, 1945–70s

Since World War II peace has been maintained in South America, initially under the aegis of the U.S. hegemony (Pax Americana) and later on, in the 1970s, in spite of the U.S. decline and the predominance of geopolitics and national security doctrines among the major South American powers as an omen of renewed tensions and potential wars. Three distinctive themes dominated the agenda of this period: (1) the U.S. hemispheric hegemony and the building of Pan-American institutions such as the Organization of American States (OAS) in the late 1940s and 1950s; (2) the emergence of schemes for regional economic integration, as a counterpoise to Pan-American institutionalization and as a way to strengthening the ISI economic policies in the late 1950s and 1960s; and (3) the prevalence of geopolitical national security doctrines, which coincided with military authoritarian regimes in the 1970s.

From the middle of World War II and throughout the mid 1960s, the United States was the dominant actor in the Western Hemisphere, the largest trading partner and capital investor, and the dominant force behind Pan-American initiatives and its military, economic, and political institutions. Between 1945 and 1948 the inter-American system was institutionalized through the Chapultepec Act of 1945, the Inter-American Reciprocal Assistance Treaty of 1947 (Rio Treaty), and the Bogotá Conference of April 1948, which created the OAS. A regional system of military and political cooperation was established under the leadership of the United States. It was designed to formally promote the peaceful settlement of international disputes and to encourage intraregional trade. But the different priorities of the United States and those of Latin America quickly became evident: for the United States, the OAS was a useful regional mechanism of collective security to pursue its global fight against communism; for the Latin Americans, the new Pan-American institutions were supposed to promote economic growth and development in the Americas.

Between 1945 and 1960 an outside power—the United States—played a powerful role as the economic engine of the region, just as it did in Europe; a normative and cultural affinity among the Latin American states reflected a common idea of regional solidarity, and there were domestic pressure groups within the different countries that promoted the idea of integration, both economic and political, alongside an emergent epistemic community in the form of the UN Economic Commission for Latin America (ECLA) in favor of regional autarky, developmentalism through ISI, and regional integration (see Bawa 1980, 116). As a result, in the late 1950s and 1960s Latin America experienced a strong wave of integration schemes. In 1960 the Latin American Free Trade Association (LAFTA) was established, contributing to the expansion of reciprocal trade and the promotion of regional markets to support ISI. The subsequent disappointment involving LAFTA led to further attempts to salvage integration through the formation of subregional groups. The most ambitious and interesting scheme among those was the Andean Pact (ANCOM), established in 1969 by Peru, Chile, Ecuador, Colombia, and Bolivia, and later on joined by Venezuela. The same year Argentina, Bolivia, Brazil, Paraguay, and Uruguay organized the La Plata Basin Group (Cuenca del Plata), for the purpose of developing subregional hydroelectric power and water resources. In July 1978, Bolivia, Brazil, Colombia, Ecuador, Guyana, Peru, Suriname, and Venezuela signed the Amazon Cooperation Treaty in order to promote the scientific and economic cooperation of the contiguous Amazon basin territories of the eight signatory countries. In August 1980, the moribund LAFTA was replaced by the Latin American Integration Association (LAIA), instituting greater flexibility and differentiating among diverse levels of economic development. However, its basic economic philosophy did not reveal substantial changes as compared to LAFTA. This long wave of economic integration did not fulfill the promised goals of economic development and growth, political coordination, and autarky vis-à-vis the developed countries.

Since the mid 1960s the hemispheric position of the United States was increasingly challenged, especially in the South American region, resulting in a relative decline of U.S. influence and a growing pluralism in the distribution of power. South America gradually recaptured its contours as an independent subsystem (Atkins 1989, 42–43). In domestic terms, many of the South American countries experienced military coups and experienced authoritarian governments dominated by the armed forces. The continuing ideological impact of the United States and the Cold War was expressed in the adoption of a doctrine of national security, according to which the local armed forces should include among their duties internal warfare against "subversive" agents, and a leadership role in the development of the national economy (see O'Donnell 1976, 1986, 1988).

In international relations, the "low politics" agenda of the 1950s and 1960s was replaced in the 1970s by a "high politics" diplomacy of national security. Once the armed forces "defeated" the internal (real or supposed) subversion and ran into serious difficulties with their expanded political and economic roles, they turned their internally oriented doctrines outwards, leading to the intensification of interstate disputes. Thus, under the influence of geopolitical ideas, many South American armies in the mid 1970s returned to their traditional missions of external defense, focusing upon their neighbors as rivals for regional leadership, natural resources, market outlets and investments, and the control of strategic borders (Ronfeldt and Einaudi 1980, 195; and Selcher 1984, 110–11). This was a particularly dangerous period in which the regional peace was at best precarious, and war remained a real possibility. Several militarized crises affected the major countries of the region, including a possible military confrontation between Chile and Peru in 1975 and an almost-certain war that was narrowly avoided by serendipity and bad weather in December 1978 between Argentina and Chile over the Beagle Channel. "Conflict hypotheses" (war plans) and arms races were widespread throughout the region, reviving the old balance-of-power alignments of one hundred years earlier. The countries with the largest military budgets were Brazil, Argentina, Chile, Peru, and Venezuela. Argentina and Brazil engaged in an arms race that included the development of ballistic missile technology and nuclear potential. Similarly, an accelerated buildup of Soviet military arms in Peru was regarded with considerable alarm by Chile and Ecuador, leading to intensive modernization plans, indigenous arms industries, and diversification of military supplies. The possibility of armed conflict over the disputed territories contributed in itself to the acceleration of this arms race. However, the regional negative peace proved to be resilient, with two exceptions: First, there was another round in the Peruvian-Ecuadorean unresolved territorial dispute in the Cordillera del Cóndor, which escalated into a brief outbreak of fighting in January–February 1981. Two hundred soldiers were believed to be killed, and there was a further impasse. Second, there was the Falklands/ Malvinas War of April–June 1982, involving Argentina and an extraregional power, the United Kingdom. Interestingly enough, most of the analysts who wrote about South America in the early 1980s predicted widespread armed conflagrations throughout the region. They were proved wrong. They probably overemphasized the pernicious aspects of geopolitics and national security doctrines, while ignoring the enduring factors that kept a precarious peace among the South American nations amidst domestic violence and militarized crises.[11]

The Contemporary Period: Democratization, Integration, the End of the Cold War, and the Advent of Stable Peace, 1980–96

The period of national security doctrines and militarized interstate disputes lasted for only a decade. By the late 1970s and early 1980s, a widespread process of democratization swept away the military governments in the entire region, with the exceptions of Paraguay and Chile (until 1989). The security dilemma was partially resolved through the democratization process, leading to a quantitative and qualitative improvement of the bilateral relations, especially those between Argentina and Brazil, and between Argentina and Chile.[12] With the advent of democratization, a second wave of integration revamped old schemes of regional integration (like the Andean Group) and created new and promising ones (foremost among them, the Common Market of the South [MERCOSUR] of Argentina, Brazil, Paraguay, and Uruguay). The concomitant end of the Cold War signaled the triumphal return of liberalism, the renewed focus upon economic growth and development, and a new regional security agenda including issues such as drug traffic, environmental problems, and migration flows (see Hirst 1994, 73–79).

Democratization in South America was a result of a series of factors, such as the delegitimization of the military regimes, serious economic crises, the resurgence of civil society, the support of socioeconomic elites, the external blessing of the United States and the Western European countries, and a kind of "domino democratic effect" that spread from Ecuador and Peru to the other Southern Cone countries. The return of civilian regimes signified a clear retreat from the pernicious geopolitical bases of foreign policy; instead, regional cooperation and integration were favored. In the Southern Cone the initial Argentine-Brazilian rapprochement of 1979 was enlarged after both countries returned to democracy, leading to bilateral economic integration and later on to the establishment of MERCOSUR. The new democratic government in Argentina also managed to resolve its long dispute with Chile over the Beagle Channel in 1984. But these new democracies are still fragile and the question for the late 1990s remains whether the political gains of the 1980s can be consolidated in face of the lingering domestic problems. Nowadays, Colombia and Peru face internal wars like those that had led to the militarization of nominally civilian re-gimes. Guyana and Suriname are still experiencing painful transitions to democracy amidst ethnic cleavages. The rest of the countries of the region, however, have managed to keep and expand their political liberties, though they have to cope with serious socioeconomic grievances due to their macroeconomic reforms.[13]

If the 1970s were characterized by tensions and militarized disputes, the 1980s and early 1990s have witnessed a new impetus to regionalism, both in political and economic terms. In political terms, the Central American crisis of the 1980s led to attempts at regional political consultation and consensus *(concertación),* such as the Contadora Group, the Group of Eight, and the contemporary Group of Rio, which includes most of the South American countries, plus Mexico and Panama. In economic terms, the latest wave of economic integration recreated the Andean Group of 1969 and the Amazon Pact of 1978, while creating MERCOSUR on the basis of the Argentine-Brazilian Integration Program of July 1986. Nowadays, we have at least twelve schemes of integration in the Americas, seven of them involving South American states: (1) LAIA, since 1980; (2) the Andean Group, since 1969; (3) MERCOSUR, since March 1991; (4) Chile-Mexico Free Trade Agreement, since 1991; (5) the Group of Three (Colombia, Venezuela, and Mexico), since 1993; (6) the Colombian-Venezuelan Free Trade Agreement, since 1992; and (7) Chile-Venezuela Free Trade Agree-ment, since 1993. The reasons for this "integrative fever" have been vari-ous: the increase in intraregional trade; the fear of the uncertain future of the international political economy and the formation of regional blocs; the Initiative for the Americas of President Bush in 1990; the establishment of NAFTA; the improvement in the political climate regarding the resolution, if not management, of outstanding territorial disputes; and political motivations, including the need to enhance the democratization process. Hence, we have not seen in South America a unilinear progression or a "spillover" process, but rather a "spill-around process" of overlapping bilateral and multilateral agreements. An impasse in one scheme of integration typically led to the creation of yet another scheme (Klaveren 1993, 118).

The establishment of MERCOSUR in 1991 has been by far the most important and promising scheme of regional integration in the whole of Latin America. If it succeeds, it would become one of the most important economic foci of the developing world, with half of the population of Latin America (about 195 million), a GDP of $785 billion in 1994, and over $100 billion in total foreign trade (Bouzas 1995, 3).

The antecedents of MERCOSUR can be traced back to the early 1980s, when Argentina and Brazil had adopted a series of accords aimed at promoting bilateral cooperation in such areas as nuclear development, military exchange, and transport communications. In 1986 Presidents Alfonsín and Sarney signed the Argentine-Brazilian Economic Integration Program (ABEIP). The ABEIP represented a breakthrough in their bilateral relations, after a century-long struggle for subparamountcy in South America. Its significance was primarily political, not economic: setting aside decades of rivalries and competition in order to create the basis for a long-term cooperation. There was a period of economic instability in the second half of the 1980s, but in July 1990 Presidents Menem and Collor signed the Buenos Aires Act that broadened the scope of this integration effort. Finally, on 26 March 1991, the foreign ministers of Argentina, Brazil, Paraguay, and Uruguay signed the Treaty of Asunción, which called for the creation of the Common Market of the South (Mercado Común del Sur - MERCOSUR) by December 1995. MERCOSUR was created as an instrument to facilitate the consolidation of democracies at home and the productive transformation and economic liberalization of each country, together with its competitive entry into the world markets (Peña 1995, 115).[14] Furthermore, MERCOSUR, as the largest customs union in the developing world, might become an important locomotive of growth for the entire region. It could also become the basis on which to build SAFTA, the South American Free Trade Area, as a counterweight to NAFTA (Naím 1995, 56).

Recap: Negative Peace, Stable Peace, and a Pluralistic Security
Community in South America

In the last one hundred years only two serious wars were fought in South America, and only one of these, the Chaco War of 1932–35, could be compared in duration and intensity to a European one. At the same time, numerous territorial disputes and rivalries have taken place, some of them lingering at the time of this writing, such as those between Venezuela and Guyana, Venezuela and Colombia, Bolivia and Chile, and Peru and Ecuador. The Peruvian-Ecuadorean dispute in particular has been characterized by cyclical escalations around the anniversary of the Rio Protocol by the end of January, such as in January 1981 and, most recently, in January 1995. Notably absent from this contemporary list are the century-old rivalry between Argentina and Brazil that ended in the 1980s and the long territorial dispute between Argentina and Chile that had led the two countries to the verge of war in several occasions (in November 1878, September 1898, December 1901, and especially in December 1978), until they peacefully resolved their dispute over the Beagle Channel in their peace treaty of 29 November 1984.

Among the South American international disputes the Argentine-Brazilian rivalry was the longest and most deeply rooted, and the one most influenced by geopolitical doctrines (Child 1984, 33; 1985, 99–100). It had important reverberations in the domestic and international politics of the region as a whole and a direct impact upon the three buffer states—Uruguay, Paraguay, and Bolivia—in particular. From the second half of the nineteenth century to the late 1970s, the relationship between the two major powers of the region was a complex mixture of conflict and cooperation. In the bloody Chaco War Argentina and Brazil supported opposing sides. Since the early 1920s and especially after World War II, the two countries have often been immersed in an arms race that included the development of nuclear technology, have adopted diametrically opposed positions regarding the role of the United States in the region, and have engaged in a fierce competition over resources such as Paraguayan hydroelectric energy and Bolivian oil and gas. The possibility of an armed conflict remained a very tangible element in the military planning of the two countries until the late 1970s. The Argentines regarded Brazil as an expansionary military, economic, and demographic power that threatened areas to its south, west, and southwest (see Guglialmelli 1979). Conversely, the Brazilians regarded their smaller neighbor with suspicion and uneasiness, fearing the kind of volatility and aggressiveness that Argentina demonstrated in its invasion of the Falklands/Malvinas in April 1982 (see Selcher 1985, 29-30). At the same time, the Argentine-Brazilian rivalry never escalated into militarized crises such as those between Argentina and Chile; moreover, their enduring rivalry did not include opposing claims to a disputed territory, such as that between Peru and Ecuador. Furthermore, the two countries sustained a long history of cooperation on regional and functional issues. A turning point occurred in 1979, when their respective military regimes came to a resolution of the hydroelectric conflict over Paraguay and a gradual rapprochement that included economic and military cooperation. The launching of the ABEIP in 1986, which epitomized the upgrading of their bilateral relations in the direction of stable peace, was followed by the signing of the Mendoza Agreements of September 1991, which banned chemical and biological weapons in Argentina, Brazil, and Chile, and by the Foz do Iguaçu Declaration of 12 December 1991, which established a binational cooperative organization of nuclear cooperation (a Brazilian-Argentine Agency for the Accounting and Control of Nuclear Materials, ABACC). There came to be a high number of institutionalized military exchanges and mutual visits between the two armies. As Thomas A. O'Keefe, president of Mercosur Consulting Group, cogently summarized, "The whole hypothesis of war between Argentina and Brazil has been junked. . . . I don't think that anyone in the Argentine military or in the Brazilian military still sees the other as a potential threat."[15] Thus, stable peace has become firmly established between these two core countries of South America.

In contrast to the Brazilian-Argentine quest for prestige and influence, Argentina and Chile confronted the problems of one of the longest land frontiers in the world and a history of territorial disputes and militarized crises, leading to occasional armed clashes that always stopped on the verge of war. Throughout the nineteenth century, both Chile and Argentina claimed the southern Patagonia region. After concluding a boundary agreement in 1881 they resolved most of their territorial differences, though the conflict over the Beagle Channel lingered until 1984. The long Beagle Channel dispute revolved about the issue of how and where to define the dividing line between the South Atlantic (Argentina's sphere of influence) and the South Pacific (Chile's sphere). The dispute turned into a serious international crisis in 1978, following Argentina's rejection of a British arbitration award giving three Beagle Channel islands to Chile. Argentina's military government adopted a hard-line policy that included military moves and serious threats of war. In December 1978 war was narrowly avoided, perhaps providentially, by a severe South Atlantic storm that prevented a naval confrontation between the two countries, and by a last-minute papal diplomatic intervention. After intense negotiations that lasted for five years, Argentina and Chile finally signed the Treaty of Peace and Friendship on 29 November 1984, which was endorsed by a vast majority of Argentine citizens in a plebiscite. In the treaty, Chile's sovereignty over the Beagle Channel islands was recognized, though there was an explicit limitation about projecting its sovereignty beyond a surrounding twelve-mile-wide zone. The 1984 treaty signaled an important improvement in their bilateral relations, which were further strengthened after Chile's return to democracy in 1989. In 1990, both countries signed an agreement of economic integration (Acuerdo de Complementación Económica) that included the construction of a gas pipeline from Neuquén (Argentina) to Santiago (Chile). In 1991, Chile and Argentina settled several minor border disputes by negotiations and tripled their bilateral trade. Chilean investments in Argentina have jumped from about $100 million in 1989 to $2 billion in 1994 (Brook 1994). As in the Argentine-Brazilian case, stable peace has become an enduring reality across the Andes, in spite of lingering territorial disputes, such as the Laguna del Desierto arbitral award (this time in favor of Argentina). Since August 1988, Chile and Argentina have held joint naval exercises in the Beagle Channel area. Although the Argentine military have probably reached a better understanding with their Brazilian colleagues than with their Chilean counterparts, Chilean officers have participated as observers since 1992 in the military meetings and exchanges of the four MERCOSUR countries (see Hirst and Rico 1992, 30–40). Moreover, together with Argentina and Brazil, Chile contributed to the reform of the Tlatelolco Treaty on the prohibition of nuclear weapons in the region and became a signatory in January 1994. It also ratified the Mendoza Declaration banning other weapons of mass destruction.

   This improvement in the bilateral relations has not been restricted only to the ABC countries. For instance, Paraguay and Bolivia, the former enemies of the Chaco War, have recently embarked on common developmental projects, including the construction of a trans-Chaco highway. After the return of democracy in 1989, Chile notably improved its relations with Peru. In the Northern Tier, Colombia and Venezuela established with Mexico the "Group of Three" in 1993, a forum of political consultation and economic integration. The bilateral trade between Colombia and Venezuela has increased notably, reaching $1.6 billion by 1993 and doubling since their free trade agreement of 1992. Despite their long-time border dispute, officials of the two sister republics promise that they will settle their differences through dialogue, thus adopting a "make talk, not war" policy that notably contrasts with the policy of their Peruvian and Ecuadorean neighbors. Yet it would still be premature to characterize the Colombian-Venezuelan relations as a firmly institutionalized stable peace. In March 1995, following the cross-border attacks by Colombian guerrillas on Venezuelan soldiers posted at the frontier, both countries increased their military presence along their common border, so that an armed conflagration between them still remains a possibility.

In sum, while in the mid 1970s all the foreign relations among the South American countries could be at best considered as a reality of negative peace (mere absence of war), by the mid 1990s we find a more diversified zone of peace, with an array of different relations: an active focus of conflict between Peru and Ecuador; a core of stable peace among the ABC countries, including also the buffer states of the Southern Cone (Uruguay, Paraguay, and Bolivia) and the bilateral relations between Brazil and its neighbors, with the possible exceptions of its relations with Suriname, Venezuela, and Colombia; and several foci of negative or unstable peace, such as between Chile and Bolivia, Venezuela and Guyana, Guyana and Suriname, Chile and Peru, and Colombia and Venezuela. This complex set of relationships is summarized in figure 3.1.

From the reading of this figure, we can draw several conclusions. First, active and potential conflicts in South America have been refocused in the Northern Tier of the region; they are linked to new security issues such as illegal drug traffic, transnational guerrilla movements, and domestic political instability. Second, the Peruvian-Ecuadorean territorial dispute is the only one in South America that has moved back and forth between negative peace and armed conflict. Third, stable peace characterizes the relationships among the three major powers of the region: Argentina, Brazil, and Chile. Their improved relations have also affected the other countries

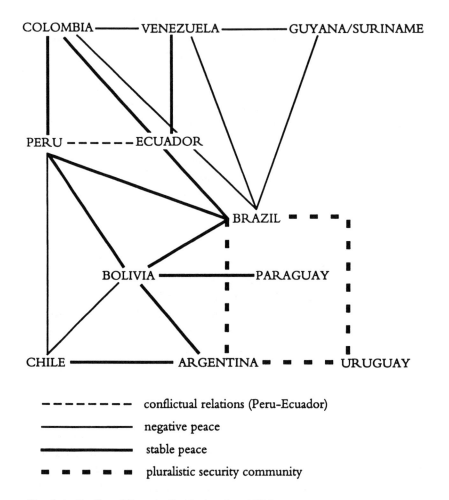

COLOMBIA——————VENEZUELA——————————GUYANA/SURINAME

PERU ——————— ECUADOR

BRAZIL

BOLIVIA——————————PARAGUAY

CHILE————————————ARGENTINA——————URUGUAY

——————————— conflictual relations (Peru-Ecuador)
———————————— negative peace
———————————— stable peace
■ ■ ■ ■ ■ pluralistic security community

Fig. 3.1. Quality of Peace in South America, 1996

of the Southern Cone: Bolivia, Uruguay, and Paraguay. In this sense, we can refer to Brazil and Argentina as the core of an incipient pluralistic security community.

EXPLAINING THE SOUTH AMERICAN LONG PEACE, 1883–1996

According to the theoretical framework depicted in chapter 2, the different explanations for the maintenance of the South American peace can be grouped into three clusters: (1) realist and geopolitical explanations (the pacifying roles of the United States and Brazil; a regional balance of power; external threats to the South American countries; and geographic isolation, irrelevance, and impotence to fight wars); (2) liberal explanations (the effects of democratization; the quest for prosperity and economic development; economic interdependence and integration; and a common normative consensus about conflict management); and (3) satisfaction with the territorial status quo, derived from both domestic and international sources.

Realist and Geopolitical Explanations

(1) The Pacifying Roles of the United States and Brazil
The realist theory of hegemonic stability can be applied to understand the maintenance of peace in South America. According to this theory, peace should be understood as an extension of the hegemonic position of the United States in the Americas. However, unlike the U.S. role in Central America and the Caribbean, this hegemony has been steadily declining in the last thirty years in South America, with the consolidation of local powers such as Brazil, Argentina, Chile, and Venezuela, and the diversification of foreign links between the South American countries and Europe, Japan, China, and the former Soviet Union (see Poitras 1990; Pastor 1992). Moreover, in regional rather than systemic terms it can be argued that Brazil has played a more preponderant role as a potential hegemonic power than the United States. Thus, it was the Brazilian power and its artful diplomacy that avoided the outbreak of violence in the region. Despite the traditional Brazilian-Argentine rivalry between the 1820s and the 1970s, the maintenance of peace in South America has remained a primary and constant goal of Brazilian foreign policy since its independence in 1822.

The pacifying role of the United States seems to offer a plausible explanation why South America has been more peaceful in the twentieth century than throughout the nineteenth century, especially at the zenith of the Pax Americana, between 1945 and the mid 1960s. The United States had both the motive and the capacity to deter wars among the South American countries (McIntyre 1993, 3–4). But this argument cannot explain why no wars occurred between 1883 and 1930, when the United States competed with the still large economic influence of the United Kingdom in the region, as well as with that of Germany and France. Moreover, the two exceptional South American wars of the twentieth century did occur at the time of U.S. preponderance. Thus, although there seems to be a correlation between U.S. hegemony and the maintenance of negative peace, it is far from perfect, and there is not necessarily a causal relationship. For instance, once the United States started its hegemonic decline after the mid 1960s, we witness, as expected from the theory, a period of heightened tensions in the Southern Cone. Yet negative peace was preserved throughout the 1970s. Moreover, with the advent of democratization in the region since the late 1970s there has been a movement from negative to stable peace in the Southern Cone, unrelated to the influence of the United States. Hence, from the perspective of the major South American powers, it seems that the U.S. role in keeping the peace has been quite negligible.[16]

The Brazilian role in maintaining the South American peace has been far more consequential. Throughout the twentieth century, Brazil has played the role of a benign potential hegemon and guarantor of the international stability and regional status quo. Since Brazil has common borders with all but two of the South American states (i.e., Chile and Ecuador), its foreign policy has had a great influence in keeping the regional peace. Brazil's traditional foreign policy has endeavored to guarantee both the territorial status quo and the balance of power vis-à-vis Argentina, based on the principle of maintaining the independence of the buffer states—Paraguay, Uruguay, and Bolivia. Despite its military, economic, and demographic superiority over Argentina and the rest of South America as a whole, the Brazilians chose not to fulfill a coercive hegemonic role in the region. This pacific (not pacifist) orientation is the result of the extraordinary territorial gains of Brazil through the last part of the nineteenth and the beginning of the twentieth centuries, which transformed it into the quintessential status quo power. In strategic, as well as in economic terms, a cooperative attitude toward the rest of South America did make a lot of sense. The last thing the Brazilians were interested in was the formation of a countercoalition led by their archrival, Argentina. By the beginning of the 1980s, the Argentines finally became aware of the futility of continuing their enduring rivalry, and thus came to recognize the power asymmetry between the two countries. The road was finally open toward rapprochement and improvement in their bilateral relations, and it led to the formation of MERCOSUR in 1991.

Brazil's rejection of the use of force in its relations with the neighboring states, especially after World War II, helped to shape the character of South America, which is distinct from that of other regions of the Third World, such as South Asia or the Middle East. The Brazilian "diplomatic way" remains a keystone in its foreign policy, whether the government be authoritarian or democratic.[17] The Brazilian pacifying effect is also relevant in understanding the movement from negative peace to stable peace and regional integration, and from there to an incipient pluralistic security community. This conclusion is reflected in the following excerpts from an interview with the Brazilian president, Fernando H. Cardoso:

> Question: Despite its strategic size and resources, Brazil has been viewed as a relatively passive leader within its region. Is that changing? Is Brazil prepared to be more assertive?
> Answer: Certainly regarding economic integration efforts, there is no doubt. My first presidential visits were to Argentina and Chile, and I am travelling to Bolivia, Colombia, and Venezuela. Brazil has excellent relations with its neighbors. We view them as partners with whom we resolve issues and set directions through negotiations. The diplomatic way is a Brazilian heritage and will remain at the heart of our role on the continent. However, I will employ diplomacy vigorously and with urgency when necessary. That is why I acted directly to help resolve the recent border conflict between Ecuador and Peru [in January–February 1995]. Maintaining Latin America as a peace zone gives the continent an enormous advantage. The key equation goes as follows: Brazil is a country of great regional importance but without hegemonic aspirations. (Quoted in Hoge 1995, 65–66)

(2) A Regional Balance of Power

An alternative realist explanation depicts the long South American peace as a function of a balance-of-power system involving a complex and interrelated set of diagonal alliances and perpendicular antagonisms. The regional balance of power has been represented by the following alignments and configurations: Chile and Brazil against Argentina and Bolivia; Chile and Ecuador against Peru; Argentina, Bolivia, and Peru against Chile; Guyana and Brazil against Venezuela; and Colombia and Brazil against Venezuela. The two major diagonal alliances in the Southern Cone have been, therefore, Brazil and Chile versus Argentina and Peru. Colombia, Venezuela, and the Guyanas do not actively participate in this system; likewise, the role of Ecuador has been minor. This convoluted system is depicted in figure 3.2.

A comprehensive regional balance of power existed only during two specific historical periods: in 1883–1919 and in the national security decade of the 1970s, when the military regimes in the Southern Cone rediscovered the old logic of geopolitics. The struggle for subparamountcy between Argentina and Brazil continued after 1920, even though Argentina gradually decayed between 1930 and the mid 1980s. The logic of the balance of power, quite irrelevant between 1945 and the 1960s, lost its significance completely with the decline of the geopolitical national security schools and the advent of democratic regimes throughout the region. Hence, its limited validity refers to the emergence and maintenance of negative peace from the end of the nineteenth century until the early 1920s. Interestingly, it was the recent Argentine recognition of an *im*balance of power vis-à-vis Brazil that contributed to the transition to stable peace between the two countries since the early 1980s.

As the theory of balance of power predicts, the equilibrium of forces that characterized the relations among Argentina, Chile, Peru, Bolivia, and Ecuador between 1883 and 1919 inhibited their use of force. The flashpoints on the frontiers between Peru and Chile, or between Chile and Argentina, had failed to ignite in part because of the logic of this balance of power. It was made up of three components: (1) the West Coast, engaging Peru, Chile, and Bolivia; (2) the East Coast, confronting Argentina and Brazil; and (3) a belt of the three buffer states—Uruguay, Paraguay, and Bolivia— acting as strategic pivots between Portuguese and Spanish South America (Parkinson 1993, 246). The alliance relationships tended to overlap with the border conflicts between the individual states. Peace was indeed maintained, though it was merely an armed (negative) peace.

In the 1970s, with the relative decline of the U.S. influence in the

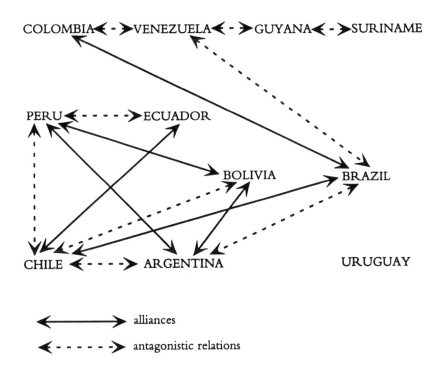

COLOMBIA ◄ - ► VENEZUELA ◄ - ► GUYANA ◄ - ► SURINAME

PERU ◄ - - - - ► ECUADOR

BOLIVIA   BRAZIL

CHILE ◄ - - - - ► ARGENTINA   URUGUAY

◄————————► alliances

◄ - - - - - ► antagonistic relations

Fig. 3.2. A Regional Balance of Power, 1883–1920s

region and the spread of authoritarian regimes in the Southern Cone, the old regional balance of power had an ephemeral comeback. The three major territorial disputes in the region—the Beagle Channel, between Argentina and Chile; the counterclaims of Peru and Ecuador in the "Oriente"; and the revisionist claims of Peru and Bolivia against Chile over the Atacama desert—seemed to converge again into a single confrontation between two blocs or alliances: Chile and Ecuador against Peru, Bolivia, and Argentina. Brazil, in spite of its historical competition with Argentina, acted now as a balancer. Moreover, unlike the original balance of power, the resurrected system of power politics in the 1970s was greatly affected by the prevailing doctrines of geopolitics, emphasizing concepts such as the organic state, the living frontier, and the laws of valuable areas and discontinuous borders (see Child 1985). The inherent fragility of the system resided in the fact that the escalation of one territorial conflict could rapidly lead to a conflagration in the entire region. In military terms, this was translated into three parallel arms races: Argentina and Brazil, Chile and Peru, and Colombia and Venezuela (see Astiz 1969, 14). Despite the pessimistic forecasting about escalation of conflicts into wars in the 1980s, this balance of power helped to keep the negative peace, or at least it did not disturb it.

The attraction of geopolitics lost force in the 1980s due to the softening of many of the rivalries and disputes, especially those between Argentina and Chile, and between Argentina and Brazil. Two factors contributed to its gradual disappearance: first, the growing imbalance of power between Brazil and the rest of the countries of the region; and second, the political transitions from authoritarian to democratic regimes.

(3) *External Threats to the South American Countries*
A third realist argument that addresses the maintenance of regional peace derives from a simple logic of alliance formation. According to this rationale, Bolivarianism—that is, Bolívar's basic conception of a loose confederation of Hispanoamerican states—derived from the external threat of Europe's great powers to the independence of South America. According to this view, the political solidarity, cooperation, and integration among the South American states has been inherently defensive and externally driven. In the 1820s, Bolívar called for the establishment of an international or supranational entity that would "serve as a council in great con-

flict, as a point of contact in common dangers, and as a faithful interpreter of public treaties where difficulties occur, as a conciliator, in short, of our differences" (quoted in Perera 1985, 133). However, the 1826 Congress of Panama convened by Bolívar was ultimately a failure, so that the political union among South American nations never materialized.

By the turn of the century, the external European threat was replaced by the aggressive foreign policy of the United States toward Latin America, especially regarding Central America and the Caribbean. The role of the United States in the Western Hemisphere did cause mixed feelings of fear and hatred for a coercive hegemon and predator, together with admiration and need for its protection and leadership (Tulchin 1994, 289). The vision of the United States as an external threat was clearly articulated by the Argentine writer Jose Ingenieros in 1922 in his essay about imperialism, as follows:

> We must recognize that in the few years of this century [i.e., 1900–1922] events have occurred in Latin America which demand serious, even gloomy reflection. We are not, we no longer want to be, we no longer can be Pan-Americanists. The famous Monroe Doctrine, has gradually proved to be a declaration of the American right to protect us and to intervene in our affairs. . . . Growth in voracity of the American privileged caste . . . has increasingly pressed for an imperialist policy, and has converted the government into an instrument of its corporations. "America for the Americans" actually means "America—our Latin America—for the North Americans. . . ." (Quoted in Tulchin 1994, 310)

As a perceived external threat, the United States fulfilled an *indirect* pacifying role in the region. The U.S. threat of intervention had the effect of inhibiting the South American nations from using force to settle their international differences. Many precepts of international law that were developed by South American jurists, such as the Calvo and Drago doctrines, defended the principle of nonintervention and peaceful settlement of disputes as a response of the weak South American powers to the possibility of forcible interventions by extraregional powers, especially the United States. Yet, in the 1930s and early 1940s Bolivia and Paraguay, Peru and Ecuador, and Peru and Colombia did not seem to have been deterred from their bellicose actions by the possibility of U.S. intervention. Likewise, it does not seem plausible that Peru and Chile in 1975, or Argentina and Chile in

1978, stopped their conflict short of war because they feared a North American intervention. Even if that external threat objectively existed, it played no part in their perception of the situation.

In sum, no serious extraregional threat affected South America after the turn of the century, and especially after World War II.[18] Conversely, military security threats usually came from a nation's immediate neighbors, or from the long rivalry between Argentina and Brazil. For the smaller South American countries, especially the buffer states, Argentina and Brazil were regarded as the powers that posed serious threats to their autonomy.

(4) Geographic Isolation, Irrelevance, and Impotence to Fight Wars
In addition to the three realist explanations presented so far—a Pax Americana or Brasiliana; a regional balance of power among Argentina, Brazil, Chile, and Peru; and the fear of extraregional intervention—the absence of war in South America has been related to the geographic isolation of many South American countries, their mutual irrelevance and lack of interactions, and their material incapacity, even impotence, to fight international wars.

According to this argument, peace was the result of the lack of interaction among the South American countries, at least until the 1960s. Scarcity of interstate transportation linkages, low levels of technology, and the fact that many of the territorial boundaries run through remote and sparsely populated areas, across the high mountains of the Andes, and in the midst of the Amazon jungle, created conditions that deterred wars of conquest and expansion. As a result, the South American peace has been a "peace of irrelevance" (see McIntyre 1993, 5–8). Following this realist logic, independence and geographic isolation, rather than interdependence, explain peace. However, although the increase of interaction after the 1960s was reflected in heightened tensions in the 1970s, as expected from this theory, there were two "anomalies." First, negative peace was maintained, with only one exception (Peru–Ecuador, in 1981 and again in 1995). Second, in the 1980s, increasing levels of interaction did not lead to more conflict, but rather to political cooperation, integration, and the deepening of the regional peace.

In historical terms, South American countries have neither traded with nor invested in each other significantly. The major economic, political, and cultural interactions occurred between South American countries and several developed nations on a vertical basis. In geopolitical terms, geographic factors affected the costs and possibility of aggression by influencing the protection and mobility of armies. There have been relatively few areas in the region where major interstate war, involving large-scale movements of ground forces, was probable or even possible (McIntyre 1993, 6; Kemp 1973, 216–17). Moreover, their large territories with relatively small populations and the emptiness of their border regions tended to insulate the countries of the region from both trade and the possibility of armed conflict (Bolin 1992, 170; Agor 1972, 19). This Rousseaunian autarky ended in the 1960s with progress in communications and transportation, the search for economic prosperity and technological advancement, and the need to develop and control the borderlands (Hazelton 1981, 66).

Furthermore, geographic isolation and economic and political irrelevance were complemented by a third and crucial factor related to the national characteristics of many South American states. Despite the absence of ethnic conflicts and the unique combination of early and uninterrupted political independence, together with a substantial incorporation into the international capitalist economy, the South American countries have remained in general weak military powers and underdeveloped economies. Thus, they lack the material basis, and sometimes even the political legitimacy, to fight international wars. Even if they wished to use violence to manage their international relations, as they usually did in domestic politics, they did not have the means to do so across their borders. Given the nature of the offense-defense balance in South America, no state, even Brazil, possessed sufficient capabilities to defeat its adversaries (see McIntyre 1993, 12). Again, this argument is plausible only with reference to negative peace: wars are not fought not because of lack of will but because of lack of money or infrastructure.

This concatenation of geographic isolation, political and economic irrelevance, and material impotence has created an interesting paradox with reference to the traditional role played by national armies in South America. As Edward Glick (1965) and Stanislav Andreski (1992) cogently suggest, South American armies have played, at best, a limited role in the strategic (i.e., external) defense of their countries, because of the lack of external threats, lack of means, or both. Military regimes in the region were specially vulnerable in international relations, since there is an inherent incompatibility between the internal and external use of the armed forces. If they were used for internal purposes (repression and civil wars), they tended to become ineffective for their professional, external role.[19] Therefore, military regimes tended to be cautious in their relations with their neighbors and usually did not escalate their international conflicts.

Liberal Explanations

(1) *Political Regimes, Democratization, and Regional Peace*
Since the last wave of democratization in the late 1970s and 1980s, most of the countries of the region have become democracies, which has contributed notably to stable peace, especially in the Southern Cone. Yet, in itself, the process of democratization cannot be considered as the only explanation for this peace, which had preceded the transition from authoritarian to liberal/democratic regimes.

In general terms, there is a high degree of indeterminacy in South America between the level of political stability of the domestic order, including the degree of national consensus, and the level of escalation of international conflicts. Democracy and political stability are not always coterminous; nondemocratic regimes, for instance, can be very stable if they reach a substantial level of national consensus and become embedded within relatively strong states, as they have been in Chile and Brazil throughout most of their political history. Conversely, unstable or new and fragile civilian regimes can be involved in armed disputes, as was the case in Peru and Ecuador in January 1981. According to this view, the relationship between the type of political regime and foreign policy behavior is at best contingent, or nonlinear. On the one hand, authoritarian regimes ruled by the military can be more peaceful than democracies in their external relations. For instance, the momentous rapprochement between Brazil and Argentina was initiated in 1979, when both regimes were still under military control. Similarly, meaningful negotiations to resolve the Bolivia-Chile-Peru dispute took place during 1975 to 1978, when all three countries were under authoritarian regimes. On the other hand, domestic instability might be expected to lead to very conservative foreign policies in order to avoid external intervention and focus upon domestic crises and conflicts.[20] The most we can say, therefore, is that in spite of the cyclical patterns of dictatorships and elected regimes in South America throughout the twentieth century, negative peace has been maintained irrespective of the different types of political regime. Even in the period of heightened tensions of the Bureaucratic Authoritarian (BA) regimes in the 1970s and early 1980s, war was avoided among the South American nations, with the exception of the January 1981 brief round between Peru and Ecuador, which in both countries involved newly established democratic regimes .

Democratic regimes and democratization processes cannot explain the maintenance of regional peace since 1883. At the same time, they are crucial in defining the *quality* of that peace. The importance of the last wave of democratization for domestic and international politics has been recognized by researchers and practitioners alike. According to the Brazilian president, Fernando H. Cardoso, "the most important change in Brazil and Latin America [has been] the implantation of freedom and democracy" (quoted in Hoge 1995, 64). Democratization has had a crucial role in the movement from negative peace to stable peace in the Southern Cone and a direct impact upon the level of regional cooperation—as measured by the quantity and quality of declarations, statements, and agreements among the political and economic elites of the ABC countries (see Schmitter 1991, 108). In particular, democratization has been an important factor in the emergence of subregional economic cooperation and integration, especially between Brazil and Argentina. The prospects for economic integration came to depend upon the existence of democratic regimes open to cooperation. At the same time, the democratic consolidation of the new civilian regimes was contingent upon the economic growth that could be facilitated by regional integration (Barletta 1994, 33; and Hurrell 1994a, 178).

To sum up, the transitions to political democracy in South America and Latin America as a whole have laid the foundations for the deepening of the regional peace even at the hemispheric, inter-American level. The promotion of democracy has became a major goal for the OAS, so that the inter-American system is nowadays being recaptured as a liberal pacific union stretching from Alaska to Tierra del Fuego. As Argentine's ex-president Raúl Alfonsín wrote in 1992:

> The reorientation of the [Argentine] foreign policy occurred within a regional framework of democratization and a common interest in avoiding conflicts between neighboring states. . . . The return to democracy in Chile and the end of the Stroessner's dictatorship in Paraguay strengthened a common concept of regional peace, relying on the capacity of

civilian governments to enhance their policies of cooperation and to overcome old [territorial] conflicts. Hence, South America is becoming a real
Zone of Peace. . . ." (Alfonsín 1992, 27; my translation)

(2) Economic Development, and Prosperity
Although South America as a whole cannot be considered economically
developed, the three major countries of the region—Argentina, Brazil, and
Chile—have reached significant levels of development. Their sustained
commitment to growth, development, and prosperity has been a contributing factor in maintaining their regional peace. Moreover, the absence of
wars in South America has been directly related to the political economy of
the region since the 1870s. Its dependent position vis-à-vis the international markets of the developed nations have determined in great part the
character of its international relations. The economic entry into the international economy after 1860 *demanded* both domestic and international
peace to promote growth, development, and prosperity. Thus, both
neocolonialists among the developed nations and local political and economic elites had a common interest in keeping the regional peace.[21]

Dependency theories were formulated in the 1960s and 1970s to explain the lack of economic development in Latin America, rather than to
understand Latin American foreign policy and the long South American
peace. But we can conjoin this approach with a liberal economic one to
analyze the maintenance of regional negative peace. The empirical results
fit the theoretical assumptions: between 1880 and the 1920s, and again
between 1945 and the 1960s, periods of economic dependence upon the
British and U.S. (economic) hegemonies have coincided with absence of
wars and a certain equilibrium, according to which local territorial disputes
seldom got out of control, though they also seldom died or were actively
resolved (Escudé 1988, 265).

Moreover, even without the external pressures, the pursuit of economic growth and development has had a pacifying effect. As Helio Jaguaribe
argues, there was a general acknowledgment by all concerned countries
about the comparative advantages of regional peace for their reciprocal
development.[22] In the first place, the goals of economic development and
nation-building are closely interdependent, and both require stability at
home and across the borders (see Anderson 1967, 48). Second, in the long
run, there seems to be a correlation between economic development and

democratization. Since both of them need a certain degree of rationalization, they together create favorable conditions for the maintenance of peace. Third, the higher the levels of economic development and prosperity, the better the prospects for political cooperation, *and vice versa*. For instance, since 1990 the bilateral trade between Argentina and Brazil, and between Chile and Argentina, has more than tripled. At the same time, the annual military spending of the ABC countries has dropped from $4.9 billion in 1985 to $3.7 billion in 1992 (Brooke 1994). Finally, decision-makers in the region appear to view war, because of its disruptive effect upon the development effort, as an all but unthinkable policy instrument—unless the survival of the state is at stake. This explains why military regimes committed to the goals of national development and growth did manage territorial disputes without escalating them into wars. In conclusion, the resumption of economic growth in the region in the early 1990s has further improved the prospects for continuing and enhancing regional cooperation and integration, soothing national and international tensions, and moving South America in the direction of stable peace and a pluralistic security community.

(3) Economic Integration and Increasing Interdependence
Different frameworks of trading groups and subregional economic integration have coexisted in South America in the last thirty years or so. Their impact as a force for the maintenance of regional peace is moot. As with the democratic factor and the level of economic development, however, it is clear that some of these subregional groupings—such as MERCOSUR and the older Andean Pact—have increased the links of economic, social, and even political interdependence among the countries of the region.

Although the quest for economic development and prosperity has been constant since the early nineteenth century, the achievement of South American economic interdependence and integration is only recent. While dependent upon external economic powers, the economic interactions among the countries of the region until the 1960s were almost null. Hence, independence, rather than interdependence, did characterize intra–South American relations. With the exception of buffer states such as Uruguay and Bolivia, which heavily depended on intraregional trade, the intraregional concentration of the large countries has been low, ranging from 20 percent to 30 percent (Haggard 1994, 22).

Recent state-led cooperation and the emergence of integrative frameworks were designed to promote interdependence, not only to manage it. For political rather than economic reasons, such as the need to legitimize and enhance the new democratic regimes, states decided to create economic interdependence through the institutionalization of mutual cooperation. In contrast to the common theoretical assumption, the order of causality has been reversed in South America: economic interdependence became the consequence, not the cause, of political cooperation and economic integration. As a result, between 1985 and 1991, intraregional exports significantly grew in Argentina, Brazil, Paraguay, Uruguay, Colombia, Chile, and Ecuador. Between 1991 and 1994, trade among the largest economies grew by 50 percent (see Naím 1995, 48; and Inotai 1994, 55).

Once economic interdependence grew as a result of political cooperation and elite-led integration, it affected the quality of regional peace. Thus, after the ABC countries became so interdependent, a war between Argentina and Chile, or between Argentina and Brazil, came to seem unprofitable, if not unthinkable.

(4) A Common Cultural Framework and Normative Consensus
A fourth different liberal argument can be made to explain the long South American peace as unrelated to the changing type of their political regimes and their quest for economic development, prosperity, economic integration, and interdependence. The South American countries, through a gradual historical and learning process, have managed to establish a unique Latin "diplomatic culture" that has helped their governments to resolve their international conflicts short of war (see Holsti 1993, 19; 1996). The South American nations succeeded in developing a theory and practice of exceptionalism regarding their recourse to international law—arbitration of disputes, mediation, bilateral negotiations, and other techniques for the peaceful settlement of international disputes—rather than the use of force in their international relations. Based upon a common historical and cultural framework, the South American nations have built a strong normative consensus that has been institutionalized in legal instruments such as the 1967 Treaty of Tlatelolco, which was supposed to transform the whole of Latin America into a zone free of nuclear weapons. Yet this normative and legal reluctance to engage in war against fellow South American nations never implied a lack of serious interstate disputes throughout the entire region. Thus, this common cultural framework and normative consensus

gives us a serious clue about the reticence of the South American states to engage in war, without discerning the quality of their peace.

In contrast to other regions of the Third World, the basic social, political, and economic values of South America directly derive from the European tradition; its values are part of the Western Christian culture. The diplomatic system of South America has developed a culture of legalism imbued with legal norms, including a specifically Spanish American international law and diplomacy. In addition, the South American elites have held common perceptions as to a distinctive regional identity and regional solidarity.[23]

From the time of their independence, the Latin American nations in general, and the Hispanoamerican states of South America in particular, have sought to build a structure of political cooperation on the basis of their common historical, cultural, and institutional heritage. Schemes of political integration, such as Bolívar's dream of a South American political union, or even more modest confederations such as Gran Colombia (Colombia-Venezuela-Ecuador) and Peru-Bolivia broke down a couple of decades after independence. However, the idea(l) of a South American consciousness, of a distinctive regional identity based on common history, culture, and language, never disappeared. When Bolívar gave up his dreams, he declared that "to govern Latin America is like trying to plow the sea." Yet, Bolivarianism never died with him; it was resurrected after World War II in the regional efforts of economic integration, and more recently, in the adoption of a regional strategy of political *concertación* regarding the resolution of conflicts such as the Central American crisis of the 1980s, and through the political activity of the Rio Group.

This common cultural framework, with the development of a distinctive regional identity and solidarity, helped to consolidate the basis for a normative consensus related to the way international relations should be conducted among the South American nations. A series of norms and principles of international law have been adopted by the South American countries since independence, including: (1) *uti possidetis* (recognition of the former colonial borders); (2) peaceful international coexistence (the principle of *convivencia*); (3) nonintervention and mutual respect of national sovereignties; and (4) peaceful settlement of international disputes, including the recourse to arbitration, mediation, and other similar juridical and diplomatic techniques.[24]

In principle, these four norms embody a formidable consensus that seems to explain the peaceful predisposition of the South American nations. But there are two serious problems with this argument. First, if these norms were adopted in 1810 or soon after that, how can they explain the maintenance of peace *since* 1883 but not before? After all, South America was a typical zone of conflict between 1810 and 1883, despite the existence of some, if not all, of these norms. Thus, the normative argument cannot explain the variance and transformation from war to negative peace and, later on, from negative to stable peace. Second, we should be aware of the divergence between rhetorics and reality; there is a gap between the formal adoption of these norms and the common practice of states in favor of ad hoc and bilateral solutions to international disputes (see Puig 1983; Payne 1994, 27–28).

In formal terms, in all the Latin American political congresses that took place in the nineteenth century, beginning with that of Panama in 1826, the issue of the maintenance of peace was addressed and formalized in a series of treaties—such as at Lima, 1848; Santiago de Chile, 1856; and Lima, 1865. Before World War II, a series of multilateral treaties were signed regarding the peaceful settlement of disputes, such as the Anti-War Treaty of Non-Aggression and Conciliation (Saavedra-Lamas Treaty) of 1933. The Pan-American movement propelled by the United States since the end of the nineteenth century also incorporated this normative consensus in the form of twelve treaties signed between 1890 and 1945, dealing with good offices, mediation, investigation, conciliation, arbitration, and judicial settlement (Bailey 1967, 75). Especially after World War II, these norms were institutionalized in three major legal instruments: the Inter-American Treaty of Reciprocal Assistance (Rio Pact) of 1947; the Charter of the Organization of American States (OAS) in 1948; and the American Treaty on Pacific Settlement (the Pact of Bogotá) of 1948.[25]

Many border disputes throughout the nineteenth century and the first two decades of the twentieth century were resolved peacefully, leading to some cession or exchange of territories. The basis for a peaceful settlement of those disputes was established through the principle of *uti possidetis, ita posideatis* (as you possess, so you may possess). This principle did not preclude the emergence of boundary disputes among the South American states, since uncertainty characterized the demarcation of frontiers of the new states. Yet, by recognizing the same norms of international law, the parties at least managed to resolve their disputes peacefully. Between 1851 and 1922 at least fourteen peaceful cessions and exchanges of territory took place in South America.[26] Eight of these disputes were resolved following arbitration; the rest through direct negotiations, good offices, and mediation. In many cases, the arbitration award was followed by further negotiations about its implementation. Thus, in practice, the South American nations have shown a consistent preference for noncompulsory, ad hoc recourse for the management and resolution of their conflicts. Furthermore, they seem to have preferred the continuation of the status quo, even if it led to continuing tensions, rather than escalating the dispute into full-scale wars.

Satisfaction with the Territorial Status Quo

Irrespective of the changing nature of their political regimes throughout the twentieth century, the rise and decline of balance of power configurations and geopolitical doctrines, and the progression from independence towards interdependence, most of the South American countries have been satisfied with the territorial status quo, following their national consolidation in the last decades of the nineteenth century and the first two decades of the twentieth. Nowadays, the two clear exceptions are Bolivia, regarding the loss to Chile of its outlet to the sea *(salida al mar)*; and Ecuador, which has rejected the Rio Protocol (1942) that was supposed to settle its border dispute with Peru. Traditionally, Argentina has been a revisionist power vis-à-vis the British occupation of the Falklands/Malvinas since 1833, and regarding the Chilean claims to the Beagle Channel. But with the return of democracy in 1983, and especially since the advent of the Peronist government of President Menem in 1989, Argentina has also become a satisfied power.

Satisfaction with the territorial status quo has been a crucial factor, though not the sole one, in the maintenance of peace in South America. It has been linked to the widespread recognition of the principle of *uti possidetis*, to the terms of the settlements completed after the conclusion of the six nineteenth-century and the two twentieth-century regional wars,[27] and especially to the fact that South America has had the lowest number of ethnic, irredentist, and transnational conflicts of any region in the world (see Gurr 1993). Moreover, we should examine the two main sources of satisfaction: domestic and international. The domestic sources derive from the type of state, the type of regime, and the link between the two in South America. The international sources stem from the position the South American states occupy in their regional hierarchy of power and prestige.

(1) The Domestic Sources of Satisfaction
As argued above, South American foreign policy has been linked indissolubly not only to the dynamics of domestic politics, such as the regime changes from authoritarian to democratic polities (and back), but also to the preponderant and even paramount role played by the state in the political and economic development of the region. In South America, the establishment of the state nearly always preceded the development of its corresponding national, social, and economic systems. Because of the lack of serious ethnic conflicts, with the exceptions of the nonintegrated indigenous populations of Peru, Bolivia, and Ecuador and the ethnic cleavages within Guyana and Suriname, the adoption of the territorial form of the European state did succeed in South America. By the turn of the century, with a few exceptions such as Colombia and Bolivia, most of the states had consolidated internally, providing a more or less stable framework of reference for domestic and international politics. Internationally, these states had resolved and stabilized most of their political boundaries. Internally, they began to expand the representative nature of their regimes and governments. Thus, the state in itself became more or less politically stable and stronger than its societal entourage.[28]

The process of state-building in South America in the first half of the nineteenth century was long and painful. As a consequence, there has been a clear tendency on the part of weak and insecure state elites to substitute control for authority, and domination for effective policy and legitimacy (Diamond and Linz 1989, 27). The result has been praetorianism, authoritarian regimes (civilian and military), populist-corporatist regimes (such as those of Perón in Argentina and Vargas in Brazil), and political disarticulation. Similarly, until the recent wave of democratization, the mobilization of civil society has been sporadic and defensive, oriented toward protest rather than toward alternative governing projects, and is thus symptomatic of weakness instead of strength.

Following the period of national consolidation, the South American states have become stronger in comparison with their governments and societies. As Barry Buzan suggests (1983, 67), by the turn of the century the idea of the national state, its formal political institutions, and its geographic territory were all clearly defined and stable. At the same time, in terms of degrees of autonomy vis-à-vis their societies, the South American states have been subject to constant pressures from within and without. With the possible exception of Chile and Uruguay throughout most of their political history as stable polyarchies, and Colombia and Venezuela after 1958 as semiconsociational democracies, most of the states were captured by exclusive and restricted groups (such as the military and the oligarchic upper classes, ruling by force rather than by legitimacy) at the expense of the rest of their societies. For instance, many of the authoritarian regimes, such as the so-called Bureaucratic Authoritarian states of Argentina (1966–70; 1976–83) and Uruguay (1973–85), proved to be relatively weak states due to their excluding and nondemocratic character, their repressive methods, and their general lack of legitimacy. In comparison to West Africa, the state in South America has been stronger; but in comparison to East Asia or Southeast Asia, it has been weaker. In sum, the state in South America seems to occupy a middle way in the weak/strong state continuum: it has been strong enough not to fall apart as in other postcolonial situations (like those in Africa). At the same time, it has been weak enough to find it hard to mobilize its society for war and conquest.[29]

Since the turn of the century the state in South America has played a paramount role in politics and economics, while at the same time political regimes have cyclically changed, sometimes strengthening (in the case of democracies) and sometimes weakening (through authoritarian regimes) the structure of the state. In the last few years, following democratization, economic liberalism, and structural economic reforms, many analysts have referred to the "retreat of the interventionist state" and the dismantling of the state apparatus (see Hagopian 1994; Nef and Bensabat 1992). However, despite privatization and the overemphasized celebration of civil society, the state has kept its formidable role vis-à-vis its society. Turning to the issue of the domestic sources of satisfaction, we find examples of the four possible ideal types presented in the last chapter, as follows:

(a) Strong states with democratic regimes. The ABC powers between the end of the nineteenth century and the 1930s belong to this category, coinciding with the emergence of liberal regimes throughout the region. Furthermore, Chile and Uruguay have been for most of the twentieth century strong states with democratic regimes. In addition, since the political democratization

in Brazil and Chile in the 1980s, these two states have managed to keep their central and even authoritarian role vis-à-vis their societies and economies. If we narrow the definition of strong states to include all those states characterized by lack of ethnic conflicts and domestic threats, then several of the current regimes in the region belong to this category, with the exceptions of Colombia, Peru, Guyana, Suriname, and Bolivia. Most of these states are actively satisfied with the territorial status quo and with the regional order.

(b) Strong states with nondemocratic regimes. Chile until the 1890s and between 1973 and 1989, and Brazil for most of its political history until 1984 belong to this category. Unlike what the theoretical framework predicts, these two countries were not revisionist troublemakers, but rather the champions of conservatism and regional peace since the beginning of the twentieth century. Their external postures were a reflection and an extension of both domestic conservatism and their territorial gains from past military and diplomatic victories. Brazil traditionally occupied a quasi-hegemonic position in the regional order, especially after concluding its territorial aggrandizement in 1910. Chile was a local hegemon in the South Pacific area, and after the 1920s remained self-enclosed and conservative in its relations with its immediate neighbors.

(c) Weak states with democratic regimes. The current regimes of Bolivia, Colombia, Ecuador, the transitional regimes of Guyana and Suriname, and Peru after the elections of spring 1995 might belong to this category. The democratic regime of Argentina between 1983 and 1989 under President Alfonsín can also be considered as a new democratic regime within a weak state. Unlike the positive satisfaction that characterizes the strong and democratic states, the degree of satisfaction is mostly passive. Due to their historical legacies, Bolivia and Ecuador have remained revisionist in their territorial demands.

(d) Weak states with nondemocratic regimes. Many of the authoritarian (civilian and military) regimes in South America belonged to this category, with the exceptions of the Bureaucratic Authoritarian regimes of Chile (1973–89), Brazil (1964–85), and to some extent Peru (1968–80). Here the logic of militocracies explains their satisfaction with the territorial status quo. As Alain Rouquié (1973, 7–8) argues, the emphasis placed on internal security and the fight against subversion, at the expense of the usual defense policy directed against external enemies, have transformed the military in-

stitutions in the region into conservative forces. Their political attitude has also been extrapolated across borders, resulting in at least a passive acceptance of the status quo. In this regard, the Argentine invasion of the Falklands/ Malvinas in April 1982 represents a deviation from the expected behavior of weak and nondemocratic states. To understand this Argentine peculiar revisionist posture, we should examine the international sources of satisfaction.

(2) The International Sources of Satisfaction
While the domestic sources of satisfaction emphasize the role of the state in South America and its changing political regimes, the international sources refer to the position the South American states have occupied in the regional hierarchy of international power and prestige. This position has been dynamic from a diachronic perspective, following the rise and decline of several regional actors, such as Argentina (decline between 1930 and 1983), and Venezuela (rise and decline between the 1970s and late 1980s). When there has been a positive correspondence between degree of power and degree of status (as in the case of Brazil), the result has been active satisfaction. Conversely, a discrepancy between power and status might have led to revisionist postures, like those adopted by Argentina between the 1930s and its return to democracy in the 1980s.

The international order in South America in the last fifty years can be considered as both stable and mature, even as seen independently from the larger inter-American system of collective security. In contrast to its convoluted domestic political changes, some of them very bloody and violent, this regional order has been characterized by the maintenance of the territorial status quo and the normative commitment of the majority of the states to uphold it. It has been organized around a clearly established hierarchy of power, consisting of four echelons. At the top in terms of military and economic power we find Brazil and Argentina (in that order), which traditionally have behaved like great powers toward their neighbors. The second rank has been traditionally occupied by Chile and Peru as middle powers (at least after Chile declined in military power compared to Argentina and Brazil in the 1920s). Immediately after them come the two sister republics of the Northern Tier, Colombia and Venezuela. Finally, at the lowest level we find the three buffer states of the Southern Cone (Bolivia, Paraguay, and Uruguay) and the peripheral states (Ecuador, Guyana, and Suriname).[30]

Despite the existence of an objective hierarchy of power, the scales of prestige and status are complicated to determine. On the one hand, it is easy to identify the "high class" of countries that are big, are relatively developed, and have some military leverage, such as Brazil and Argentina, in contraposition to a "low class" of nations such as Bolivia or Paraguay. On the other hand, the hierarchy of prestige is less evident regarding "middle class" powers such as Colombia, or even small countries like Uruguay, which traditionally enjoyed a higher status relative to its small power due to its high level of political development.

By juxtaposing the objective hierarchy of power with the more subjective or intersubjective hierarchy of prestige we obtain four possible combinations that explain satisfaction with the territorial status quo in South America as follows:

(a) The powerful and high-status states. By definition, those states tend to be satisfied with the status quo. The ABC powers between 1883 and the 1920s belonged to this category; they stood at the apex of the South American hierarchy and managed the region in a kind of condominium, concert, or institutionalized balance of power. As mentioned, after the 1920s Chile's power decreased relative to Argentina's and Brazil's. Moreover, Argentina's political decay between 1930 and 1983 directly affected its power and prestige. After 1930, therefore, only Brazil has kept its position at the top of the region's hierarchy of power and prestige.

Among all the South American nations, *Brazil* has been geopolitically the most satisfied country. The reasons for that are threefold: First, it has the most to lose from a violent disruption of the regional status quo, which could damage its international prestige, economic prosperity and development, and its control of the Amazon borderlands. Second, it has the necessary military, economic, and even demographic power to project its influence across the region. Third, any change in the territorial status quo might affect the existing structure of prestige, which underlines Brazil's superiority over Argentina and the rest of South America. Brazil's pacific foreign policy tradition has reflected an artful policy of a state that, though much weaker in domestic and fiscal areas, enjoys a clear but not overwhelming lead in power resources over its neighbors. Thus, Brazil has enjoyed regional predominance, rather than hegemony.[31]

(b) The powerful and low-status states. This category of states includes

relatively strong powers that do not enjoy the status they think they deserve. In the South American scene, three countries can be classified in this category: Argentina between 1930 and the 1980s; Peru, until 1968; and Venezuela, during the 1970s and early 1980s.

Between the 1860s and the end of the nineteenth century, *Argentina* gradually emerged as a strong power in South America that came to compete with Chile and Brazil. Yet, the mainstream foreign policy elite was far from being revisionist at that time. As Argentine president Carlos Pellegrini declared in 1881:

> It is enough to look at the map of the Argentine republic in order to understand its foreign policy. It has an enormous territory from the tropics to the pole. What can it gain from war? Territorial expansion? Glories? It cannot be an Argentine policy. (Quoted in Lascano 1938, 164; my translation)

This conservative position changed after the first two decades of the twentieth century, when Argentina became the most advanced South American country and among the richest nations of the world. Argentina sustained territorial ambitions regarding the "lost" territories of the Viceroyalty of the Río de la Plata, including Uruguay, Paraguay, and parts of Bolivia. Furthermore, in terms of prestige, between the two world wars the Argentines regarded themselves as political and ideological rivals to the United States in the leadership of the whole Western Hemisphere, so that they identified Brazil as a "subimperialist" U.S. proxy (see Barclay 1971). Argentina was the most threatened South American state and at the same time one of the most threatening powers (McIntyre 1993, 13). On the one hand, it maintained serious territorial disputes with two of the most powerful states in the region: Chile and Brazil. On the other, it was a constant menace regarding the smaller buffer states in the Southern Cone. The political and economic decay after 1930 exacerbated a sense of lost status, fueled by a territorial nationalism that contrasted with a long diplomatic tradition of extreme caution, international law, and even moralism. Political instability and economic decline damaged the Argentine status in regional terms, leading to revisionist foreign policies. This revisionism was expressed in the crisis with Chile in 1977–78 over the Beagle Channel and escalated into a full-fledged war with Great Britain over the Falklands/

Malvinas in 1982. With the return of democracy, a new equilibrium was found between power and status that turned Argentina into a conservative power vis-à-vis the regional order, with the exception of its continuing claims over the Falklands/Malvinas.[32]

Despite its position as a middle-range power in South America, *Peru* played no significant role in the international scene until the advent of the progressive military regime of Velasco Alvarado in 1968. Between 1968 and 1975, Peru narrowed the gap between its low status and its own perception of power by increasing its military strength in comparison with its immediate neighbors, Chile and Ecuador. For a short period of time the military regime gained both power and status, overcoming almost a century of national trauma caused by its defeat in the War of the Pacific. Even after the decline of prestige during the "Phase Two" of the military government (1975–80) and the return to civilian rule in the 1980s, Peruvian foreign policy toward Chile remained strongly influenced by considerations of national power and prestige (St.John 1992, 224). At the same time, relations with Chile have improved steadily, although similar efforts of rapprochement with Ecuador were complicated by domestic political calculations in both countries. Nowadays, Peru obviously supports the status quo of its borders.[33]

Venezuela entered the ranks of the middle-range powers in the 1970s, thanks to its strategic location in the Northern Tier/Caribbean region and its strength as a major oil exporter. Its rapid military expansion in the 1970s was oriented toward external rather than internal wars. Against the background of enduring territorial disputes with both Colombia and Guyana, Venezuela could be regarded as a dissatisfied power, enjoying a status inferior to its own perceived power and unable to resolve old border conflicts with its neighbors. Despite these two serious boundary disputes, Venezuela has been the only South American country that never has gone to war with a neighbor. The explanation for this peaceful disposition is related to the relative success of the Venezuelan democracy since 1958 and its emphasis upon political and economic development.[34]

(c) Weak powers with high status. These states tend to be satisfied with the territorial status quo. In regional terms, we can include in this category Uruguay and Chile since the 1920s.

Despite its small size and weakness in military terms, *Uruguay* stands out among the South American countries as the best example of a strong but small democratic state. Uruguay has played a significant and constructive role in regional international relations, despite its insignificant power, due to its high level of political and economic development. Since its creation in 1828, and for obvious reasons such as the enduring rivalry between Argentina and Brazil, Uruguay has had a vested interest in promoting the pacific settlement of international disputes and upholding the territorial status quo and the regional order in active terms.[35]

Like Uruguay, *Chile* has been a strong and democratic state for most of the twentieth century, except for a turbulent period between 1924 and 1932 and the Pinochet military dictatorship of 1973–89. Until the 1920s, Chile was one of the ABC powers, leading the other South American states together with Argentina and Brazil. In the South Pacific area, throughout the nineteenth century Chile was the paramount power and the military victor of two wars against Peru and Bolivia, and after that a formidable rival to Argentina. Following the War of the Pacific (1879–83), Chile opted for an armed peace regarding its three neighbors (Peru, Argentina, and Bolivia) and upheld the postwar territorial status quo. Despite its relative military decline since the 1920s, Chile has managed to maintain a high status and prestige, linked to its long political stability, national cohesion, and more recently, the success of its economic plans.[36]

(d) Weak powers with low status. In this final category we find six South American states: Guyana, Suriname, Colombia, Ecuador, Bolivia, and Paraguay. Among them, Bolivia and Ecuador are dissatisfied weak powers, while the rest of the countries are at least passively satisfied with the territorial status quo. All of these states, with the possible exception of Colombia as an original sponsor of the Contadora group, have a low status that corresponds to their low degree of military, economic, and diplomatic power. Moreover, all these countries have been traditionally weak states and, with the exception of the Colombian consociational democracy since 1958, their political changes in the direction of democratization have been very fragile (such as in Bolivia), recent (in Paraguay), or currently unfolding (in Guyana and Suriname).

Satisfaction with the territorial status quo has been directly associated with the results of the settlements following the last war fought by the relevant countries. Accordingly, Bolivia and Ecuador remain the two revisionist countries in the 1990s. As the loser of both the War of the Pacific against Chile, and the Chaco War against Paraguay, *Bolivia* has lost considerable parts of its ex-colonial territory. Consequently, Bolivian claims to an "out-let to the sea" *(salida al mar)* has remained a parameter in its diplomacy for the last one hundred years, with the issue still unresolved, as reflected in the lack of diplomatic relations with Chile.[37] Similarly, since 1960 *Ecuador* has maintained the thesis of the nullity of the Rio Protocol signed with Peru (1942), which has led to subsequent armed rounds in the Peruvian-Ecuadorean dispute in the Cordillera del Cóndor, especially in 1981 and in 1995. The dispute still remains unresolved.[38]

Paraguay, another buffer state, did emerge victorious from its war against Bolivia in the 1930's, after suffering a catastrophic debacle in 1870 against a coalition of Argentina, Brazil, and Uruguay. Its historical trajectory and geopolitical position have led Paraguay, a quintessential weak state domi-nated by a patrimonialist dictatorship, to seek support of international law and the upholding of the territorial status quo in its relations with its mighty neighbors. Cleverly, Paraguay has followed since World War II a "pendulum diplomacy" that oscillates between Brazil and Argentina in order to keep its independence and relative autonomy vis-à-vis its powerful neighbors.[39]

The Northern Tier states—namely, Colombia, Guyana, and Suriname—are at least passively satisfied with the territorial status quo. *Colombia* is a particularly interesting case: it has been traditionally a very weak state, even after its early democratization in the late 1950s, despite its potentialities as a middle-range power in terms of military and economic power and some diplomatic latitude derived from its recent regional efforts at the Andean Group and the Contadora Group. At least until the 1960s Colombia has traditionally followed a low profile in its foreign policy, despite its territo-rial dispute with Venezuela. The "Tibet of South America," as it has been called, has been too immersed in its domestic problems to embark in revi-sionist adventures toward its neighbors.[40] The same can be said regarding the two former European colonies of Guyana and Suriname. They dispute their common border, while Venezuela still claims about half of Guyana's territory. These two small powers and weak states (ethnically divided) have been experiencing significant transitions towards democracy.

After reviewing both the domestic and the international sources of satisfaction, we can draw the following conclusions:

First, the current democratic regimes in the region are satisfied with the territorial status quo, with the exceptions of Bolivia and Ecuador. Since the return of democracy in 1983, and especially since 1989, Argentina has also become satisfied with the territorial status quo, with the exception of the Falklands/Malvinas issue.

Second, the two traditional strong states in the region, Chile and Brazil, have clearly expressed a normative (active) commitment to the maintenance of peace in the region, irrespective of their different and changing political regimes throughout their political history.

Third, as the case of Brazil clearly implies, there seems to be a clear correlation between domestic and international stability, and between the strength of the state and its degree of international power and status.

Fourth, as the cases of Uruguay, Chile, and Argentina demonstrate, there is no clear link between the objective military and economic power of a state and the status it enjoys in the hierarchy of prestige. Despite the Chilean relative military decline after the 1920s and the complete lack of military power in the case of Uruguay, both countries have enjoyed a relatively high status due to their high level of political and economic development. Conversely, Argentina, a strong military and economic power, enjoyed only a low level of prestige between 1930 and 1983, due to the weakness of its state and its low level of political development.

Fifth, weak and nondemocratic states and powers, as well as weak and democratic ones, tend to support the territorial status quo, at least in passive terms, as in the cases of Colombia, Paraguay, Guyana, and Suriname.

Sixth, weak states and powers might remain revisionist in their territorial claims, irrespective of their changing political regimes. Thus, Bolivia and Ecuador continue to be dissatisfied with their territorial status quo as a direct consequence of their territorial losses in the past. While Bolivia has adopted a certain political/diplomatic posture to reflect its lingering dissatisfaction vis-à-vis Chile, Ecuador did escalate its territorial conflict with Peru into military confrontations in 1981 and again in 1995.

Seventh, a discrepancy between objective power capabilities and a relative low status might result in a dissatisfaction with the status quo and revisionist policies geared toward closing this gap between the level of status and the level of power. This point has been illustrated in the cases of Peru (1968–80) and Venezuela (1970s–80s). Once these two countries relatively declined in terms of their power capabilities a new equilibrium was found to express their passive satisfaction with the status quo.

Eighth, in contrast to alternate cycles of political transitions from and to democratic regimes, the international relations of South America have been characterized in the last sixty years by a high level of conservatism and continuity, as a reflection of the widespread satisfaction of most of the countries with the territorial status quo.

CONDITIONS FOR THE MAINTENANCE OF REGIONAL PEACE IN SOUTH AMERICA

What have been the necessary, sufficient, and favorable conditions for the maintenance of peace in South America? How and when did negative peace move in the direction of stable peace? Are the Deutschian conditions for pluralistic security communities present in the case of the Southern Cone in the mid 1990s?

(1) Negative Peace, 1883–1980s

Regional peace, at least in its primitive, negative phase, preceded the development of stable peace in the mid 1980s and the emergence of an incipient security community in the 1990s. Despite the intentions of the OAS Charter and other regional legal instruments to turn Latin America in general, and the South American region in particular, into a zone of stable peace, the South American countries until a decade ago were only part of a zone of negative peace.

Negative peace has been maintained by the fact that the majority of the South American states—with the exceptions of Bolivia and Ecuador— have been actively or passively satisfied with the territorial status quo. Moreover, this was also facilitated by the presence of at least some strong states and some democracies in the region; a common cultural framework and a normative consensus of peaceful resolution of disputes; the pacifying presence of Brazil in the region, as the champion of the status quo since the beginning of the century; the lack of interaction among the South American states until the 1960s; geographical isolation and irrelevance, tied to their domestic constraints (economic and institutional) against fighting external wars; and their constant quest for economic development and prosperity, related to their subordinate position vis-à-vis the major economic powers. Interestingly, realist arguments such as the paramount U.S. presence in the region, the emergence of a balance of power from 1883 to the 1920s and again in the 1970s, and the reference to the United States as a common external threat have been less convincing in illuminating the reality of negative peace.

(2) Stable Peace in the Southern Cone Since the Early 1980s
With the spread of democracy in the region after the late 1970s, the South American countries—especially those in the Southern Cone—have been moving in the direction of stable peace, enhancing their economic interdependence and furthering their economic and political integration. In the case of the relationships among Argentina, Brazil, Paraguay, Uruguay, and even Chile, the outbreak of an international war has become unlikely, if not impossible. Moreover, with the resolution of pending disputes between Argentina and Chile (the Beagle Channel), and the end of the enduring rivalry between Argentina and Brazil, all the countries of this subregion have become satisfied with the territorial status quo, with the exceptions of Bolivia and Ecuador.

Following the return to democracy in Argentina (December 1983), and Brazil (March 1985), a notable improvement in their bilateral relations has taken place in the last decade. Since these two countries are also the major actors of the region, their political, economic, and even strategic cooperation have immediate repercussions for the Southern Cone and the whole of South America. A core of Brazilian-Argentine economic cooperation has set the parameters for the development of MERCOSUR, including also Uruguay and Paraguay; moreover, this development has also directly affected the revival of another important integrative scheme in the region, the Andean Pact. Their common democratic regimes and their enhanced economic interdependence guarantee the maintenance of a zone of stable peace.

Since the rapprochement between Argentina and Brazil begun in the late 1970s, the spread of democracy throughout the Southern Cone constitutes a sufficient, albeit not a necessary condition for stable peace. Thus, irrespective of the democratic character of the regimes, the necessary conditions are a continuing satisfaction with the territorial status quo, together with a common normative framework that expresses the predilection for peaceful change and peaceful settlement of international disputes. In addition, economic factors such as enhanced economic interdependence, subregional cooperation and integration, and the quest for economic development and prosperity have contributed to the maintenance and enhancement of stable peace, without being either necessary or sufficient.

(3) A Pluralistic Security Community in the Southern Cone, 1991–?
The highest level of peace South America can expect to achieve is through the formation and maintenance of a pluralistic security community. It is nowadays debated whether the Southern Cone countries have moved even beyond stable peace and in the direction of a security community, focusing around the recent MERCOSUR institutional framework (see Castañeda 1994; Holsti 1996; Hurrell 1994b; Kacowicz 1994b; Lowenthal 1994, 242–43; and Hirst and Rico 1992).

Has the Southern Cone of South America transformed itself into a pluralistic security community, in relation to which not only common threats but also shared perceptions and a common identity may be identified? In the economic sphere, MERCOSUR since 1991 epitomizes a serious effort at institutionalizing economic cooperation, increasing interdependence, and moving in the direction of economic, if not political, integration. In the security field, the level of cooperation regarding nuclear proliferation and banning chemical and biological weapons, as well as conventional arms control and reductions, has been notable among the ABC countries. Therefore, it seems that dependable expectations of peaceful change characterize today the relations among Argentina, Brazil, Uruguay, and Paraguay. At the political level, however, it becomes more difficult to talk about the Southern Cone as a consolidated pluralistic security community. For instance, in the last five years we have seen a growing divergence in the foreign policies of Brazil and Argentina vis-à-vis the United States, showing an interesting reversal in their traditional roles. These differences reflect unlike conceptions of national and regional identity. Argentina has reverted to its nineteenth-century image of a Western, almost European, country; while Brazil emphasizes its Latin American reach and Third World pedigree.

In their seminal work, Deutsch and his associates (1957) identified fourteen different conditions (two "essential" and twelve "helpful") for the development of pluralistic security communities. Most of these conditions are currently present in South America, especially in its Southern Cone, as follows:

(a) Compatibility of major values. According to Deutsch et al., there has to be a compatibility of the major values held by the relevant political strata of all the countries in the region. It is clear that today's value is democracy, although it is not the only one. Even before the latest advent of democratization in the region, the South American countries already shared com-

mon values and normative theories regarding the development of a specific Latin American international law and diplomacy.

(b) Mutual responsiveness. This condition refers to the "capacity of the participating political units to respond to each other's needs, messages, and actions quickly, adequately, and without resort to violence" (Deutsch 1957, 129). In other words, there should be a sense of community.

In the South American case, this sense developed with the rebellion against the domination of the Iberian colonial powers in the early nineteenth century and the subsequent wars of independence. In 1826, Simón Bolívar convened the First International Congress in the Colombian province of Panama. Bolívar referred to an Iberoamerican type of community, linked to the United Kingdom rather than to the United States. However, in the latter part of the nineteenth century, this Bolivarean idea coalesced with larger efforts of Panamericanism, which found expression after World War II through the Inter-American Treaty of Mutual Assistance and the Organization of American States, both sponsored by the United States. On the surface, adherence to the written principles of the OAS provided the basis for a viable hemispheric security community. But the actual work of the OAS did not entirely fulfill these expectations. The development of Panamericanism revealed an inherent ambivalence between the concept of belonging to the Western Hemisphere and the sense of a more exclusive community of Latin American nations. Despite this contradiction, mutual responsiveness persists, at least in rhetorical terms, at the bilateral and multilateral levels among the countries of the region, as illustrated by the current role of the Rio Group.

(c) A distinctive way of life. A strong strain of South American exceptionalism runs through the theory and practice of diplomacy among the countries of the region. South American diplomats and international lawyers usually assert that they have managed to develop a distinctive way of managing international relations in a peaceful way and much better than their European and Third World counterparts (see Jones 1991, 111).

(d) Development of core areas. The notion of core areas or regional hegemony seems to challenge the traditional concept of the balance of power. In this regard, Brazil's potential to exert influence throughout South America has been a key factor in maintaining the regional peace. A core of Brazilian-Argentine economic, political, and military cooperation have set the parameters for the development of MERCOSUR since 1991.

(e) Superior economic growth. According to this condition, the area's economic statistics should show a markedly superior economic growth, either as measured against the recent past of the region to be integrated or as against neighboring areas. The data regarding South America's economic performance in the early 1990s, as compared to that of the "lost decade" of the 1980s, is very encouraging: there has been an estimated average regional GDP growth between 3 percent and 5 percent, with inflation well under control, except in Brazil until 1997.

(f) Expectations of joint economic reward. The expectations of joint economic reward have been instrumental in the formation of MERCOSUR in March 1991 and in the revamping of the Andean Group. Economic incentives, as well as political ones, have pressed in the direction of political and economic cooperation, rather than any particular sense of "we-feeling."

(g) Wide range of mutual transactions. Unlike the peace of irrelevance of the past, the intraregional contacts have been expanding, intensifying, and increasing in importance. These interactions have diversified at a rapid pace, including nowadays flows of people, communication, intraregional trade, and investment in neighboring countries.

(h) Broadening of elites. This condition implies an expansion of the political, social, or economic elites. It has been effected, at least at the political level, through processes of liberalization and democratization that have taken place since 1978.

(i) and (j) Links of social communication and greater mobility of persons. Cooperation based on bilateral contacts and multilateral schemes of economic integration have enhanced the links of social communication among the countries and peoples of the region. These links include increased migration flows, cultural events, academic contacts, periodic meetings of regional and subregional organizations, and mutual visits by heads-of-state.

(k) Reluctance to wage "fratricidal" wars. Traditionally, South American forces had a reputation for close involvement in their countries' internal affairs, including recurrent coups d'état and civil wars. But they have not been actively involved in fighting each other. With democratization, the absence of international war has been extended also to the domestic scene, with the exceptions of Peru and Colombia.

(l) Outside military threats. In contrast to Central America and the Caribbean region, it is difficult to single out a tangible external threat to the countries of the region, especially since the end of the Cold War.

(m) Strong economic ties. As mentioned above, the relations among the South American countries until the early 1990s were *not* characterized by strong economic ties. Today the picture has changed radically, with high levels of intraregional trade and mutual investments, such as in the cases of Argentina and Brazil, Argentina and Chile, and Colombia and Venezuela.

(n) Ethnic and linguistic assimilation. With the exception of Brazil, the former British colony of Guyana, and the former Dutch colony of Suriname, the countries of the region had experienced the effects of three hundred years of Spanish colonial rule. Moreover, the social cohesiveness of the region has been enhanced by a common religion—Roman Catholicism. In contrast to other developing regions, South America has been quite homogeneous in terms of culture, faith, and language. Hence, the region has spared the traumatic experiences that have characterized ethnic conflicts in Africa, Asia, and even in some countries of Central America such as Guatemala.

In sum, most of the necessary and helpful conditions for the development of pluralistic security communities in South America in general, and in the Southern Cone in particular, have been present, some of them even before the last wave of democratization in the 1980s. Regarding the helpful conditions, we should underline the positive role played by Brazil and Argentina in developing the core of a potential security community in the region. Other favorable conditions, especially in the economic, social, and transnational realms, remain so far incipient. As a consequence, it is still premature to talk about a mature sense of community and shared identity ("we feeling") among the members of the region, including mutual sympathy and loyalties. Argentina and Brazil, as well as the other members of MERCOSUR and other subregional integrative schemes, still have a long way to go in terms of articulating common foreign policies, as well as coordinating their macroeconomic policies above and beyond the continuing development of their national economies.

CONCLUSIONS

In this chapter, I have analyzed the long South American peace since 1883, which incudes the period of stable peace among the countries of the Southern Cone and the emergence of a potential security community in the Southern Cone since the early 1990s.

To understand the maintenance of regional peace for more than one hundred years I have assessed nine alternative explanations: (1) the pacifying roles of the hemispheric hegemon, the United States, and of the potential regional hegemon, Brazil; (2) the formation of a regional balance of power between 1883 and 1930 and again between 1970 and 1980; (3) common external threat/s to the South American countries, especially the perception of the U.S. role; (4) geographic isolation, lack of interactions (irrelevance), and material impotence to fight international wars; (5) the effects of democratization upon regional peace; (6) the quest for prosperity and economic development, linked to the dependent position of the countries of the region vis-à-vis the major economic powers; (7) economic interdependence and integration; (8) a normative consensus about conflict management, based upon a common cultural framework; and (9) satisfaction with the territorial status quo, derived from both domestic and international sources. From the analysis of these alternative explanations, several conclusions can be elaborated:

First, some of these explanations obvious overlap and complement each other. For instance, satisfaction with the territorial status quo has been directly linked to the economic weakness of many South American states, as well as to their common normative framework in favor of *uti possidetis*.

Second, a distinction should be drawn between explanations that underline the mere existence of regional peace and those that emphasize its maintenance and persistence. For instance, normative consensus, democratization, and economic integration refer more to the quality of the peace to be maintained than to its creation. They are clearly linked to the upgrading of South America in the direction of stable peace and an incipient pluralistic security community.

Third, these explanations derive from different paradigms or worldviews regarding the reality of regional peace. While realists have emphasized factors such as balance of power or hegemony, liberals stress the effects of norms, democratization, international institutions, and economic interdependence. Yet this theoretical dichotomy is more apparent than real. For instance, a strong core or regional hegemon can coexist and even encourage the spread of norms of peaceful coexistence.

Fourth, the South American case is a vivid example of how non-democracies can establish and maintain peaceful relations among themselves and with democracies as well, including zones of negative and even stable peace. The liberal approach might explain the quality of that peace, and the transition from negative to stable peace and even to pluralistic security communities, as it is clearly demonstrated by the Southern Cone experience. Although democracy does not seem to be a necessary condition for the establishment of stable peace and pluralistic security communities, in the long run democratic regimes are the best guarantee for their maintenance and endurance. At the same time, negative peace (mere absence of wars) can be maintained if the majority of the countries of the region are or become satisfied with the territorial status quo. That satisfaction can be reached by both weak states, immersed in domestic security dilemmas and unable to fight external wars; or alternatively, by strong states, especially if they also sustain democratic regimes, such as Chile between 1883 and 1973, and since 1989. Strong and nondemocratic states can even be the staunchest champions of the regional status quo, as was the case with Brazil before its return to democracy in 1985.

Fifth, since satisfaction with the territorial status quo is not the only necessary condition for the maintenance of peace (it is sufficient for negative peace, but necessary for stable peace and for pluralistic security communities); it has to be complemented by other, related explanations. Hence, the South American case shows clearly the overdetermination of causes.

Finally, the South American case has demonstrated that nondemocratic regimes can maintain peace among themselves, if they are satisfied and embedded within strong states. Moreover, if democracies are peaceful in a region because they are satisfied, then nonsatisfied democracies might be revisionist, even turning to the use of violence. Conversely, not only strong and democratic states but also weak and nondemocratic ones might be satisfied with the territorial status quo. The logic seems to be that well-established democracies are at peace with one another, in part because their territorial ambitions are limited or satisfied, and so too are some nondemocratic states, although for very different reasons. Thus, satisfaction with the territorial status quo becomes an intervening variable for which we must look for deeper and perhaps multiple causes, both domestic and international.

In the South American case we have witnessed an interesting transition from negative to stable peace, and even from stable peace to an incipient pluralistic security community among the MERCOSUR member states. In terms of political regimes and types of states, all of the possible variations have been represented in the diplomatic history of this region. In the next chapter I turn to the analysis of a second zone of peace in the developing world: West Africa since 1957. Unlike South America, as we shall see, West Africa can at most be considered only as a zone of negative peace.

CHAPTER 4

WEST AFRICA, 1957–1996
International Peace and Domestic Wars

West Africa stands out as the only zone of negative peace in Africa since the beginning of the decolonization process after World War II. With the exception of the brief and inconsequential war between Mali and Burkina Faso in December 1985, there have been no international wars among the sixteen member states of the Economic Community of West African States (ECOWAS) that comprise West Africa. This condition of negative peace is quite remarkable, given the multiethnic and multinational character of the member states and the persistence of numerous territorial disputes. Moreover, this lack of international wars starkly contrasts with widespread domestic violence, military coups, and virulent civil wars, such as the Nigerian-Biafran conflagration of 1967–70; that of Liberia in 1990 to 1996; and that of Sierra Leone since 1992. The convoluted reality of West Africa, then, can be characterized by relative international peace and by domestic war. In the following pages, I analyze these two dimensions by addressing a similar question to that formulated in the preceding chapter: Why there have been no wars *between* states in the region, while so much domestic violence has taken place *within* them?

West Africa as a region is circumscribed by political factors such as diplomacy and former colonial administration, rather than by geographic or ethnographic characteristics. Fortuitously, West Africa was able to reach political independence without the complication of racial problems and the presence of white settlers, unlike East Africa or Southern Africa. Yet like other African regions it has suffered seriously from the political fragmentation created by the colonial powers (Adedeji 1970, 214–15; see also Simmons 1972, 296–97; and Cantori and Spiegel 1970, 48). In terms of cultural background, this region presents the most heterogeneous conglomeration of states in Africa, due to their diverse colonial trajectories. Four states were part of former British West Africa: Ghana, Nigeria, Sierra Leone, and The Gambia. Half of the West African states belong to the former French colonial empire in West Africa (AOF): Guinea, Benin, Ivory Coast, Mali, Mauritania, Niger, Senegal, and Burkina Faso. A third category of states includes Liberia, formally independent since 1847; Togo, a former

French and German colony; and Guinea Bissau and Cape Verde, which
won independence only in the mid 1970s after a long war of decolonization
against Portugal.

The sixteen states of West Africa occupy an area of about 6.1 million
square kilometers, with a population of about 200 million people. Although
the region has been endowed with many mineral and agricultural resources,
such as petroleum, iron ore, tin, lead, bauxite, gold, diamonds, cocoa, cof-
fee, and groundnut, it is considered one of the poorest and underdeveloped
of the world, with an annual average GNP per capita of less than $600. All
the ECOWAS states, including the relatively developed among them such
as Nigeria and Ivory Coast, are in the bottom 30 percent of the Human
Development Rank (Okolo 1985, 123–24; Shaw and Okolo 1994, 3;
Griffiths 1994, 217–19; Ezenwe 1983, 18–22). In domestic political terms,
only The Gambia and to a lesser extent Senegal were democracies before
1991. Most of the inept regimes of the region have been characterized as
either one-party regimes or military authoritarian ones. In a comparative
perspective, it seems that West Africa has experienced the greatest number
of military coups among the African regions (Grundy 1985, 108).

There are important differences among the West African states despite
their economic, social, and political commonalities. There are sharp inequalities in resources and sizes; there are maritime and Sahelian states; and
there is a divergence in their monetary systems. The most striking differentiation is that between Nigeria and the other fifteen members of ECOWAS.
Nigeria has a population and a GNP that are roughly equal to those of its all
West African neighbors together. This has affected the numerous attempts
of intraregional cooperation and integration, including the establishment
of ECOWAS in 1975 and the West African peacekeeping force in Liberia
in 1990 (ECOMOG).

At first sight, it would appear that there is a substantial potential for
violent interstate conflict, due to the artificiality of the political boundaries
and the transnational ethnic links that transcend the former colonial political divisions. And yet, irredentism on ethnic or historical grounds has been
almost nonexistent in the region, with the exceptions of Ghana against
Togo, Ghana against Ivory Coast up to 1966, Burkina Faso against Mali
until 1986, and Senegal against Mauritania in 1989–90. Moreover, West
Africa has experienced long-standing disputes among countries on several
issues: frontier disputes between Ivory Coast and Ghana, Nigeria and Benin,

Dahomey and Niger, and Mali and Burkina Faso; traditional rivalries between Guinea and Senegal and between Senegal and Mali; and long-standing suspicions between Nigeria and Ghana (at least until 1966), between Nigeria and Ivory Coast since the 1960s, Ghana and Ivory Coast in the 1960s and again in the 1980s, and Burkina and Ivory Coast in the 1980s (see Agymean-Duah 1990, 558). Among all these disputes, only Burkina Faso and Mali engaged in a brief war (in December 1985), while Senegal and Mauritania sustained a long militarized dispute in 1989–90 without escalating it into a full-fledged war (see Kacowicz 1997).

This negative regional peace has been the result of a rational policy adopted by the West African states to respect their international borders and to avoid the implementation of separatist, irredentist, and self-determination claims on a national (i.e., ethnic) basis. Moreover, it has been the by-product of their preoccupation and even fixation with domestic problems, leaving no motivations or means to fight external wars. Although the political boundaries were determined by colonial administrators arbitrarily, they have been thoroughly respected by the new independent states. In West Africa, as in South America, the principle of *uti possidetis* has been adopted partly as a response to the institutional, economic, social, and political weaknesses of the new countries, which were states-nations rather than nation-states, having to govern multiethnic populations and to deal with mostly domestic security threats. Since the West African states had to define themselves according to the preexisting colonial boundaries, most of them realized that they had a reciprocal interest in respecting their international borders (see Herbst 1989; Herbst 1990, 117–19; and Jackson and Rosberg 1982). This commitment has been furthered by the norms of behavior developed by the Organization of African Unity (OAU) and by the legal framework of the international community that upholds the "juridical" sovereignty of all African states, notwithstanding their empirical conditions (see Jackson 1987). Furthermore, the juxtaposition of Anglophone, Lusophone, and Francophone states has tended to harden the formal borders between them (Asiwaju 1993, 78). This recognition of the international borders masks the fact that these boundaries have been very permeable since precolonial times. In the words of Robert Kaplan (1994, 46): "There is no other place on the planet where political maps are so deceptive as in West Africa." This permeability has been manifested through transnational transactions involving people (labor and refugee migrations, guerrilla fighters), and commodities (smuggling and "unofficial" trade). The effect of these transactions has been mixed: positive, with respect to the maintenance of peace *across* borders; and detrimental, by the exacerbation of domestic conflicts, as in the cases of the civil wars of Liberia and Sierra Leone.

In the following pages I examine several explanations for the regional negative peace that characterizes West Africa. First, I succinctly narrate the diplomatic history of the region since 1957. Second, I examine realist arguments such as Nigerian hegemony and a regional balance of power. Third, I refer to several liberal explanations. Fourth, I address the "satisfaction" argument, emphasizing its domestic and international dimensions. Finally, I speculate about the prospects for the emergence of stable peace and a pluralistic security community in the future.

THE HISTORICAL RECORD: A NARRATIVE OF WEST AFRICAN INTERNATIONAL RELATIONS

Because of its relative marginalization and isolation from the East-West struggle during the Cold War, West Africa, unlike other African regions such as the Horn or Southern Africa, has been understudied in terms of international relations and diplomatic history, with a few exceptions concerning ECOWAS and the relationship between the Francophone states and their former colonial power, France. Yet the West African negative peace should be comprehended not as a mere by-product of the area's marginalization from the mainstream events in international relations, or as a French artifact, but mainly as a result of the evolving intraregional relations since the formal independence of Ghana in 1957.

The historical record of West Africa can be divided into the following periods: (1) a *preindependence* period, including precolonial times and the colonial rule between 1883 and the early 1960s; (2) the *formative period* of 1957–66, characterized by the emergence of new independent states and a turbulent phase of multiple alliances and rivalries (1960–63), followed by the formation of the OAU in 1963; (3) the *external consolidation* period, defined by intensive domestic turmoil—military coups, the Nigerian civil war of 1966–70—as opposed to the ulterior emergence of Nigeria as a regional power in the early 1970s; (4) the *ECOWAS* period of 1975–89, defined by the formation and evolution of the regional organization and its relative failure in economic terms ("the lost decade"); and (5) the *contemporary* period of 1989–96, which includes the Senegalese-Mauritanian conflict of 1989–90, the civil war in Liberia and Sierra Leone that led to the formation of ECOMOG in 1990, the democratization wave of the early 1990s, and the end of the Cold War and its effects upon the region.

The Preindependence Period: Precolonial Wars and Peaceful Decolonization, Up to 1957

In precolonial times West African politics were regulated by complex norms, rules, and institutions, including the peaceful settlement of disputes and norms for the limitation of war (Bull 1984, 106). With the exception of the Islamic revolutions, African wars were not ideological, but rather fought for material and territorial reasons (see Smith 1976). They were an important part of the life of loosely defined political entities—sometimes extended kinship systems, sometimes more established kingdoms and communities—that preceded the emergence of the colonial states at the end of the nineteenth century (see Jackson 1993, 138–40).[1]

In the 1880s the scramble for Africa accelerated. The Berlin Conference of 1884–85 epitomized the emergence of the modern state system, which was copied from the European metropolitan model and featured clearly defined political boundaries and territoriality. It was this new colonial state system, rather than the old, precolonial model, that after 1957 would provide the juridical and territorial basis for the African postcolonial system of independent states. The "political balkanization" of West Africa by European colonialism, and the failure of the colonial system to find a delicate equilibrium between the colonial state and the precolonial African societies, left a long-term heritage of domestic instability and external peace for postcolonial Africa. This colonial heritage is the necessary point of departure for any analysis of contemporary African international relations, including its regional negative peace and the rigidity of its international borders (see Bull 1984, 114; Young 1995, 23–24; Lamouse-Smith 1992, 70–71; Young 1988, 32–52; and Boyd 1979, 1).

The colonial period culminated with the postwar interregnum of 1945–60, during which peaceful decolonization took place, with the exceptions of the Portuguese colonies of Guinea Bissau and Cape Verde. At its beginning, colonialism seemed impregnable and destined to last for ever; fifteen years later it was almost completely liquidated. The protagonists of this impressive process of peaceful change were both the colonial powers (Britain and France), and the "local heroes." In the British colonies, the pace was set partly by Kwame Nkrumah, leading to the independence of Ghana in 1957. In French West Africa, Sekou Touré of Guinea openly defied President De Gaulle's colonial policy by opting for immediate independence in 1958. Of the fifteen West African colonies, eleven gained political sovereignty by 1960 (nine in that very year), the next two between 1961 and 1965, and the last two (Guinea Bissau and Cape Verde) in 1973 and 1974, respectively.

In contrast to decolonization processes in other developing regions, the British and French-ruled territories of West Africa became independent through constitutional negotiations rather than through revolution and war. The end of the British and French empires was rapid and smooth, although the effects were in the long term pernicious for economic development and domestic politics. For instance, the "Loi Cadre" (Outline Law), enacted by France in 1956, divided French West Africa into a semifederal framework of eight colonies with an autonomous status, leading to the creation of eight different weak states. Although the borders of these states were arbitrarily drawn by the French, they have been solemnly kept until the present day.[2]

The Formative Period: New Independent States, Ideological Alliances and Splits, and the Formation of the OAU, 1957–66

According to I. William Zartman (1966, 1), the international relations among the states and states-to-be in West Africa were directed toward the achievement of three concurrent goals: political independence, regional unity, and economic development. At the domestic level, the first few years of independence were characterized by systematic efforts on the part of the new political leaders to build the state and the nation by concentrating power at the political center, by overcoming the constraints of the colonial heritage through the reorganization of public institutions, and by trying to create a nation out of the multinational colonial framework (see Chazan et al. 1992, 46). Conversely, at the international level, the new states of West Africa embarked in a series of alliances, counteralliances, and attempts at regional unity between 1957 and 1963. This active drive for political, or at least functional, cooperation was motivated by a Pan-African ideology of continental unity and by the desire to avoid isolation (Zartman 1966, 17).

During this early period, the new West African states successfully passed the test regarding the stability of their national frontiers. A kind of equilibrium was achieved between a relative failure in creating or consolidating larger political groupings beyond the former colonial state, on the one hand, and on the other a relative success in preventing the disintegration of the basic territorial units—the colonial states—established during the colonial period. For instance, the Ghana-Guinea Union of November 1958 died of inaction; the Mali Federation composed of Soudan (later Mali) and Senegal, founded in January 1959, broke up by August 1960; and even the radical Union of African States of December 1960—including Ghana, Guinea, and Mali—was later absorbed into the Casablanca bloc by January 1961. This Casablanca group, under the leadership of Kwame Nkrumah of Ghana, put political unity first and looked forward to the liquidation of the former colonial boundaries and the establishment of a pan-African state or states. In contrast, the Monrovia group led by Ivory Coast and to a lesser extent Nigeria gave priority to economic cooperation instead of political association. By the time the OAU was established in 1963, the Union of African States had disintegrated, while the Monrovia group's position was ultimately vindicated through the OAU Charter (see Oliver 1992, 231; Thompson 1972, xvi; Griffiths 1994, 76–77; Williams 1961; and Welch 1966, 340–41).

Between 1957 and 1961 the emergent Francophone states of West Africa were split over the issue of "balkanization." Leopold Senghor of Senegal agreed on the separation of Francophone West Africa from France, but as a single political unit. By contrast, Houphouet-Boigny of Ivory Coast urged France to grant independence on an individual basis, while maintaining strong ties between the metropolis and its former colonies. At the same time, Houphouet resented Sekou Touré's newfound stature as the leader of independent Guinea after 1958 and his budding alliance with Nkrumah of Ghana. As a reaction to the political radicals and unificationists led by Ghana, Guinea, and later Mali, Houphouet-Boigny formed the Conseil de l'Entente in October 1958, which included Ivory Coast, Dahomey, Upper Volta, and Niger. The Entente states constituted the core of the conservative Brazzaville Group (1960), later regrouped in the

UAM (the Union Africaine et Malgache de Cooperation Economique), the OCAM (the Organization Commune Africaine et Malgache), and the larger Monrovia group that ultimately set the tone in the formation of the OAU in 1963 (see Post 1968, 166–73).

In this initial period Ghana played a preponderant role in the international relations of the region, while Nigeria played only a minor one. Through the charismatic leadership of Nkrumah, Ghana successfully diffused the ideas of African unity and a distinctive "African personality" (see Timothy 1981, 228). By contrast, Nigeria under the civilian rule of Prime Minister Tafawa Balewa (1960–66), focused upon the cultivation of a "special relationship" with the United Kingdom at the expense of an active regional role. Moreover, the diametrically opposed attitudes of Balewa and President Nkrumah regarding which strategy of African unification should be adopted explain the difficult relations between these two key countries until 1966 (see Akindele 1973, 58–59; Ihonvbere 1991, 517; and Stremlau 1977, 17–20).

By 1962 a series of state visits among Senegal, Guinea, Mali, and the Ivory Coast led the way to reconciliation among the Francophone states of the region. Ghana became isolated, especially by the military coup in Togo of January 1963. By the beginning of 1963, it became clear that the functionalist, nonpolitical path to regional and continental unity was the one to be followed, instead of the political path sponsored by Ghana. The Addis Ababa Conference of May 1963, which established the OAU, marked the end of the alliances and counteralliances in the foreign relations of the West African states. The Charter of the OAU, signed on 26 May 1963, represented a clear victory of the moderates over the radicals in the debate about the nature and form of international relations to be followed (see Rubin and Weinstein 1974, 238–39; Sessay et al. 1984, 1–5; and Post 1968, 175–76). Like Bolívar before him, Nkrumah had his dreams of political unification on a supranational framework under his leadership shattered by the pragmatism and political realism of his neighbors. The OAU Charter itself included only a formal institutionalization of the elusive slogan of unity, while sanctioning the independence of the postcolonial states. At least in formal terms, the chaotic and frantic search for alliances and ideological counter-alliances of 1957–62 was now replaced by a "concert" system that promoted sovereign equality, noninterference in domestic affairs, and respect for the sovereignty and territorial integrity of all African states.

The Period of External Consolidation: Domestic Turmoil, Nigerian Civil War,
and the Emergence of Nigeria as a Regional Power, 1966–75

During the years 1966–75 three major events took place in the region, which affected the course of its international relations: the replacement of democratic regimes by military coups and civilian authoritarian regimes; the Nigerian civil war of 1966–70; and the emergence of Nigeria as the preponderant regional power in the early 1970s.

The replacement of formal democracy by single-party and military rule in the mid 1960s transformed the politics of West Africa. The emergence of one-party systems of government and the recurrence of military coups (with the subsequent establishment of military governments) became widespread, with very few exceptions, such as The Gambia and Senegal. African leaders were looking for suitable political institutions and arrangements to secure their control of state power. It was assumed that the West African states were affected by similar problems, such as inter- and intraelite conflict, ethnic strife, collapsing institutions, economic collapse, and corruption. Almost all the military leaders who brought about "coups galore" in 1966–70 claimed that the previous civilian government was corrupt, the economy was in disorder, and the masses should be mobilized for national reconstruction and development (see Wiseman 1990, 18; Jackson and Rosberg 1985, 297–98; Feit 1968, 180–81; Bienen 1985, 358; and Charlton 1983, 284–85). Interestingly, the new military regimes did not change the course of their foreign policy as compared to their civilian predecessors, with the exception of the military government that replaced Nkrumah in Ghana in 1966. A list of military coups that took place in the region between 1963 and 1975 is summarized in table 4.1.

The second major event that took place in this period was the Nigerian civil war of 1967–70. This was a long domestic crisis, with serious international repercussions. It started with the Ibo military coup of General Ironsi on 15 January 1966, which deposed the civilian federal government in Lagos. In July 1966, after anti-Ibo riots took place in the north, Ironsi was overthrown in an anti-Ibo coup that brought to power Colonel Gowon, a northern Christian. Gowon attempted to solve the constitutional problem of having only three regional governments—in the North, West, and East— by breaking up the three regions into twelve states. At this point, in July

Table 4.1. Successful Coups d'Etat in West Africa, 1963–75

Year	Country	Leaders	Civilian/Military
1963	Benin	Ahomadegbe	Civilian
1963	Togo	Grunitzky	Civilian
1965	Benin	Soglo	Military
1966	Burkina Faso	Lamizana	Military
1966	Ghana	Ankrah	Military
1966	Nigeria	Ironsi	Military
1966	Nigeria	Gowon	Military
1967	Benin	Alley	Military
1967	Sierra Leone	Juxon-Smith	Military
1967	Togo	Eyadema	Military
1968	Mali	Traore	Military
1969	Benin	De Souza	Military
1972	Benin	Kerekou	Military
1974	Niger	Kountche	Military
1975	Nigeria	Murtala Mohammed	Military

Source: Griffiths (1993, 210–15).

1967, the military governor of the eastern region took the fateful decision of resisting the division of the East into three states, leading to Biafra's secession from Nigeria and detonating a virulent civil war. It lasted until January 1970 and cost almost two million lives. After an initial Ibo advance through the Mid-West region was repulsed, the military outcome was already clear, though it took the federal forces two more years to defeat Biafra, because of the support of the latter by external powers including France, Portugal, and South Africa.

The Nigerian civil war, though formally a domestic affair, had important international repercussions. From a regional perspective the OAU was caught in a dilemma of attempting to manage the conflict and to promote peace, on the one hand, while condemning the Biafran secession and not wanting to interfere in the domestic affairs of Nigeria, on the other.[3] The vast majority of the West African states, with the exception of Ivory Coast and Benin, remained hostile toward the attempt at secession by Biafra. In the African continent, Biafra gained diplomatic recognition only by Ivory

Coast, Gabon, Tanzania, and Zambia. The rest of the African states officially supported the Nigerian government and criticized the four countries
that challenged the orthodox interpretation of the principle of national
self-determination, according to which the legitimacy of an established state
and its territorial borders should not be challenged by force.

After the attempted secession of Biafra was suppressed by force, the
process of peaceful reconciliation between the Ibos and the federal government proceeded smoothly, to the amazement of many political observers
(Lawler 1976, 1). Nigeria emerged from its virulent civil war as a single
state and as a major political force in West Africa. Politically, Nigeria became a more united, stable, and confident country. Due to the astonishing
expansion of its oil production and rising prices, a relatively strong and rich
state emerged from the ashes of the civil war. This economic bonanza led
to significant changes in the degree of state authority, state intervention in
the national economy, and especially in the relations between Nigeria and
its neighbors (see Gambari 1975, 161–62; Griffiths 1994, 86–90; and Williams and Turner 1978, 152–53).

Among the lessons Nigeria learned from its civil war was the need to
have friendly governments among its neighboring countries to protect its
national security both externally and internally. With its increased financial
power and substantial economic growth, Nigeria was in a strong position
to push its claims as the paramount regional power. Its post–civil war regime decided to become active in the promotion of economic assistance to
its neighbors. It used its economic prosperity through "spraying diplomacy"
by fostering bilateral and multilateral frameworks of cooperation in the
region. The political and economic goal was to create a framework of
regional integration—an economic community of West African states.

In April 1972, General Gowon of Nigeria and President Eyadema of
Togo signed a treaty providing for the establishment of an "embryo" of
ECOWAS. According to Gowon's diplomatic strategy of bandwagoning,
it was clear that a Nigerian-Togo economic community would also bring
sandwiched Benin to the fore. Once Benin joined the economic community, Niger would have little choice but to follow suit. After Niger, isolated
Guinea would come, and then the rest of the Francophone states. In seeking the support of these countries, Nigeria pursued a carefully planned
strategy of persuasion, offering interest-free loans, grants, concessionally
priced oil, and equity investments in common ventures. These efforts finally

bore fruit. Following meetings in Accra in February 1974 and Monrovia in January 1975, the treaty establishing ECOWAS was adopted by a ministerial meeting at Lagos on May 28, 1975 (see Okolo 1985, 123–28; Huxtable and Hobson 1994, 8–10; Ojo 1980, 590–91; Lancaster 1995, 195; Inegbedion 1994, 222; and Bach 1983, 617).

The idea of ECOWAS offered the promise of political stability and economic development beyond the scope of preexisting functional and integrative efforts at the subregional level, such as the Organization of Senegal River States, the River Niger Commission, the Mano River Union, the Conseil de l'Entente, the Customs Union of West African States (UDEAO), and even the large Francophone Economic Community of West Africa (CEAO). In this sense, ECOWAS was the latest and most significant effort to integrate all the states of the region into a viable economic framework. It was regarded as necessary to reduce dependence upon the developed countries, to foster economic development, and to improve collectively the bargaining position of West Africa vis-à-vis the industrialized states.

The ECOWAS Period: Economic Failures and Political Successes, and the
"Lost Decade" of Growth, 1975–89

The ECOWAS's long decade of 1975–89 was defined by the creation and institutionalization of this regional integration scheme, its ambiguous economic record, and its more promising political setting. The 1980s witnessed the relative decline of the Nigerian preponderance in economic and political terms, the clustering of regional conflicts around radical military regimes in Burkina Faso, Ghana, and Liberia, and the only significant interstate war that took place in West Africa, involving Burkina Faso and Mali in December 1985. In economic terms this period was characterized as the "lost decade" because of its negative economic growth and lack of development.

Nigeria played a pivotal role in the creation of ECOWAS in 1975. ECOWAS reflected Nigeria's attempt to transcend the rivalry with France and the Francophone states, which had established a more exclusive integrative scheme back in 1970. Although the conflict between Nigeria and its Francophone neighbors moderated, some distrust remained. Nonetheless, all the states of West Africa remained formally committed to a regional economic integration. In the first few years of its existence, ECOWAS organized its regional bureaucracy and negotiated tariff-reduction schedules and a common industrial policy (see Bach 1983, 605–17; and Huxtable and Hobson 1994, 11–13).

ECOWAS failed to fulfill its ambitious economic goals. The consolidation of customs procedures was not implemented. Moreover, trade liberalization was postponed again and again. The protocol on the free movement of labor was finally signed in 1986, but few states actually ratified it. Mostly important, the proportion of intraregional trade remained very low, just over 5 percent of their total trade (Lancaster 1995, 196). The economic stagnation of ECOWAS coincided with a decline of Nigerian political and economic influence in the early 1980s following the end of the oil boom and serious domestic political problems. Nigeria's foreign policy became more a matter of rhetoric and propaganda than a consistent program for advancing Nigeria's interests in a regional framework (see Ihonvbere 1991, 524–25). Nigeria preferred its narrow national interests to the welfare of the regional community and ordered the closure of its land borders in April 1984. It expelled hundreds of thousands of illegal immigrants from the country in May 1985.

In political terms, ECOWAS fulfilled a more positive role as a kind of reference group or "club" for the West African heads of state to manage conflicts and to institutionalize clear rules of the game, including basic norms of peaceful coexistence and continuing commitment to the goals of the organization (see Lancaster 1995, 196–97; Agyeman-Duah and Ojo 1991, 299). The 1980s witnessed the emergence of a second generation of military leaders, more radical and populist, who deviated from the consensus institutionalized in ECOWAS: Jerry Rawlings in Ghana after 1979; Thomas Sankara in Burkina Faso between 1983 and 1987; Samuel Doe in Liberia between 1980 and 1982; and Mathieu Kerekou in Benin after 1972. These military leaders stood at the center of most of the region's conflicts in the 1980s, which were not allowed to degenerate into open warfare, with the exception of the brief war between Mali and Burkina Faso in December 1985.

This shooting war between Mali and Burkina Faso escalated from a long dispute over the allegedly mineral-rich Agacher Strip along their common border. Some journalists and scholars refer to this conflict as a "war," though it hardly merited the name, since combat ended in a few days and casualties were light (about sixty to one hundred men). The dispute was exacerbated by the ideological animadversion between the parties, since Sankara in Burkina Faso had launched a challenge to the conservative Francophone countries. The war ended inconclusively after five days through the intervention and mediation of Houphouet Boigny of Ivory Coast and other Francophone states of West Africa through their common defense pact (ANAD). The Burkina-Mali armed conflict vividly demonstrated the extreme sensitivities of West African states —such as Mali—to radical or revolutionary regimes on their borders.[4]

The 1980s were characterized not only by ideological and territorial conflicts but also by a catastrophic economic crisis that affected most of the countries of the region—negative growth, stagnation, declining rates of agricultural growth and declining volumes of exports, worsening income inequality, more extensive absolute poverty, and a serious gap in their balance of payment. This economic crisis was accompanied by a political crisis, including political decay, corruption, immobilism, domestic violence, and instability (see Sandbrook 1985, 1993; Kraus 1994, 247–52; Adedeji 1993, 4). This was a "lost decade" in which the region became more marginalized, and at the same time, more dependent upon the international political economy. Africans themselves began to realize the seriousness of their economic crisis when they signed a continental plan of economic reform at Lagos in 1980. Only in the early 1990s, did the economic situation of several West African countries—such as Ghana—start to improve.

The Contemporary Period: The Senegal-Mauritania Conflict, the Liberian Civil War and ECOMOG, Democratization, and the End of the Cold War, 1989–96

Since 1989 the West African region has been immersed in a series of conflicts that highlight its dual condition of international peace and domestic war. In 1989–90, Senegal and Mauritania became locked in a serious confrontation that led them to the verge of war. By the end of 1989, Liberia faced an invasion by dissidents located in Ivory Coast; it triggered a long and virulent civil war that spilled over into Sierra Leone in 1992–93. In spite of the end of the Cold War and a widespread wave of democratization initiated by Benin in 1990–91, it seems that the region is experiencing more violence nowadays than it did in previous periods. At the same time, the civil wars in Liberia and Sierra Leone, although they had important international ramifications, did not escalate into armed conflicts involving the different states of West Africa. To the contrary, since 1990 we have witnessed the deployment of ECOMOG, a regional peacekeeping (or peace-enforcing) military force under the auspices of ECOWAS and the Nigerian leadership; it has intervened to stop the carnage in Liberia and in Sierra Leone.

The Senegal-Mauritanian border tensions, which led to the fatal incident at Diawara Village on 9 April 1989 and to subsequent mass killings, pogroms, and deportation of Senegalese in Mauritania and of Mauritanians in Senegal, were rooted in a long history of land disputes among individuals and communities living along both banks of the River Senegal. It was desertification that pushed nomadic Arab herders into the territory of sedentary black African farmers who inhabited both banks of the river, which divides the two states. A series of border incidents between Senegalese and Mauritarian farmers and border police across the valley rapidly precipitated riots and bloodshed within both states, leading to a massive population transfer. It has been estimated that about twenty-two hundred people died in Mauritania and about sixty in Senegal as a result of ethnic riots (Bluwey 1994, 97). At the intergovernmental level, Mauritania and Senegal severed diplomatic relations in April 1989, militarized their common borders, and prepared for a war that never took place. After two years of negotiations and the mediation of the OAU, the two countries agreed to reopen diplomatic relations. This dispute did lead to the worst intercommunity violence that has ever taken place between Moors and Africans *within* Senegal and Mauritania. Moreover, the sense of good neighborliness that characterized the relations of two states close to each to other geographically, historically, and ethnically has completely disappeared.[5]

The crisis involving Senegal and Mauritania in 1989–90 was not very significant in comparison to the civil wars that have taken place in Liberia and Sierra Leone since December 1989 and 1992, respectively. Initially, the invasion of Liberia by a small band of rebels led by Charles Taylor, crossing into the Nimba County from neighboring Ivory Coast, seemed a minor affair. Yet the rebel forces managed to control most of the country within months, taking advantage of the animosity toward the dictatorship of Samuel K. Doe. Thousands died and many more fled across the borders into Guinea, Ivory Coast, and Sierra Leone. Another rebel group under

Prince Johnson challenged both the beleaguered government in Monrovia and the forces of Taylor. In August 1990, a number of West African countries, under the leadership of Nigeria and the formal auspices of ECOWAS, decided to send a peacekeeping force (ECOMOG) to Monrovia to broker a peace among the armed factions. ECOMOG grew to 7,000 troops by the end of 1990, and reached more than 11,500 by 1993. It protected the "Interim Government of National Unity" of Dr. Amos Sawyer by securing Monrovia and its immediate surroundings.

The civil war in Liberia spilled over into neighboring Sierra Leone through rebel incursions by the NPFL forces of Charles Taylor. About six hundred thousand Liberians (out of a population of about 2.5 million) were displaced by the war and fled to Sierra Leone, Guinea, and Ivory Coast. The civil war posed a serious threat of destabilization to the regional security, since many of the West African states harbored similar ethnic cleavages within their own national territories. Moreover, the war created a serious humanitarian and economic burden to the neighboring states through the overflow of refugees into adjacent countries and the return of repatriated nationals. In the words of President Babangida of Nigeria,

> It appears that events occurring in other parts of the world have rapidly upstaged the problem of crisis of Africa. Nowhere is this development more observable than in Liberia where the complete breakdown of law and order, the killings, the starvation, the general suffering of Liberians and other Africans go almost unnoticed by the international community. . . . The clear lesson that is evolving is that the time has come for Africa to take its destiny in [sic] its own hands. We can no longer abandon the management of crisis in Africa to external actors
> . . . Instability in any of the countries of West Africa affects the stability of West Africa, as well as affect [sic] the lives of thousands of our people [living abroad]. The experiences of other regions of the world prove that economic development can only be promoted in a stable and secure political environment. (Babangida 1991, 9)

The formation of ECOMOG underlined the extent to which Nigeria reasserted itself as the leading power in the region, at least in military terms. The ECOMOG force was initially manned by contingents from The Gambia, Ghana, Guinea, Sierra Leone, and Nigeria. Ivory Coast and Burkina Faso, and to a lesser extent Togo and Benin, initially opposed its deployment. Senegal and Mali contributed some contingents after 1993, while

Niger, Cape Verde, Mauritania, and Guinea Bissau were inactive throughout the Liberian conflict (see Best 1991, 41; Nwokedi 1992, 3–5; Burguess 1995, 9; Smock 1991, 15–16; Akinrinade 1992, 47–48; Da Costa 1993, 19–20; Clapham 1994; and Ero 1995, 1–6).

The ECOMOG operation in Liberia went through four distinct phases. In the first phase, from August to November 1990, ECOMOG played the role of peace enforcement rather than peacekeeping, directly confronting the rebel forces of the NPFL until an initial cease-fire was agreed to and a semblance of order was restored in and around the capital, Monrovia. In the second phase, between November 1990 and October 1992, ECOWAS was involved in peacemaking, orchestrating several peace negotiations among the warring factions (the series of "Yamousoukro agreements" [I to IV], under the sponsorship of Houphoue-Boigny of Ivory Coast). With the spillover of the war into Sierra Leone and the breakdown of the cease-fire in October 1992, ECOMOG renewed its use of force against the forces of Taylor and instituted economic sanctions and an arms embargo on Liberia. Finally, the last phase since 1993 has witnessed a widening of peacemaking efforts, this time involving the United Nations and the OAU. The Cotonou Agreement of 25 July 1993 and a series of cease-fires "officially" ended the war by September of 1995 with a cost of at least 150,000 people dead. On 6 April 1996, the civil war was reignited for several weeks with renewed clashes between the governmental forces (this time including Charles Taylor as a prominent member of the transitional government) and the armed faction of Prince Johnson.[6]

Has the ECOWAS action in Liberia been a success or a failure? Probably both. On the positive side, it stopped the carnage that had been rampant in Monrovia previous to the presence of ECOMOG. Moreover, it somehow prevented the continuation of anarchy in the country and led to the peace agreements of 1993 and 1995. As the Ghanaian foreign minister stated in 1990, "For the first time, African countries are prepared to take on very heavy responsibilities in terms of finance, men, and other things, to try to help another African country to get back on its feet. It is a very useful development, and it does mean a certain reinvigoration of ECOWAS" (Asomoah, quoted in Novicki 1990, 20). On the negative side, the ECOMOG intervention did prolong the civil war for five long years, even though the rebel forces of Charles Taylor already controlled two-thirds of the country. Moreover, it epitomized an initial cleavage between Anglophone and Francophone states and was ultimately regarded as an instrument of a renewed Nigerian bid for hegemony. In any case, the ECOMOG operation did eventually reinforce the importance of ECOWAS as a political forum for negotiations and mediation, in contrast to its failure to fulfill the economic goals of the integration.

While the Liberian civil war was unfolding, a more promising process was taking place in the region: democratization. Between 1989 and 1991 political demonstrations and riots rocked several one-party states and military regimes in the region. This political movement, coupled with economic reform and liberalization, has become the focus of what Africans call their "second independence" and has marshaled the support of the international community since the end of the Cold War (see Sandbrook 1993; Harbeson 1995; Legum 1990, 130–34; and Ake 1993).

Only eight years ago there were only two countries in West Africa with reasonably open political systems: The Gambia and Senegal. Since 1989, however, most of the countries in the region have experienced at least some degree of democratization. Benin was one of the fist authoritarian regimes to be replaced by a democratic multiparty system. Military leaders were also deposed in Mali, and transitions to civilian rule were negotiated successfully in Niger, though unsuccessfully in Nigeria and Togo. Cape Verde and Guinea Bissau experienced in the early 1990s successful transitions toward multiparty systems. Flawed elections, still considered representative, have taken place in Ghana, Ivory Coast, Burkina Faso, and, most recently, in Sierra Leone. Political liberalization has occurred in Guinea and Liberia, and to a lesser extent in Mauritania. Although this wave of democratization seems to be very popular in West Africa, as elsewhere, it has to cope with the difficult social and economic environment that characterizes this region, including economic underdevelopment and ethnic cleavages. The fragility of this process has been clearly demonstrated in recent coups in The Gambia, Niger, and Sierra Leone, and in the continuing military rule of General Sani Abacha in Nigeria (see Allen 1992, 25; Raynal 1991, 3–4; and Cohen 1995, 286–88).

It is evident that the rhetorical support of the West for democratization and liberalization in the region has been linked to the end of the Cold War and to the increasing marginalization of West Africa in economic, political, and strategic terms. As the intrinsic importance of West Africa gradually decreased, the West could relax, allowing itself a greater latitude to conduct a more principled foreign policy (Ake 1993, 71). The African countries may perceive this attitudinal change as a new, and more pervasive, form of *political* conditionality and intervention in their domestic affairs, alongside with the persisting economic conditionality that had already imposed reform and radical adjustment of their national economies.

As compared to other regions in the African continent, West Africa has been less affected by the end of the Cold War, since it had been relatively isolated from it. Yet the threat of increasing marginalization—as evidenced by the French gradual withdrawal from its economic and military commitments toward its former colonies—has posed new challenges and opportunities to the member states of ECOWAS. The dual reality of regional peace and domestic war might continue in the near future, though it might be affected, or distorted, by the diminishing prospects of economic aid and new investments from extraregional sources. We might witness a trend toward greater regionalism in West Africa as characterized by the imperative of economic cooperation and a more intensive bid for political domination and regional competition. In the West African theater the major actors will probably remain Nigeria and Ivory Coast, though Ghana, Senegal, and even Burkina Faso and Benin will seek at least a prestigious role to play.

Recap: Negative Peace and Territorial Conflicts in West Africa

This brief narrative illustrates the contradictory situation in West Africa, characterized by the absence of international wars and by virulent domestic conflicts. With the exception of the Burkina-Mali war of 1985, all interstate conflicts have not escalated to the degree of full-fledged wars. Instead, the countries of the region have chosen among a wide repertoire of foreign-policy measures to express their conflict behavior, including: breaking diplomatic relations, closing of borders, disruption of economic relations, support for another regime's internal enemies, official statements criticizing other governments, and troop mobilization and militarization of their frontiers (see Agyeman-Duah and Ojo 1991, 306–7). Despite the distrust and the acrimonious competition among several states in the region, including covert belligerent interventions across borders, open war has been considered an aberration in terms of normal or expected foreign policy (see Bozeman 1976, 45).

While West Africa has been marred by innumerable conflicts, both domestic and international, negative peace has prevailed at the regional level. Civil wars have spilled over into neighboring countries, if only because of the transnational ethnic connections. Yet the transformation of a civil war (such as Liberia's) into a regional imbroglio has not changed that war into an international conflagration involving several states.

The West African states have been highly interactive and interdependent among themselves, to the extent that nearly all of them have been involved in a conflict with a neighboring or distant state. The motives for these conflicts have been multiple. Among them are: (1) decolonization power struggles; (2) new independent consolidation; (3) leftover liberation movements; (4) ill-defined territorial boundaries; (5) structural rivalries, in terms of regional power distribution; (6) ideology, personal rivalries, prestige, and bid for regional subparamountcy, as in the fluctuating relations between Nigeria and Ghana; (7) refugee issues and migrant populations, as in the case of the Nigerian expulsion of about one million Ghanaians in 1982; and (8) the harboring of opposition and dissident forces across borders, such as the Guinea Bissau's support for the Casamance guerrillas against Senegal, and the notorious support of Nkrumah's Ghana of several radical groups against Nigeria and other conservative regimes in the early 1960s. Some border disputes have been economically motivated, such as the Mali-Burkina Faso conflict over the Agader Strip, Senegal-Mauritania in 1989–90, and Senegal-Gambia. Some other conflicts have been precipitated by sociopolitical problems, such as the spillover of civil war from Liberia to Sierra Leone and of Chad into Niger and Nigeria; the irredentist claims of Togo over Ghana and vice versa; and the irredentist claims of Ghana over Ivory Coast. Maritime frontiers have been also a source of interstate conflicts, as in the case of the dispute between Senegal and Guinea-Bissau, recently resolved by an International Court of Justice decision. In addition, some of the West African states have had serious border disputes with extraregional members: Nigeria with Cameroon (1981), Chad (1983), and Equatorial Guinea over the island of Fernando Po; and Mauritania with Morocco over the Western (Spanish) Sahara. In the Nigerian case, the fact that Nigeria has strained relationships with its non-ECOWAS neighbors (i.e., Chad, Cameroon, and Equatorial Guinea) partly explains its more accommodative disposition toward its West African partners (see Asiwaju 1993, 85).[7]

Most of the international conflicts in West Africa have been related to territorial disputes, usually associated with the demarcation of the colonial borders. Only a few territorial disputes have been linked to irredentist claims on historical and ethnic bases, such as the mutual claims of Ghana and Togo over the Ewe homeland, the claims of Ghana over Sanwi in Ivory Coast, and the Senegal claims over the Senegal Valley, party occupied by Mauritania. A comprehensive list of territorial disputes and other, nonterritorial conflicts is summarized in table 4.2.

Table 4.2. Territorial Disputes and Nonterritorial
Conflicts in West Africa

	Years of Dispute	Countries Involved	Issue(s)
A. *Territorial and Border Disputes*			
1.	1963	Dahomey-Niger	Lete Island
2.	1959–66	Ghana-Ivory Coast	Sanwi (Ivory Coast)
3.	1958–66	Ghana-Togo	irredentism (Ewe)
4.	1963–66	Ghana-Upper Volta	border demarcation
5.	colonial–1958	Guinea-Liberia	claims near Nimba
6.	colonial–1960	Liberia-Ivory Coast	Cavally River
7.	1960–63	Mali-Mauritania	Eastern Hodh
8.	1960–86	Mali-Burkina Faso	Agacher strip
9.	1960–85	Senegal-Gambia	border demarcation
10.	1960–64	Niger-Upper Volta	border demarcation
11.	1960–92	Senegal-Mauritania	Senegal Valley
B. *Non-Territorial Disputes*			
12.	1957–66	Nigeria-Ghana	ideological rivalry
13.	1957–66, 1980s	Nigeria-Ivory Coast	status rivalry
14.	1966	Ghana-Guinea	ideological rivalry
15.	1983–87	Burkina-Ivory Coast	ideological rivalry
16.	1957–63	Mali-Senegal	personal rivalry
17.	1957–96	Senegal-Ivory Coast	status rivalry

To cope with this vast array of territorial and nonterritorial disputes the West African states have skillfully established institutional mechanisms within the OAU, ECOWAS, and the CEAO. This has been furthered by the

ECOWAS Protocol Relating to Mutual Assistance (1981), which establishes a mechanism of collective security, including cases of internal conflict that might endanger the security and peace of the West African region (see Omede 1995, 47).

What are the prospects of West Africa to move ahead from this dual condition of domestic wars and negative regional peace in the direction of stable peace and the formation of a security community? The answer is at best ambiguous, depending upon many unpredictable variables, such as the extent to which Nigeria will democratize or not in the near future, or the continuing pace of economic growth of Ivory Coast and Ghana. It is evident, though, that economic growth and emerging democratic regimes in the region might contribute to the upgrading of the quality of peace among states, as well as within them. At the same time, Africa's "second independence" (i.e., democratization) might result in the revitalization of ethnicity and politicized tribal identity, as well as the emergence or resurgence of civil society (see Mazrui 1993, 34), leading to claims of national self-determination. While optimists will argue that the existing international boundaries will remain protected by the same norms that have kept those borders since independence, pessimists hold that the existing disparity between Africa's de jure and de facto political map will increase markedly, resulting not in a movement from negative to stable peace but in a reversal from negative peace to active interstate conflict (see Kaplan 1994; Ravenhill 1988).

Explaining the West African Negative Peace, 1957–96

According to the framework developed in chapter 2, the alternative explanations for the West African negative peace are clustered in three groups: (1) realist and geopolitical; (2) liberal; and (3) satisfaction with the territorial status quo.

Realist and Geopolitical Explanations

To understand the maintenance of regional negative peace four alternative realist explanations can be mentioned: (1) the presence of a hegemon— either extraregional or regional—that imposes and maintains the regional peace; (2) the formation of a regional balance of power; (3) a third-party threat against the countries of the region; and (4) lack of material means, and/or irrelevance. According to these explanations, much of intra-African and even extra-African foreign policy has little to do with domestic needs or purposes. Moreover, despite the low levels of military and economic power, some evident principles of national interest have affected certain states. For instance, the landlocked West African states—Mali, Burkina Faso, and Niger—need good relations with their maritime neighbors. Similarly, the smaller states, such as Togo or Dahomey, need good relations with their more powerful neighbors (such as Ghana or Nigeria) to counterbalance threatening neighbors (see Zartman 1965).

(1) The Pacifying Roles of France and Nigeria
Three countries can aspire to the role of hegemon: France as an extraregional hegemon; Nigeria, which has partially fulfilled that function as the dynamic force behind ECOWAS and as the sponsor of ECOMOG; and Ivory Coast, which competes with Nigeria in the economic realm.

France has maintained a strong presence in its former colonies in West Africa, sometimes preventing the outbreak of serious civil or interstate wars. Its postcolonial commitment to its former dependencies is based upon cultural, economic, strategic, and prestige considerations (Zartman 1984, 40). Thirty-six years after independence, France continues to play a dominant role in the formulation of economic and monetary policies through the franc zone. Similarly, Francophone states still rely upon it for military security through bilateral military assistance agreements, including the eventual deployment of French troops to assist the local governments, with the exception of Guinea (see Martin 1995; Kraus 1994). Interestingly, the most virulent civil wars in West Africa have taken place outside of the French neocolonialist reach—in Nigeria, Liberia, and Sierra Leone.

This "French connection," "frequently tutelary, often intrusive, and sometimes overly interventionist" (Young 1995, 30), has complicated the relations between Francophone and Anglophone countries in West Africa. While France has considered Nigeria as a potential threat to its interests in West Africa, the Nigerians, in turn, have perceived France as a source of danger and as an obstacle to the expansion of their regional influence. France may have played a pacifying role vis-à-vis the relations among the Francophone states, but it was more of a negative factor in the international relations among the sixteen states of the region. It exacerbated the mutual suspicion and competition between Ivory Coast, Senegal, Burkina and Mali, on the one hand, and Nigeria and Ghana, on the other (see Olaniyan 1986, 148; Nwokedi 1985, 198; and Akinterinwa 1990).

The obvious candidate for subparamountcy at the regional level has been Nigeria. On any measure of objective factors such as population and military and economic power, it should dominate West Africa. But internal problems (ethnic cleavages and political decay) have bedeviled the country since independence, precluding a clear fulfillment of its hegemonic role. As with Brazil in South America, Nigeria has played a positive and preponderant role in keeping the regional peace. This has become evident with the launching of ECOWAS in 1975, and especially with the ECOWAS intervention and deployment of ECOMOG during the civil war in Liberia. At the same time, the Nigerian dominance has been traditionally disputed by other states that regard themselves as alternative candidates for regional leadership, including Ghana, Ivory Coast, and Senegal.

Nigeria is immediately surrounded by Benin, Niger, Cameroon, and Chad. Its relations with its West African neighbors have been far more cordial than with Cameroon and Chad. Particularly since the end of its civil war, Nigeria has recognized the need to maintain good relations and to "build bridges" across to the rest of West Africa. Its foreign policy has always rested upon five basic principles that overlap with the regional normative consensus: sovereign equality, respect for independence, respect for boundaries, noninterference, and functional cooperation (Akinrinade 1992, 49). Nigeria did play successful roles of mediation in the dispute between Guinea and Senegal, and between Dahomey and Niger. Instead of using its size and resources to threaten its neighbors, it has preferred diplomatic negotiations and economic inducements.

Nigerians have always regarded themselves as having a "manifest destiny" to fulfill in the African continent. They consider the pursuit of peace and functional cooperation as a function of their historical role by virtue of the fact that they are the largest black country in the world. Hence, they have created a "Father Christmas" image for themselves as a result of their apparent goodwill toward their neighbors (Moyosore 1990, 33–34). This image goes all the way back to the initial foreign policy, as stated by Prime Minister Balewa in 1964:

> All that we pray for the African continent is that there will be peace and stability. If there is to be peace and stability the countries in Africa must

maintain the closest friendly relations with one another. I see no point at all in Nigeria having to station troops along the border with Dahomey, Chad, and Niger. . . . (Balewa 1964, 80)

This "Father Christmas" image was reflected in the early 1970s in the Nigerian efforts that successfully led to the formation of ECOWAS in 1975. This was achieved primarily through petrodollars (or petro-nairas) and massive Nigerian aid to its neighbors. Despite the collapse of the oil market in the early 1980s and its domestic political turmoil, Nigeria continued to collaborate with its neighbors, especially following the rise of Ibrahim Babangida in August 1985. Nigeria's eagerness to reassert itself as the major peacemaker and political influence in the region became evident with the ECOMOG initiative of August 1990. The Liberian civil war has become a kind of test case to assert the degree to which other states in the region are ready to accept Nigeria's new prominence. The ECOMOG operation also illustrates the inherent contradictions and the dilemma of Nigeria's potential hegemony. On the one hand, Nigeria has been always preoccupied with finding ways of cooperating with its neighbors, including its Francophone rivals. On the other hand, it has constantly attempted to have its prestige acknowledged by the other West African countries. As President Babangida recognized, Nigeria considered itself "duty-bound" to influence and affect any event "which threatens to jeopardize or compromise the stability, prosperity, and security of the subregion" (quoted in Adibe 1994b, 2–3).

(2) A Regional Balance of Power
An alternative realist explanation depicts the West African negative peace as a function of a balance-of-power system involving a set of informal and formal alliances that developed in the initial phase of independence until 1963. Yet, given the general low level of power of the West African states and the preponderance of Nigerian military power after 1970, it seems quite irrelevant to refer to a concrete regional balance of power as having a pacifying effect upon their international relations.

Between 1957 and 1963 the new West African states involved themselves in a frantic drive for alliances and regional unity, stemming from both the pan-African ideology of unity and the desire to avoid isolation (Zartman 1970, 117). As a result, a Kautilyan pattern of checkerboard links emerged, with the interlocked alliances of the radical countries—Guinea,

Ghana, and Mali—in opposition to the conservative Conseil de l'Entente grouping of Ivory Coast, Upper Volta, Niger, and Dahomey. Soon this primitive and local checkerboard was replaced by a more sophisticated and larger balance of power in which the Casablanca (radical) group opposed the Brazzaville/Monrovia (conservative) group. Ultimately, this balance of power proved to be ephemeral, being dissolved into a "concert" system institutionalized through the formation of the OAU in 1963 (see Zartman 1970, 123–26).

Beyond this short period of formal alliances until 1963, the only balance of power that comes to mind after 1970 is a veiled competition for regional military and economic supremacy between France and Nigeria, despite their considerable economic ties and potential for bilateral cooperation. Nowadays, since Ivory Coast has become the largest intraregional trading partner, another informal equilibrium might be evolving between Nigeria and Ivory Coast in geopolitical and geoeconomic terms.

(3) External Threats to the West African Countries
A third realist argument links the maintenance of regional peace to a simple logic of alliance formation. According to this logic, the ideology of pan-Africanism has been conceived as a defensive response to the colonialist and postcolonialist threats of France and other colonial powers or surrogates (such as South Africa). Yet, with very few exceptions, the security of the new states of West Africa has been endangered by neither extraregional threats nor the threats from their own neighbors. The major source of insecurity has been and remained *domestic*—threats by the army (or factions within it), political opponents, and ethnic conflict. In turn, the threats to regional security can most often be traced to a wide variety of deprivations (such as famine, disease, and pestilence) exacerbated by domestic conflicts (see Keller 1996, 5).

While there have not been clear external threats to the region as a whole, threat *perceptions* have shaped the relations among the major countries of the region. For instance, while Nigeria never proved to be a source of external threat to the independence of its Francophone neighbors, countries such as Ivory Coast, Burkina, Senegal, and Mali usually regarded Nigerian activist foreign policy with some degree of fear and suspicion, as in the case of the ECOMOG operation. Conversely, Nigeria traditionally considered the French connection in West Africa as a considerable source of danger. Yet, these mutual perceptions of threat have been relatively minor in comparison to the serious domestic problems that affect the internal fabric of the West African states and that might spill over boundaries, such as in the case of the Liberian civil war.

(4) Irrelevance and Impotence to Fight Inter-State Wars
The most important sources of threats to the West African states have been indeed *domestic*, rather than international. Since they have been so immersed in dealing with their own domestic problems, they have been quite impotent to fight outsiders. Their regional negative peace has not been a mere consequence of French or Nigerian hegemony, or of a fortuitous balance of power or third-party threats. Instead, this negative peace is also explained by their domestic wars and by their lack of power and resources to escalate their international disputes.

The postindependence period in West Africa has been characterized by an intense concern with nation-building within the borders of the colonial state. National integration of diverse ethnic subgroups and the concern with economic development and growth have removed from the agenda the question of external borders, which have been generally accepted as given by the vast majority of the new states. Therefore, interstate war, conquest, and even widespread external violence have been always considered outside of the West African normative consensus. Moreover, wars were also considered as an irrelevant option, since there have not been many West African "powers" (in terms of military, economic, scientific, technological, and industrial capacities) to carry them out. In simple material terms, the typical military forces in West Africa have been very weak, organized for neither border defense nor for aggressive attacks. This weakness has been a direct result of the underdeveloped state of the economies. As a result, territorial expansionism has been very rare, in Africa in general, and in West Africa in particular, leading to the widespread respect, if not satisfaction, with the territorial status quo.[8]

Liberal Explanations

The extent to which the liberal explanations have been relevant to understand the maintenance of negative peace in West Africa has been at best limited. In the first place, the democratic peace argument has been irrelevant;

authoritarian regimes have kept the regional negative peace. Second, the countries of the region are economically underdeveloped; prosperity and development remain a major goal in the articulation of their foreign policies. Third, since 1975 ECOWAS has fulfilled a positive role as a force for the maintenance of regional peace. Yet ECOWAS has been more relevant as a political and security forum than as an economic framework for integration. Finally, Pan-Africanism and the support for *uti possidetis* have been important consensual norms that have articulated the peaceful international relations of the region and supported the territorial status quo.

(1) Political Regimes and Democratization

As mentioned above, most of the countries of the region, with the exceptions of The Gambia (until 1994), and Senegal (since the end of the 1970s) have not sustained democratic regimes. There have been a vast array of nondemocratic regimes in the region, including: (1) party-mobilizing regimes, such as Ghana under Kwame Nkrumah, Mali under Modibo Keita, and Guinea under Sekou Touré; (2) party-centralist regimes, such as the "Afro-Marxist" states of Guinea-Bissau and Benin; (3) personal-coercion regimes, such as Liberia under Samuel Doe (1980–90); (4) populist regimes, such as Ghana under Jerry Rawlings since the mid 1980s, and Burkina Faso under Thomas Sankara in the mid 1980s; (5) plebiscitarian one-party systems, such as President Eyadema's regime in Togo; (6) military oligarchies, such as President Babangida's in Nigeria; and (7) competitive one-party systems, such as the regime of Houphouet-Boigny of Ivory Coast (see Chazan et al. 1992, 142–48; Bratton and Walle 1994, 474–83).

The most distinctive political feature of West Africa in the last forty years has been the occurrence of military coups and the lack of full-fledged democracies, linked to the weaknesses of its state structures and the multinational character of its societies. The 1963 coup in Dahomey initiated a long series of military takeovers. One civilian regime after another soon succumbed to the new political consciousness of the armed forces, with the exceptions of Ivory Coast, Senegal, Cape Verde, and The Gambia (until 1994). Despite some obvious political changes in the domestic arena, what is striking is the degree of continuity in foreign policy, with the possible exceptions of Ghana before and after 1966 (following Nkrumah's deposition) and the military populist regimes of Ghana, Liberia, and Burkina Faso in the mid 1980s. Furthermore, the innumerable military coups have had only most indirect links with the "outside world." Contrary to what the diversionary theory of war might predict, internal instability in West Africa has not been translated into aggressive foreign policies, so that militocracies have managed to keep a negative peace among themselves (see Wright 1992, 337; Matthews 1970b, 484; and Bienen 1980, 180–86).

Whether civilian or military, most African regimes have been authoritarian. The near universal failure of democracy in the new states of West Africa has been directly related to a general weakness of state authority and the absence of basic conditions for institutional governance. However, since the beginning of the 1990s West Africa has witnessed an impressive wave of liberalization and democratization as part of a continental trend that is currently sweeping Africa. These political transitions have adopted four basic forms: (1) normal transformations from military dictatorships to civilian regimes via national conferences, as in Benin, Mali, and Niger; (2) managed military transitions, in which the military regime still retains complete control over the political process, as in Burkina Faso, Ghana, Guinea, and Mauritania; (3) extreme cases of authoritarian military reaction, in which the process has been truncated by the military, as in Nigeria, Togo, and Sierra Leone; and (4) co-opted transitions, in which the civilian executive gradually allows the opening of the political system, as in Ivory Coast and Senegal (Martin 1995, 179).

These democratization processes are at best protean and uncertain. Elections have taken place in several countries, including Ghana, Nigeria, Ivory Coast, Senegal, Mali, Benin, Cape Verde, and Sierra Leone. At the same time, there have been some serious reversions to authoritarianism, such as in Nigeria, the Gambia, Niger, and Sierra Leone. Even in Senegal, where multiparty elections have been held several times, civil unrest broke out following the secessionist struggle of the Casamance. It is unclear whether the "Western" form of democracy will succeed in the region, beyond its mere formalistic expression. The future of this fragile wave of democratization seems to depend upon two interrelated trends: the strengthening of the state and the consolidation of its civil society.[9]

To what extent will this political wave lead to a deepening of the regional peace? According to the democratic peace theory, one can expect that as the number of consolidated democracies increases, the quality of their international relations will change accordingly in the direction of stable peace and the emergence of security communities. In the long term, democratic rule is essential to guarantee domestic peace, and domestic peace in itself is a prerequisite to reach stable peace and integration at the interstate level. Conversely, in the short term, these processes might have destabilizing effects upon the domestic and international arena by increasing political pluralism and exacerbating possible ethnic and separatist claims, with possible irredentist and transnational claims that spill over international borders.

(2) Economic Underdevelopment and (Lack of) Prosperity
In terms of the necessary economic preconditions for the establishment of democracy, it is clear that the West African region is truly disadvantaged, with one of the poorest records of economic underdevelopment. At the same time, the demand for economic development has become synonymous with the need for successful government, so that the democratization wave can be considered partly as a result of the "lost decade" of negative economic growth in the 1980s.

Economic development and prosperity in themselves cannot explain the negative peace in West Africa, since they remain wanting. Yet as paramount goals in the national agendas of the new states since 1957, they provide a rationale for maintaining the regional status quo and promoting economic cooperation on functionalist terms. For instance, international river and lake basins in West Africa have been the subject of joint interstate actions and integrated development plans, including irrigation projects, hydroelectric power exploitation, fisheries development, improved transportation involving navigation and ports, and the promotion of intraregional trade (Ofoegbu 1971, 23-24; see also Austin 1984, 207). Furthermore, the need for development and growth has provided an *economic* justification for the formation of ECOWAS and other integration schemes through collective economic self-reliance. In this sense, the pursuit of these goals, as the liberal theory suggests, has had a pacifying effect upon the international relations of the region.

Just as South America remained dependent on Britain during the nineteenth century, so West African states have experienced formal political independence along with continuing economic dependence upon their former colonial masters—the United Kingdom and especially France. West Africa's place at the periphery of the global economy and the phenomenon of neocolonialism have had a pacifying effect in two ways: through the direct effects of dependence (metropolitan–former colony vertical relationships) and through the indirect effects upon the intraregional (horizontal) relations themselves (see Yansané 1984, 377; Aluko 1987, 661–62; Callaghy 1995, 42–44; and Shaw 1978, 231–36). For instance, among the Francophone states, key states such as Ivory Coast and Senegal have developed and maintained conservative positions regarding the territorial status quo as a reflection of their economic, and even military, dependence upon France. Moreover, the disposition of the West African states to enhance their cooperation through the OAU and ECOWAS has been justified, in both economic and *political* terms, as a need to overcome collectively the extreme dependence of their national economies on the export of primary agricultural products to the industrialized North, exacerbated by the growing imbalances between the prices of raw materials and those of manufactured products.

(3) Economic Interdependence, Integration, and Transnational Relations in West Africa
A third, related liberal explanation for the maintenance of regional peace emphasizes the degree of economic interdependence and transnational relations among the countries and peoples of the region. In the West African context, there are three relevant overlapping and contradictory characteristics. First, the degree of economic interactions and transactions at the interstate level has remained very low since independence throughout the 1990s. Second, there is an important regional institution, ECOWAS, that epitomizes the relative failure of economic integration and the relative success of political and security cooperation. Third, at the unofficial level, the region has witnessed a substantive flow of transnational transactions among peoples and across borders.

In general, the volume of interstate trade within West Africa has remained very low. Intra-West African and international trade patterns show insignificant horizontal interactions among the countries of the region, in contrast to high vertical relationships between them and the industrialized countries of the North. This has been a result of their colonial history, the lack of economic complementarity of their economies, the process of state-building and nation-building that impeded the emergence of a regional consciousness and unity, a lack of regional infrastructures in terms of transport and communication, and their divergent currency systems and linguistic affiliations. After twenty years of ECOWAS formal cooperation, intraregional trade remains less than 10 percent of their total trade (see Okolo 1985, 124; Wright 1992, 340; Good 1964, 636; Okwechime 1988, 102; and Adibe 1994, 199–201).

Against this discouraging picture, the launching of integration schemes has been justified in political and economic terms as a *means* to further economic and political interdependence among the West African states and independence from the former colonial powers. The political elites of the new states bolstered interstate integration by emphasizing their small-scale internal markets and their financial weaknesses, as a result of the colonial balkanization of West Africa. In addition to the failed federalist projects of political integration, West African states have established about *twenty-one* major economic cooperation and functionalist integration schemes, including the Francophone Community of West Africa (CEAO) in 1970 and the larger ECOWAS grouping of 1975. Unfortunately, many of these schemes have been "paper" integrations—that is, ephemeral and lacking in substance (Ravenhill 1988, 301).[10]

The establishment of ECOWAS in 1975 has been the most ambitious of recent integrative projects. The goals of this organization as stated at its inception were far-reaching and comprehensive—cooperation for trade promotion and liberalization, increased freedom of movement for its populations, transportation development and coordination, coordination of telecommunications, industrial and agricultural growth, raising the standard of living of its peoples, and increasing and maintaining economic stability. In spite of the fact that most of the economic goals have remained unfulfilled, the mere existence of an institutional framework of economic, social, and even political integration has contributed to keeping the regional peace. In this sense, ECOWAS has been by far more successful as a political forum than as an economic community.

From an economic point of view, it seems that the obstacles in the path of ECOWAS toward collective self-reliance have been many and insurmountable, related to both intraregional and extraregional developments. Among them are: (1) the differences in size of the member states, as represented by the economic predominance of Nigeria and Ivory Coast, and to some extent Senegal and Ghana; (2) the existence of other intergovernmental organizations alongside ECOWAS, such as the CEAO, with different loyalties; (3) the different political and economic orientations of the regimes and the constant changes in political leadership, coupled with a lack of democratic governments; (4) the rise and fall of the Nigerian regional leadership, following the drop in the oil market; (5) the diversity of currencies and complex exchange controls; (6) the low levels of intraregional trade; (7) extroverted, rather than introverted, communication and telecommunication links; (8) the competition, rather than complementarity, of the national economies as primary producers of similar agricultural products; and (9) different levels of economic development, juxtaposing emergent industrializing markets in Nigeria, Ivory Coast, Ghana, and Senegal with completely underdeveloped countries, such as The Gambia or Burkina Faso (see Olaniyan 1986, 143–44; Okolo 1985, 130–33; Aribisala 1985, 85–86; Lancaster 1995, 202; Kumar and Osagie 1978, 48–52; Okwechime 1988, 110; and Ezenwe 1983, 138–51).

From a political point of view, the balance sheet of ECOWAS has been more positive. To start with, "the greatest common denominator of the sixteen countries belonging to ECOWAS has been precisely that: their membership in ECOWAS" (Kornfeld 1990, 87). ECOWAS has become an important political forum, or "reference group," for the consensual behavior of its member-states. It has also contributed to the peaceful settlement of international disputes and conflicts. The relative strength of the organization has been demonstrated by the members' willingness to act collectively to maintain the stability of the region, and even to intervene in the domestic affairs of other member-states, such as in the case of the ECOMOG intervention in Liberia since 1990 and most recently in Sierra Leone (May–June 1997). The Liberian operation, despite its setbacks and the lack of consensus among its ECOWAS members, has demonstrated the possibilities of a regional collective security framework, applied as a response to a *domestic* threat to the regional security. In this sense, it can be interpreted not only as a means to bring peace to that country but also as a heroic (if not very successful) attempt to link the end of a domestic war to the maintenance of the regional peace.

In addition to the interstate level, liberal and neofunctionalist theories emphasize a second dimension of cooperation and interdependence: transnational relations among peoples rather than among states. West Africa has since colonial times been characterized by a high level of transactions across its formal political borders. Because many local border communities maintain close transnational ethnic, sociocultural, and economic ties, the West African political borders have been usually porous and pregnable.

Many ethnic groups are "vivisected" across international borders, such as the Yoruba and Baatonu across Nigeria-Benin; the Kanuri across Nigeria-Niger; the Gourmantine astride Benin-Togo-Burkina; the Akan across Ghana-Ivory Coast; the Mende of Sierra Leone, Liberia, and Guinea; the Ewe of southwestern Nigeria, southern Benin, southern Togo, and south-eastern Ghana; the Wolof of Senegal and Gambia; the Dioula across Senegal-Guinea Bissau; and the Moors and Tukulors across Senegal-Mauritania (Asiwaju 1993, 90). These transstate relations have involved people (labor and refugee migrations, guerrilla fighters), and commodities (smuggling, narco-trafficking, and other "unofficial" trade). Increased informal sector exchanges across borders have compensated for the stagnation in the official trade, including money, labor, goods, and services (Shaw and Okolo 1994, 7). The freedom of movement supposedly guaranteed by the ECOWAS Protocol is in fact a means to provide a de jure status to a preexisting situation of labor movement across borders, which dates back to precolonial times (Brydon 1985, 583).

Given the permeability of these boundaries and the impressive scope of transnational transactions, this "transstate regionalism" seems to challenge the juridical reality of existing political borders in the region (see Bach 1995). As a result, its impact upon the maintenance of regional negative peace has had contradictory effects. On the one hand, if it implies a process of deterritorialization of the "juridical" states of the region, then this situation goes far to explain the infrequency of border wars and formal interstate armed conflicts—they just do not make any sense. Moreover, these transborder transactions might contribute to the emergence of a sense of community at the subnational and transnational levels. On the other hand, the erosion or irrelevance of the political borders can also signify that domestic conflicts might easily spill over across borders, such as in the cases of the Liberian civil war being "diffused" to Sierra Leone.

(4) Cultural Framework and Normative Consensus
Like the South American countries, the West African states have developed a very specific normative consensus of their own in the form of a reciprocal respect for the norms of territorial integrity and *uti possidetis*. The norms of behavior established by the Organization of African Unity in 1964 in favor of the "freezing" of the international borders were designed to keep the international peace in the region and to delegitimize war as a

mechanism to resolve international disputes. With the exceptions of Somalia, Morocco, Ghana, and Togo, the policies of the vast majority of African states reflect their respect for their existing borders. This normative consensus has been reached in West Africa despite a heterogeneous cultural framework of distinctive French, British, and Portuguese legacies.

The importance of international norms as an explanatory factor for the maintenance of regional peace derives primarily from the fact that the principles of decolonization, colonial self-determination, and sovereign equality adopted by the international community as a whole after World War II have conferred "juridical statehood" on the new states of postcolonial Africa even if they lacked the empirical components of sovereignty. The desire to retain formal sovereignty, as recognized by international law and diplomacy, has constituted a powerful motive to respect and perpetuate the ex-colonial territorial status quo and discouraged both secessions and unifications (see Jackson and Rosberg 1982, 1985; Jackson 1993; and Young 1995, 26).[11]

In addition to the norms adopted by the international community as a whole, the West African states themselves managed to establish a structure of norms that limited intraregional conflicts and led to multilateral forms of conflict resolution. These basic norms included: (1) nonintervention in the domestic affairs of other African states; (2) nonrecourse to force in inter-African relations; namely, interstate wars were not considered legitimate policy alternatives; (3) nonrecourse to extraregional military, economic, political, and diplomatic assistance in the resolution of regional disputes; in other words, African solutions should be preferred in dealing with African problems; and (4) respect for the territorial status quo, as established by the colonial powers. This last norm has stood in direct opposition to the norm of Pan-Africanism, at least in its extreme (Nkrumah's) version of political supranationalism.

The most relevant norm to explain the maintenance of negative peace in West Africa has been the principle of the sanctity of colonial boundaries—the juridical concept of *uti possidetis*. As a result, most of the territorial disputes that have arisen in independent West Africa have been resolved by direct negotiations and mediation, applying the colonial treaties as the point of juridical reference. As with the ban against harboring other states' subversives, the doctrine of *uti possidetis* has held through a reciprocal interest not to open a Pandora's box of ethnic self-determination. This rationale has been clearly expressed by the former president of Togo, Sylvanus Olympio, as follows:

> In their struggle against the colonial powers the new African states, arbitrary and unrealistic as their original boundaries may have been, managed at least to mobilize the will of their citizens toward the attainment of national independence. Achieved at great sacrifice, such a reward is not to be cast away lightly; nor should the national will, once unified, be diluted by the formation of nebulous political units. (Quoted in Emerson 1962, 280)

In addition to article 3, paragraph 3, of the OAU Charter, which emphasizes the principle of respect for the sovereignty and territorial integrity of each African state, the OAU Cairo Declaration of July 1964 specifically refers to the respect for the existing colonial borders in very similar terms to the policy adopted by the new Latin American states in the wake of the end of the Spanish Empire in the Western Hemisphere. Thus, the Declaration expresses that "all Member States pledge themselves to respect the frontiers existing on their achievement of national independence" (Brownlie 1970, 360–61). The 1964 resolution provided the basis for a rule of regional customary international law, binding those states that expressed the acceptance of the territorial status quo at the time of their independence. Moreover, it helped to establish the primacy of a basic norm of international law over the Pan-African preindependence ideology that previously challenged existing borders (Touval 1967, 125; Young 1991, 328–35). In sum, the notion of the nation-state was replaced in favor of the state-nation, or territorial state, linking the principle of territorial integrity with the preservation of the colonial frontiers, at the expense of ethnic self-determination. At the same time, the OAU resolution did not address the problems arising from different interpretations of documents defining the border demarcations and from irredentist claims based on historical demands previous to the colonial period (as in the cases of Somalia and Morocco).

Satisfaction with the Territorial Status Quo

The majority of the West African countries, with the exception of Ghana and Togo between 1957 and 1966, Senegal in 1989–90, and Burkina Faso in the mid 1980s, have consistently adhered to the maintenance of the territorial status quo in their region.

Satisfaction with the territorial status quo has been a crucial cause, though not the sole one, of the phenomenon of negative regional peace. Certain factors peculiar to the African scene have generated this satisfaction, such as: (1) the ideological appeal of Pan-Africanism (African unity); (2) the normative consensus of the African states, manifested through the principle of *uti possidetis* and the norms of the OAU in favor of the territorial status quo; (3) the weak resource bases of most states in the region in terms of military and economic power; (4) the weak character of the regimes and states; (5) the multiethnic character of most African states and their internal lack of cohesion and stability; (6) the common perceptions of domestic threats and vulnerability, including threats of secession as in the cases of Nigeria and Congo (ex-Zaire); (7) the conservative bias of the politicians who gained power in the terminal colonial period, who ruled in the first two decades after independence; and (8) the emphasis upon state- and nation-building, based upon the former colonial state as the legitimate focus of political control.

Despite the fact that innumerable tribes and ethnic groups vivisect the borders in West Africa, irredentist claims, such as Ghanaian and Togolese mutual claims for the Ewe's homeland, have been very rare. This meager support for revisionist causes is a further evidence of the decision of the majority of the West African states to preserve their existing borders. As mentioned, this commitment has been directly related to the fear of opening an ethnic Pandora's box: once any boundary is seriously questioned, why not all boundaries in Africa? Hence, the predilection for territorial integrity over national (i.e., ethnic) self-determination has been a consequence of both political realism and the desire to develop the necessary conditions of modern nationhood within the inherited colonial boundaries (see Nzongola-Ntalaja 1987, 55). This satisfaction with the territorial status quo, however, has coexisted with more revisionist stances towards global politics and the required changes in the international political economy in terms of (re)distributive justice. To understand it, we should assess in further detail its domestic and international sources.

(1) The Domestic Sources of Satisfaction

As argued above, the peaceful foreign policy of most West African states has been linked indissolubly to their institutional weaknesses to the extent that the new states have been "states-nations," or even quasi-states, rather than full-fledged nation-states. Until recently, their political and social deficiencies have been exacerbated by domestic ethnic conflicts and by recurrent coups d'etat throughout the region. As a result, the domestic struggles to unify the various artificial political entities, to forge a national identity and ideology transcending long-standing linguistic and ethnic ties, and to consolidate the weak institutional structures of the West African states have not allowed much energy to be spent in armed conflicts between them. Since most of the states have been very weak in relation to their own societies, they have been anxious at least to gain some international legitimacy for their ex-colonial borders. Hence, they have "chosen" to remain at peace, at least in international terms (see Jackson and Rosberg 1982; Welch 1966, 357; and Matthews 1970a, 348).

In terms of state-society relations, the majority of the West African states—with the possible exceptions of Cape Verde and to a lesser extent Senegal, Ivory Coast, Guinea Bissau, and occasionally Ghana—have been very weak; they are characterized by the withering away of central governments, the rise of tribal and regional domains, and low levels of political institutionalization and legitimacy. Some of these states have even lost control over their political and economic space, as in the cases of Liberia and Sierra Leone. Other countries, such as Nigeria, Niger, Togo, and Mali currently confront serious dangers of collapsing as well (Zartman 1995, 9–10; Kaplan 1994; Clapham 1991, 95–97).

In West Africa we find the typical weak, "soft," or "overdeveloped" Third World state. This state is weak in foundations, structurally deficient, ethnically plural, lacking domestic cohesion, and without legitimacy and authority over civil society beyond its weak national center (see Chabal 1992, 69–74; Ayoob 1995, 15; Azarya 1988; Zolberg 1968, 71; and Neuberger 1991, 105). The state has been "swollen" or "overdeveloped" to the extent that it owns or controls the vast share of the national economy and consumes extensive resources. Yet, at the same time, it has been "weak" because of its inability to carry out its ambitious programs and reach society through the exercise of its authority and/or legitimacy (see Rotchild and Foley 1983, 311–15; and Diamond 1988, 20–21). Moreover, the general incapability of the West African state has to be assessed in its socioeconomic context of scarcity and underdevelopment and against the political-juridical background of its colonial legacy. That is, the West African state has been artificial, in the sense that it has not emerged as a nation-state but remains a postcolonial state without a consolidated national identity; rather, it contains many nations and ethnic groups within its ex-colonial borders (see Sandbrook 1985, 49–52; Bozeman 1976, 23; Curtin 1966, 144).

Ultimately, most of these states have confronted since their emergence the same basic problems of nation-building and state consolidation—establishing order, stability, and a semblance of civility. Many of these states have failed in these domestic tasks, as witness the high incidence of domestic political violence expressed through civil wars, ethnic strife, military coups, and the failure of democratic experiments until the early 1990s. Because many of the states have been very weak, their international boundaries have acted as external shells for their international legitimacy, protecting the juridical reality (or fiction) of their nascent and incapable political communities. Therefore, their active satisfaction with the territorial status quo has directly derived from their inherent institutional and structural weaknesses. Turning to the four possible ideal types of domestic sources of satisfaction, we find in West Africa the following distribution:

(a) Strong states with democratic regimes. Since most of the West African states are weak, and their regimes have been nondemocratic, only a few states might belong to this category: Cape Verde after 1991, and to a lesser extent Senegal after 1981 and Guinea Bissau after 1994. These states tend to be satisfied with the territorial status quo.

The distinctiveness of *Guinea Bissau and Cape Verde* as strong states is related to the fact that these two former Portuguese colonies won their independence after a long guerrilla war of liberation, during which they internally consolidated and built stable political institutions, especially their political parties (the PAIGC of Guinea Bissau and the PAICV of Cape Verde). Yet their transitions from single-partyism to multiparty democracies have been very recent.[12]

The case of *Senegal* is more ambiguous. It is a relatively strong state that has managed to develop an effective political apparatus and a certain degree of coherence due to the able political leadership of Leopold Senghor and Abdou Diouf. But the Senegalese state faces continuing disaffection and secessionist threats from the non-Wolof-speaking province of Casamance. Its political regime is also peculiar. Among all the West African states, with the exception of The Gambia, Senegal alone has maintained a limited form of polyarchy, similar to Mexico's "semidemocratic" regime; it combines multiparty elections with the continuing hegemonic rule of the Socialist

Party.[13] In its border dispute with Mauritania since 1960, Senegal has made revisionist claims over the Senegal Valley, so that on this particular issue it has *not* been satisfied with the territorial status quo, despite its satisfaction with the regional order as a whole.

(b) Strong states with nondemocratic regimes. In addition to Guinea Bissau and Cape Verde before their recent democratization processes, and to Senegal before the 1980s, we can include in this category two other states: Ivory Coast, and to a lesser extent Ghana (in the early 1960s and again since the end of the 1980s).

Ivory Coast under the leadership of Houphouet-Boigny (between 1952 and 1993) managed, like Senegal, to foster a relatively strong state (vis-à-vis its society), coupled with a "benevolent" authoritarian regime. The Ivorian state did succeed in reproducing the pattern of social relations on which it was based, while maintaining a high degree of political stability. Conservatism at home was coupled with a strong conservatism in external affairs, linked with its long-term association with France and expressed through a general satisfaction with the territorial status quo.[14]

The political situation of *Ghana* is much more complicated to pinpoint, since Ghana has experimented virtually every type of democratic and nondemocratic regime during its short existence. Furthermore, the strength of the state has varied notably, from a relative height in the early 1960s under Nkrumah's leadership to a precipitous fall from the mid 1960s until the mid 1980s, when the state started again to enhance its ability to implement its policies. In the early 1960s, Ghana adopted revisionist and irredentist policies towards its more conservative neighbors, especially Ivory Coast and Togo.[15]

(c) Weak states with democratic regimes. Since the beginning of the 1990s, Benin and Mali have experienced successful transitions to democracy. In addition, we can mention the following countries and periods of democratic rule: The Gambia, since independence until 1994; Niger, since 1991 until the coup of 1995; Nigeria, 1960–66 and 1979–83; and Ghana, 1969–72 and 1979–81. All these countries have usually adopted conservative positions regarding their international borders, including the active defense and promotion of the status quo by Nigeria during its brief periods of democratic rule.

(d) Weak states with nondemocratic regimes. The majority of the West African states, most of the time, have belonged to this category. It includes

regimes that underwent democratization processes in Burkina Faso and Sierra Leone (until May 1997), and to a lesser extent in Guinea and Mauritania; military and authoritarian governments in The Gambia, Niger, Togo, and Nigeria; and the collapsed state of Liberia. Before 1991, one could have found in this category most of the West African states, with the exceptions of The Gambia (democratic), Senegal (strong and semidemocratic), Guinea Bissau (strong), Cape Verde (strong), and Ivory Coast (strong). The majority of the weak and nondemocratic states have been at least passively satisfied with the territorial status quo, with the exceptions of Togo vis-à-vis Ghana in 1960-1966, and the dispute between Mali and Burkina Faso until the resolution of their conflict in 1986. Some of them have been also actively satisfied, including Nigeria, Togo, and The Gambia.

(2) The International Sources of Satisfaction
While the domestic sources of satisfaction in the region are related to the weakness of the West African states despite their changing political regimes, the international sources are related to the position they occupy in the regional hierarchy of international power and prestige. Due to the dual traits of the region—domestic violence and international peace—the West African states are *less* concerned about the anarchy of their international relations, and much more preoccupied with their domestic anarchy, caused by the lack of social cohesion and state's minimal capabilities to govern adequately. Paradoxically, West African states can feel more secure in international politics than in domestic politics, recreating a regional international society or "concert" system. Their "juridical statehood"—their legal, formal, and external sovereignty—has preserved their former colonial borders and also forestalled wars among them. However, this "juridical statehood" has not avoided the escalation of their domestic conflicts into civil wars (see Thomas and Mazrui 1992, 159–61).

At the same time, West African states are somewhat affected by the distribution and diffusion of power, even if it has less serious implications than in other regions of the world. There is a certain hierarchy of power. At the top, in terms of military and economic power, we find Nigeria and the Ivory Coast. The second rank has been occupied by Senegal, Ghana, and Guinea. In the third echelon we find the landlocked states (Niger, Mali, and Burkina Faso) and Mauritania. At the bottom of the power scale there are the smallest states (Cape Verde, Gambia, Guinea Bissau, Benin, and Togo) and the two that have been recently immersed in civil wars (Liberia and Sierra Leone).

Despite this apparent hierarchy, the level of power has been generally low, and the extent of influence by any West African state—even Nigeria—upon its neighbors remains limited. Moreover, there is not always a complete overlap between the hierarchy of power and the scales of prestige and hierarchy. For instance, the status of a small state such as The Gambia or Cape Verde has been higher than its objective power. By juxtaposing the objective hierarchy of power with the more subjective hierarchy of prestige we recognize four possible combinations that explain the satisfaction with the territorial status quo in West Africa as follows:

(a) *The powerful and high-status states.* Two states belong to this category in West Africa: Nigeria and Ivory Coast. *Nigeria* can be considered as "a giant among Lilliputians" in West Africa in terms of its size, population, GNP, oil wealth, and military power. The optimistic assessments of Nigerian power have overlooked the distortions inherited from its colonial legacy, the weakness of its state, the dependent structure of its economy, and its ethnic and social cleavages. Given its objective conditions relative to that of its neighbors, Nigeria tried after 1970 to exercise various types of leverage. It is evident that Nigeria has increased its influence upon its neighbors over the years, as was demonstrated in the formation of ECOWAS in 1975 and the launching of the ECOMOG operation in Liberia after 1990. At the same time, and in spite of its high status, it overemphasized and overplayed its role and importance, ignoring its fragile domestic situation.[16]

While Nigeria has been considered as the potential or aspiring hegemon of West Africa as a whole, *Ivory Coast* traditionally has had a similar role regarding French West Africa. Lacking the military or demographic power of Nigeria, Ivory Coast has successfully competed with it on economic terms. For instance, in the ten years before independence and in the dozen years after it, Ivory Coast was the most successful of the West African states in terms of economic growth. Within the framework of continued close ties with France, the Ivorian president, Houphouet-Boigny, carefully developed a zone of security and economic cooperation around his country, actively sustaining the territorial status quo.[17]

(b) *The powerful and low-status states.* There are almost no West African states in this category, with the possible exceptions of Nigeria during the early 1960s and since 1993, and Guinea in its early independence years

(1958–70). In the case of *Nigeria*, this gap reflects the disjunction between the objective power and the positive self-image of Nigeria in international relations, on the one hand, and, on the other, its lack of foreign policy activism in the early 1960s and its deteriorating prestige as a consequence of its continuing military rule after 1993. Yet Nigeria has kept its conservative posture toward its neighbors in spite of its frequent regime changes.

Guinea has been endowed with rich natural resources and initially enjoyed high status because of its early independence in 1958. But Guinea's status in the region has gradually deteriorated as a result of its ambiguous and revisionist foreign policy regarding France and its neighbors. Its economic power also steadily deteriorated in the late 1970s and early 1980s.[18]

(c) Weak powers with high status: In this category we find small states that have managed to enhance their status and prestige well beyond their objective power: Nkrumah's Ghana, between 1957 and 1966; Senegal; The Gambia; and Cape Verde.

No contemporary figure has had a greater ideological impact on the West African region than Nkrumah has had. Despite its lack of material and military resources, *Ghana* under Nkrumah enjoyed a status and prestige much higher than its real power. This discrepancy between status and power enhanced Nkrumah's revisionist appetite toward its neighbors—especially Ivory Coast and Togo. With the overthrow of Nkrumah in 1966, Ghana reverted to a more conservative foreign policy, with a concomitant lower status and a support for the territorial status quo.[19]

The prestigious leadership of Leopold Senghor (1960–80) and his successor, Abdou Diouf, have enhanced the status of *Senegal* among the Francophone West African states well above its objective power. Senegal's important role in the international relations of the region has been directly associated with its stable and open political regime. Like Ivory Coast, Senegal adopted conservative foreign policies, with the exceptions of its territorial dispute with Mauritania over the Senegal Valley, related to the status of the Fulani/ Tukulor Black African minorities and its frustration about the existence of The Gambia, a smuggling enclave within its territory.[20]

The Gambia and Cape Verde are very small and weak states that have enjoyed a respectable status in spite of their tiny size. *The Gambia* has been a bastion of multiparty democracy between 1965 and 1994. *Cape Verde* has been actively involved in international relations, promoting cooperative relations and integration within ECOWAS and within Africa in general.

Both states have successfully used their lack of power to enhance their prestige and status, being obviously satisfied with the territorial status quo.

(d) Weak powers with low status. In this final category we find the majority of the West African states: Liberia, Sierra Leone, Togo, Benin, Niger, Burkina Faso, Mauritania, Mali, Ghana between 1966 and 1985, and Guinea after 1970. Most of these countries have been actively satisfied with the territorial status quo, with the exceptions of Burkina Faso and Mali, whose border dispute was ultimately resolved in 1986. Their commitment to uphold the territorial status quo has been directly related to their weaknesses as states and to their weaknesses as powers; they have been incapable of fighting external wars because of their material and institutional impotence.

After reviewing both the domestic and the international sources of satisfaction, we can draw the following conclusions:

First, most of the current democratic regimes in the region are satisfied with the territorial status quo, with the exception of Senegal vis-à-vis its former territorial claims against Mauritania.

Second, the few strong states in the region—Ivory Coast, Senegal, Guinea Bissau, Cape Verde, and Ghana since the mid 1980s—have in general supported the territorial status quo, with the exception of Senegal vis-à-vis Mauritania in 1989–90.

Third, the strongest powers in the region—Nigeria and Ivory Coast—have usually enjoyed a high status and held conservative positions regarding the territorial status quo.

Fourth, most of the West African countries are weak states, irrespective of their changing political regimes. They have in general actively supported the territorial status quo because of their institutional weaknesses and their focus upon persisting domestic conflicts.

Fifth, most of the weak states are also weak powers. As such, their satisfaction with the territorial status quo is a reflection of their impotence in terms of material means to fight external wars.

Sixth, a discrepancy between power capabilities and status might lead countries to adopt revisionist postures, as in the case of Guinea between 1958 and 1970 (relatively high power but low status), and Nkrumah's Ghana (relatively low power but high status). Under a condition of equilibrium between power capabilities and status, states tend to be satisfied with the territorial status quo.

CONDITIONS FOR THE DEVELOPMENT AND MAINTENANCE OF
REGIONAL PEACE IN WEST AFRICA

By way of summary, we can now cluster these different explanations by referring to the reality of negative peace, and by assessing the prospects for moving in the direction of stable peace and the establishment of a pluralistic security community in West Africa.

(1) Negative Peace, 1957–96.
There have been only a few cases in which West African states feared the use of military force by their neighbors, and only one in which a territorial dispute escalated into an actual war (Burkina Faso and Mali in December 1985). Interstate violence has been almost excluded from the international relations of the region, in contrast to the widespread domestic violence.

The West African zone of negative peace has been maintained by the fact that the majority of the states—with the exceptions of Ghana and Togo in 1957–66, and, to a lesser extent, Burkina Faso in 1984–86 and Senegal regarding Mauritania in 1989–90—have been actively or passively satisfied with the territorial status quo. This satisfaction has remained more or less constant, notwithstanding the changing nature of their political regimes and linked to their military and economic weaknesses vis-à-vis their respective societies. The West African case thus comprises a group of mostly weak and nondemocratic states that have adopted a conservative attitude in their regional international relations, keeping *external* peace but indulging in *internal* conflicts and civil wars.

Moreover, this West African negative peace has been facilitated by the presence of two relatively strong and conservative Francophone states, Ivory Coast and Senegal, as surrogates if not satellites of France itself; a normative consensus associated with Pan-Africanism and the norms sanctioned by the OAU that preferred peaceful resolution of disputes over war and African solutions to African problems; and occasionally by the dense networks of migration and "unofficial trade" (smuggling). We should also mention the positive and preponderant role of Nigeria, mainly as the leader and the major contributor of the regional integration scheme, ECOWAS. This has become evident in ECOWAS's intervention and deployment of ECOMOG in the Liberian civil war since August 1990. Interestingly, other realist explanations such as balance of power, third-party threats, and geographical irrelevance have been less important in illuminating the reality of the West African negative peace.

The West African negative peace preceded the formation and institutionalization of the regional integrative scheme, ECOWAS, in 1975. Despite its inherent potential to move the region in the direction of stable peace and even to establish a pluralistic security community, over the last twenty years it has failed to fulfill its ambitious economic goals of integration and economic interdependence. At the same time, ECOWAS has managed to coordinate regional political decisions of the West African heads of state, and even to implement a common security policy toward the Liberian domestic crisis of 1990.

In spite of the incipient collective security apparatus, the regional institutionalization, and the recent wave of democratization, the West African negative peace has not become a stable peace. The international peace has not become internalized within the borders of its member states. Thus, the future of the region remains uncertain, if not ominous.

(2) Prospects for stable peace and the emergence of a pluralistic security community. At first glance, any description of the region as a zone of stable peace or even as a pluralistic security community seems an oxymoron against the background of the civil wars of Liberia and Sierra Leone. And yet, several of the conditions identified by Deutsch et al. in 1957 fall into place:

(a) Compatibility of major values. Obviously, democracy is not considered as a major value in the region. Yet, the pledge by all West African states to "respect the frontiers existing on their achievement of national independence" constitutes a common norm adopted on the basis of reciprocity. The principles of territorial integrity, peaceful settlement of disputes, and *uti possidetis* are the building blocks of at least a potential security community, and these principles guide their international relations and restrain the outbursts of violent interstate conflicts.

(b) Mutual responsiveness. A sense of community in West Africa has been expressed in general terms through the ideology of Pan-Africanism. This ideology developed and found expression through the speeches and actions of leaders such as Leopold Senghor of Senegal and Kwame Nkrumah of Ghana. Yet only with the formation of ECOWAS in 1975 did this incipi-

ent sense of community became institutionalized, overcoming language and ethnic divides that traditionally separated the countries of the region. In this way, ECOWAS gradually became an important reference group for the actions of its member states.

(c) A distinctive way of life. It is difficult to single out a distinctive way of life for West Africa, due to language and ideological differences that traditionally divided the region between the Francophone and Anglophone groups.

(d) Development of core areas. As mentioned above, Nigeria stands at the core of ECOWAS and the West African region as a whole. It was Nigerian determination, diplomatic activity, and financial support that led to the formation of ECOWAS in 1975 and ECOMOG in 1990. Moreover, on any measure of objective factors, such as population, military power, GDP, and economic strength, Nigeria *should* dominate its West African region and become what India is in South Asia, or South Africa has become in Southern Africa. However, Nigeria has been bedeviled by domestic problems since independence and marginalized by extraregional powers such as France and by the major Francophone states in the region—Senegal, Guinea, and especially Ivory Coast.

(e) Superior economic growth. Although the formation of ECOWAS led to high expectations regarding the possibility of reaching "superior" economic growth, this did not come about. Actually, most of the West African states have experienced low or even *negative* rates of growth since the early 1980s.

(f) Expectation of joint economic reward. There was a strong expectation of joint economic rewards following the formation and development of ECOWAS. The main motivations behind this integration scheme were twofold: political, as against external political dependence; and economic, as against economic dependence and as a means to overcome the disadvantages of small size by accelerating the rate of growth and development. These goals and expectations have yet to be realized.

(g) Wide ranges of mutual transactions. In the mid 1990s, relatively low levels of economic exchange exist among neighboring states in West Africa. The level of formal sector intra-ECOWAS trade, as a proportion of its total trade, remains very low (less than 10 percent). In addition, transport connections and telecommunication links continue to be poor and underdeveloped, and few currencies are easily convertible. Wide ranges of mutual

transactions have occurred only at the level of unrecorded trade flows or smuggling, and through migration flows.

(h) Broadening of elites. Until the early 1990s, the failure of democratization in West Africa implied the disaffection and even alienation of important elites from the government. The broadening of political and social elites in the region has proceeded slowly and with serious difficulties, as evidenced by Nigeria.

(i) Links of social communication. At the official level, these links have remained incipient and underdeveloped.

(j) Greater mobility of persons. According to articles 2d and 27 (1, 2) of the ECOWAS Treaty of 1975, the need to maintain and encourage intra-regional migration was recognized. Moreover, in 1979, ECOWAS adopted a protocol on the "free movement of persons, and the right of residence and establishment." As a result, migrant laborers flocked from Niger, Benin, Togo, and Ghana into the larger Nigerian economy and from landlocked Burkina Faso into Ivory Coast and Ghana. But in January 1983 Nigeria deported about two million aliens and closed its borders until January 1986. This incident demonstrates the fragility of the integration process and the vulnerability of the would-be hegemon, Nigeria.

(k) Reluctance to wage "fratricidal" wars. This condition has been adopted by the vast majority of the West African states with reference to their international relations only. It was even formalized in a nonaggression and defense treaty signed in 1980. With respect to civil wars, the intervention of ECOMOG in the Liberian civil war was justified as being a response to a threat to regional peace.

(l) Outside military threats. In contrast to other regions of Africa clearly affected by the Cold War, West Africa has been marginalized within the international system. Thus, it has been difficult to trace outside military threats to the region, although Nigeria (and to a lesser extent Guinea and Ghana) have perceived France as a potential source of danger.

(m) Strong economic ties. Despite the plethora of economic cooperation schemes that existed in West Africa even before the formation of ECOWAS in 1975, there have been no strong economic ties among the countries of the region. This lack of economic ties is related to several structural problems, such as the inequality of any potential economic partners (Nigeria, Ivory Coast, Senegal, and Ghana are well ahead the other ECOWAS members).

(n) Ethnic and linguistic assimilation. The West African countries are eth-

nically and linguistically heterogeneous. For the Francophone countries, the French colonial experience provided some cohesive effect, though this effect was later diluted by ideological differences following the independence of Guinea, the competition between Senegal and Ivory Coast, and the animadversion between Senegal and Mali and between Senegal and Mauritania. In terms of ethnic, linguistic, religious, and historical factors, West Africa is characterized by a clear lack of social cohesion.

In sum, a few necessary and helpful conditions for the formation and consolidation of a pluralistic security community are present in West Africa, mostly within the institutional framework of ECOWAS. Nigeria still has the potential, together with Ivory Coast, to act as the military and economic core of an embryonic community. There is also a strong political and economic rationale to deepen and implement the institutional framework carefully crafted by the ECOWAS Treaty in 1975 after the European Union model. Most of the member-states are satisfied with the territorial status quo, entertain similar aspirations in terms of development and growth, and share common normative assumptions, currently embarking on the twin difficult processes of liberalization and democratization. But three major stumbling blocks impede the advent of stable peace and the realization of a pluralistic security community: first, the persistence of authoritarian regimes, especially in countries like Nigeria; second, economic stagnation and marginalization, which impede the unfolding of growing interdependence following the formalization of economic and even political integration; and third, domestic violence and wars, which might spill over across borders and thus constantly threaten the delicate fabric of negative regional peace. Until democratization and economic growth take place in the whole region, West African states will remain inherently unstable, plagued by civil conflicts and wars, but probably be at peace among themselves.

CONCLUSIONS

In this chapter I have analyzed the complex reality of regional negative peace in West Africa since 1957, a period in which West Africa has been prey to virulent domestic violence and civil wars. To understand its maintenance for about forty years, I have assessed nine alternative explanations: (1) the pacifying roles of France and of Nigeria as potential extraregional and regional hegemons; (2) the formation of a regional balance of power; (3) common external threats to the countries of the region, such as the alleged French and Nigerian threats; (4) the material impotence of most West African states to fight external wars; (5) the effects of changing political regimes upon regional peace; (6) the quest for prosperity and economic development, associated with a structural dependence upon the world economy; (7) the institutionalization of economic integration, in spite of low levels of interdependence, and the existence of informal transnational links; (8) a regional normative consensus about *uti possidetis*; and (9) the widespread satisfaction with the territorial status quo, with only a few exceptions. The domestic sources of satisfaction directly relate to the weakness of most West African states. Similarly, the international sources of satisfaction involve power distribution and level of status in the regional hierarchy of prestige. From the analysis of these alternative explanations, several conclusions can be elaborated, as follows:

First, the key to understand the twin processes of regional peace and domestic war in West Africa resides in the widespread satisfaction with the territorial status quo by the majority of the countries. This satisfaction can be explained by the *weaknesses* of the West African countries as states, with reference to their societies, and as powers, regarding their foreign relations and material capabilities. These two weaknesses have led most of the states to adopt a rational policy of respecting the norm of *uti possidetis* on a reciprocal basis, despite the apparent artificiality of their borders. Hence, in the case of West Africa there seems to be a negative correlation between domestic conflict and international wars. Contrary to what the theory of diversionary war predicts, under conditions of extreme domestic instability, institutional weakness, and even violent conflict within a state, there seems to be a tendency for a more *peaceful* foreign conflict behavior than one can expect from a "direct linkage" argument (see Matthews 1970b, 484; Andreski 1992). In this sense, this active satisfaction with the territorial status quo overlaps with a "peace of impotence."[21]

Second, many of the liberal explanations proved to be unable to explain the mere existence of negative peace. For instance, negative peace has *preceded* the recent wave of democratization, the efforts of economic development and growth, and the attempts to institutionalize economic links and integration. It seems that these liberal factors might have contributed to maintaining and extending the negative peace, and perhaps to moving it in more stable directions. At the same time, normative consensus based on the mutual respect of ex-colonial borders *(uti possidetis)* and the impact of informal transnational seem to be crucial in establishing that negative peace in the first place.

Third, several of the realist claims proved also to be incapable of explaining the complex reality of domestic war and regional peace in West Africa. For instance, there have been no substantial balances of power in the region, no serious external threats, nor geopolitical relevance. At the same time, the roles of France (in Francophone West Africa) and of Nigeria after 1970 have been preponderant in leading and keeping this regional negative peace. Similarly, the material impotence of most of the West African states, linked to their internal weaknesses, has clearly indicated why most of them chose satisfaction with the territorial status quo.

Fourth, the West African case is a clear example of how nondemocracies can establish and maintain peaceful relations among themselves. This very lack of democratization, coupled with the institutional weaknesses of many states, also explains their domestic violence. In the long term, democratization might contribute to the prospects for stable peace by promoting *domestic* reconciliation within the states of the region. However, in the short term it might also adversely affect the continuation of regional peace by encouraging ethnic groups to openly question their national boundaries and to present democratic demands for self-determination and secession.

Finally, in terms of policy prescription, it seems that what West Africa needs most is not only a successful democratization process but also a strengthening of their states so that they can augment their political capacity and overcome their institutional failures (see Ayoob 1995; Holsti 1996). By definition, strong states will keep their domestic peace, while democratic regimes will keep their international peace. A combination of both stronger and more democratic states might enable the region to escape from its continuing anarchy of domestic wars. Even though I have emphasized in this chapter the importance of the political/legal (some might argue fictional or formalistic) dimension of peaceful international relations, this interstate negative peace has been dimmed by the virulent impact of continuing domestic anarchy, as demonstrated by the renewed carnage in Liberia in April–May 1996, and more recently by the events in Sierra Leone in May–June 1997. Stable peace and a pluralistic security community, which demand integration and peaceful change *within* the national community itself in addition to peaceful international relations, remain a distant dream.

CHAPTER 5

ZONES OF PEACE IN A COMPARATIVE PERSPECTIVE

After reviewing South America and West Africa, I draw in this concluding chapter comparisons between these two regions, as well as with other zones of peace, including East Asia and Southeast Asia (ASEAN), in contrast to zones of conflict such as Central America until the 1990s and most of the African continent. Since the beginning of the 1990s a few zones of conflict in the developing world—including Central America, Southern Africa, and even the Middle East—have been evolving in the direction of negative peace. In this sense, and based upon the converging processes of economic and political liberalization, globalization, and the end of the Cold War, we can express some guarded optimism about the transformation of the remaining zones of conflict into incipient zones of negative peace.

Beyond this comparative dimension one can infer some important theoretical conclusions from the South American and West African experiences. First, I assess how well the different hypotheses have fared. Second, I examine the possible links between different types of political regimes and gradations of peace, between different types of states and conditions of peace, and between civil wars and international wars. Third, I refine the theoretical model described in chapter 2 with reference to the different conditions for the three gradations of regional peace, the validity of the democratic peace theory, and the relevance of regional norms.

Moreover, some policy-oriented conclusions can be elaborated. First, it is crucial to understand how peace is maintained. Second, it is equally important to grasp the regional perspective, as opposed to the systemic and dyadic levels. Third, given the salience of satisfaction with the territorial status quo as a sufficient condition for the maintenance of regional negative peace, one has to address the question of "how to get satisfaction"—in other words, how we should turn a zone of conflict into a zone of peace.

COMPARING ZONES OF PEACE AND ZONES OF CONFLICT

In this section I draw several comparisons among zones of peace and zones of conflict in the developing world. First, I compare South America and

West Africa. Second, in the Latin American context, I draw a contrast between South America and Central America. Third, I emphasize the uniqueness of West Africa within the African continent. Fourth, I briefly refer to two other zones of peace that include developing nations: Northeast Asia and Southeast Asia (ASEAN).

South America and West Africa: Similarities and Differences
The two major case studies explored in this book are those of very different regions in the developing world that have experienced long periods of international peace. In South America, the "story" goes back more than one hundred years, encompassing different levels or gradations of regional peace: from negative peace to stable peace to the emergence of a nascent pluralistic security community in the Southern Cone. The West African story is a shorter one (since 1957) and has featured both civil wars and regional negative peace only.

In these two regions we can chronologically identify different gradations of peace. After decolonization (in both regions) and an initial period of turmoil (in South America), there had been negative peace, which was either a peace of irrelevance (lack of interaction among the new states in South America) or a peace of impotence (transnational links in West Africa without concomitant interstate interdependence). With the increase in the amount of official and unofficial transactions, the possibilities for further cooperation *and* conflict multiplied. Negative peace could then be followed and transcended by stable peace, as it happened in South America in the 1980s but *not* in West Africa. Finally, if and when stable peace becomes institutionalized at both the domestic level (democratization) and the international level (integration), we might reach the uppermost level of pluralistic security communities, in which the member states and the peoples of the region manage to develop a supranational and transnational identity. In this respect, cultural and especially normative affinities are crucial in determining the dynamics and the general direction of the region toward or away from peace.

Turning to a more detailed comparison between South America and West Africa, we can point out some obvious disparities as well as some intriguing common patterns. In terms of disparities, these two regions of the Third World reflect distinct political and economic developments in their postcolonial periods of independence. They are obviously very different in their political, economic, and social indicators. Although they have a common genesis—the breakdown of immense colonial empires into artificial new states that originally were not nations—their trajectory has been distinctive, due in the first place to their disparate dates of decolonization (in South America, more than 180 years ago; in West Africa, only about 38 years ago). Thus, a better comparison could probably be the one between the states of West Africa today and the South American states in the nineteenth century. As a matter of fact, contemporary West Africa has experienced *less* interstate war than did nineteenth-century South America, which was *not* a zone of negative peace until the mid 1880s. Before that date, South America experienced a series of "great wars," including long wars of independence that spilled over into widespread civil wars. The consolidation and pacification of the South American states occurred only in the second half of the nineteenth century. Since the 1880s, and despite the large number of militarized interstate disputes, South America has remained internationally at peace.

Another major difference between these two regions is that the growth of national sentiment in the South American states, unlike that in West Africa, was impeded by neither ethnic nor religious cleavages. The relative similarity in ethnic and cultural background diminished the perils of irredentism and tribalism. Although many South American states were initially weak vis-à-vis their own societies (as it was evident from the recurrent coups d'etat until two decades ago), they became eventually full-fledged nation-states and not just states-nations or quasi-states with a mere possession of juridical sovereignty, like some of their West African counterparts. In contrast to many African and Middle Eastern countries, the South American nations have enjoyed general acceptance of their states; that is, the legitimacy of their existence as such was not disputed. Moreover, their recognized borders corresponded on the whole to geographic barriers, in contrast to the more arbitrary and artificial nature of the African borders. However, in comparison to Western Europe and North America, the processes of state-making and nation-building remained retarded, partly due to the economic and political cultures of preindustrial Spain and Portugal (Ayoob 1991, 268).

Finally, in terms of political and economic liberalization, the wave of democratization that swept South America in the 1980s has been by far more effective and resilient than the one affecting the African continent since the early 1990s. While South America has probably reached a point of no return in which democracy is likely to take root permanently, in West Africa institutional breakdowns and plain anarchy remain real possibilities, as vividly demonstrated in the cases of Liberia and Sierra Leone. The major differences between South America and West Africa are summarized in table 5.1.

Table 5.1. Major Differences between
South America and West Africa

Variable	South America	West Africa
Level of development	NICs, high, low	very low
Decolonization	1810–20s	1950s–60s
State legitimacy	high	low
Ethnic problems	only Peru, Ecuador	widespread
Cultural heritage	homogeneous	heterogeneous
National economies	complement, competitive	competitive
Transnationalism	relatively low	high (informal)
Interdependence	after the 1980s	very low
Geographical factors	isolation	convergence
Type of borders	mostly natural	mostly artificial
Border interaction	minimal until the 1960s	permeability
Political development	all levels	usually low
Type of states	strong and weak	mostly weak
Nation-states	generally consolidated	states-nations
Democratization	widespread since 1970s	partial in 1990s
Integration	relative success	relative failure
Border prospects	pacified	might be redrawn
Sovereignty	empirical	mostly juridical
Realm of peace	domestic and international	international
Types of peace	all three gradations	only negative

Despite these vast disparities, interstate peace has persisted in both areas, and for very similar reasons, as can be inferred from table 5.2. For instance, the satisfaction with the territorial status quo has been linked to the institutional weaknesses of many states in both regions, a normative consensus regarding *uti possidetis* and the peaceful management of international disputes, the presence of an aspiring or potential regional hegemon that favors the regional status quo, and the development of institutional frameworks of economic integration to foster initial low degrees of interdependence.

Table 5.2. Explanations for the Maintenance of Regional Peace in South America and in West Africa

Explanation	South America	West Africa
Regional hegemon	yes: United States Brazil	yes: France Nigeria
Regional balance of power	only 1883–1930 and in the 1970s	1957–66
Third-party threat	no	no
Irrelevance and impotence	until the 1960s no	no yes
Democratization	since the 1970s	partially in the 1990s
Prosperity and economic development	after the 1980s	no
Integration	yes: MERCOSUR Andean Pact	yes: ECOWAS
Normative consensus	yes	yes
Satisfaction with the status quo Exceptions:	yes Bolivia, Ecuador	yes Ghana, Togo, Burkina Faso

In the domestic realm, throughout most of their independent political life the recurrent form of political regime until a decade ago was a militocracy—an authoritarian military regime that lacked the militarism of civilian regimes in Europe (Andreski 1992, 179; see also Lyon 1973, 50). The lack of international wars generally contrasted with a high level of domestic violence, in the form of civil wars and recurrent military coups. Throughout their political history, virulent civil wars took place in Argentina, Colombia, Peru, Nigeria, Liberia, and Sierra Leone. By contrast, international wars have been exceptional: Bolivia-Paraguay (1932–35) and Peru-Ecuador (1941, 1981, 1995) in South America, and only Burkina Faso-Mali (1985) in West Africa.

In the international realm, both the South American and West African states have remained peripheral geopolitically, before, during, and after the Cold War. Both regions have been relatively isolated from great power conflicts, so that their international relations should be understood mostly in *intraregional* terms. This has probably contributed to the longevity of their regional peace. Moreover, both of them have embarked upon regional and subregional integrative schemes, which have succeeded far more in their political and security dimensions than in their proper economic ones. These integrative efforts have been usually supported by a local regional hegemon (or candidate to such hegemony): Brazil in South America and Nigeria in West Africa. Furthermore, regional solidarity and the rhetoric of a community have furthered the development of regional norms of coexistence, such as *uti possidetis* and the peaceful settlement of international disputes.

To sum up, it is in the exercise of their intraregional international relations and the maintenance of regional peace—previous to the latest wave of democratization—that we can identify similar cross-regional patterns. This is possible in spite of their structural (economic, political, cultural, and social) differences and their diverging trajectories. South America has been traveling through all three gradations of regional peace, while West Africa seems to be stuck at the initial stage of negative peace.

South America as Compared to Central America

Besides directly comparing South America and West Africa, it is important to assess the uniqueness of these two regions within the framework of their broader contexts; i.e., Latin America and Africa. Within Latin America, we should contrast the South American zone of peace with the Central American zone of conflict. Similarly, we should compare the West African zone of negative peace with other zones of conflict in the African continent, including North Africa and the Maghreb, Southern Africa before 1990, East Africa and the Horn, and Equatorial/Central Africa.

In contrast to South America, Central America was a typical zone of conflict practically until the end of the Cold War in 1989. The region was afflicted by long civil wars based on ideology and several military interventions by the overwhelming hegemon, the United States. All of the countries of the region are still weak powers in international relations. Moreover, all of them, with the peculiar exception of Costa Rica, are weak states and have sustained until recently nondemocratic regimes. The end of the Cold War has notably contributed to the overall pacification and democratization of Central America, moving it in the direction of negative, if not stable peace (see Baranyi 1995).

Given the relatively small number of countries that comprise this region (Costa Rica, El Salvador, Guatemala, Honduras, Nicaragua, and Panama) Central America has experienced a larger number of international wars than the southern part of Latin America. In the last 110 years, there have been four international wars: Guatemala vs. El Salvador (1885); Guatemala vs. El Salvador and Honduras (1906); Nicaragua vs. El Salvador and Honduras (1907); and El Salvador vs. Honduras (1969). With the exception of Costa Rica, which has enjoyed both domestic and international peace for long periods of time, and Panama, which has been always a virtual U.S. protectorate, the countries have been actively involved in interstate disputes and wars, and El Salvador and Nicaragua have adopted revisionist and belligerent postures throughout their political history. Moreover, in the 1970s and 1980s the region suffered virulent civil wars that were partly internationalized, especially in El Salvador (1981–89) and Nicaragua (1983–88) (see Goldstein 1992, 210–12; Brogan 1990, 412–58). In addition, long territorial disputes antagonized El Salvador and Honduras, as well as Belize and Guatemala. The major differences between South and Central America are summarized in table 5.3.

While Central America until 1989 was a typical zone of conflict, since then it has gradually evolved into a zone of negative peace. Impressive advances have taken place: war termination in El Salvador and Nicaragua,

Table 5.3. *Major Differences between*
South America and Central America

Variable	South America	Central America
Size of countries	big and small	small
Type of states	strong and weak	usually weak
U.S. presence	quite marginal	overwhelming
Civil wars	sporadic	widespread
International wars	exceptional	unusual
Foreign intervention	almost none	yes (mostly U.S.)
Regional IR	intraregional	U.S.-dependent
Dependence on U.S.	low to medium	overwhelming
Cold War scenario	marginal	important
Political regimes	all the types	authoritarian
Local hegemon	Brazil	United States

reduction of foreign military involvement by the great powers, democratization, and even economic stabilization. The domestic peace achieved in El Salvador and Nicaragua due to the Contadora/Esquipula peace process has also had a pacifying effect upon international relations; there has been a reduction of militarized interstate disputes between Honduras and Nicaragua and a judicial resolution of the long El Salvador-Honduras conflict (Baranyi 1995, 147–52). Among the factors conducive to this auspicious evolution are: the end of the Cold War; war weariness and the exhaustion of the belligerents; active peacemaking by regional actors such as Mexico, Colombia, Venezuela, and Costa Rica, as well as international organizations; and the recent wave of democratization, which affected Central America as in the rest of Latin America. Moreover, like South America, Central America has always retained a sense of common identity and has attempted to recreate various integration schemes, following the failure of the United Provinces of Central America after 1838. This feeling of a common destiny contributed in the past to the regionalization of civil wars. Nowadays, it bolsters the expansion of both domestic and international peace.

The Uniqueness of West Africa, as Compared to other African Regions
As far as the African continent is concerned, the West African region is quite representative of other regions of sub-Saharan Africa with respect to

political, economic, and social indicators, the prevalence of juridical sovereignty over empirical sovereignty, the widespread weakness of the states vis-à-vis their (weak) societies, the persistence of Pan-Africanism and a broad normative consensus about the mutual respect for the ex-colonial borders, and a relative impotence in terms of power in international relations. At the same time, in contrast to other regions of the continent, the West African negative peace has been characterized by: a particular link to France, the Nigerian quest for subparamountcy, the relative isolation and marginalization from the Cold War confrontation, and the dearth of white settlers, in contrast to East Africa and especially Southern Africa. These important differences account for the fact that West Africa has been the only zone of negative peace in sub-Saharan Africa until the emergence of Southern Africa as a prospective area of stable peace in the beginning of the 1990s. The major differences between West Africa and other African regions are summarized in table 5.4.

Table 5.4. Major Differences between West Africa
and other African Regions

Variable	West Africa	Other Regions
Cold War relevance	not important	important
Type of peace	negative	none
French connection	very important	only in Equatorial Africa
Decolonization	mostly peaceful	peaceful and violent
Strategic role	none	yes (except for France)
Cultural variety	high	mixed
Regional hegemon	Nigeria	less clear (only South Africa)
White settlers	small minority	relevant (in East and Southern Africa)
International wars	exceptional	unusual

Conversely, West Africa epitomizes the African political and economic reality, basically characterized by internal turmoil and corruption, civil wars,

and international peace. It is no accident that the few wars that took place
in other African regions have been usually related to: (1) the overwhelming
presence of white settlers; and/or (2) the impact of the East-West confrontation, especially in the Horn of Africa; and/or (3) the revisionist attitudes
of few nation-states (historical states) in Africa, namely, Somalia, Ethiopia,
and Morocco. A list of the contemporary African international and civil
wars in Southern Africa, East Africa/The Horn, Equatorial/Central Africa,
and North Africa/Maghreb is compiled in table 5.5.

Table 5.5. Contemporary Wars in Africa

African Region	International Wars	Civil Wars
Southern Africa	Angola (1975–91) Namibia (1966–89)	Angola (1975–91) Mozambique (1979–92)
East Africa and The Horn	Ethiopia-Somalia (1964) Kenya-Somalia (1963–67) Ogaden (1977–78) Tanzania-Uganda (1978–79)	Sudan (1983–) Ethiopia-Eritrea (1970–91) Uganda (1980–) Somalia (1982–) Rwanda (1990–93) Burundi (1988–)
Equatorial and Central Africa	Chad-Libya (1978–87)	Zaire (1960–62) Zaire (1997)
North Africa and Maghreb	France-Tunisia (1961) Morocco-Algeria (1963) Saharan War (Morocco, Mauritania, Algeria, Polisario) 1975–	
West Africa	Burkina Faso-Mali (1985)	Nigeria-Biafra (1966–70) Liberia (1989–) Sierra Leone (1992–)

Sources: Goldstein 1992; Copson 1994; and Griffiths 1993.

From a reading of table 5.5 it becomes evident that most of the *international* wars in Africa have taken place in East Africa/The Horn, involving Somalia and Ethiopia; in Southern Africa, involving South Africa; and in North Africa, involving Morocco.

Interestingly, many of these wars did not take place only because of border disputes and territorial dissatisfaction with the status quo. Still, the number of international wars, as compared to domestic conflict and civil wars, has been relatively small. Some of these civil wars have spilled over transnationally, since the political borders are not significant or relevant and ethnic groups are disseminated across multinational states. There is a marked discrepancy between the juridical sovereignty accorded to the African states through the recognition of their inherited international borders and the empirical reality characterized by the permeability of their boundaries (Ravenhill 1988, 283). However, irredentist claims across borders have been usually kept under control, so that a continental peace of impotence has reigned, due to the weakness (both domestically and internationally) of many African states.

Comparing South America and West Africa with the Asian Zones of Peace
(Northeast Asia and South East Asia [ASEAN])
South America and West Africa are not the only zones of peace involving developing countries. In the Asian continent, we can identify regions also characterized by negative peace (in the case of East Asia) and stable peace (in the case of the ASEAN countries).

(1) The Northeast Asian zone of negative peace, 1953–
Since the end of the Korean War in 1953 the countries of Northeast Asia have managed to keep a fragile negative peace among themselves, interrupted only once by the Sino-Soviet border war of 1969. Until 1990, the only democracy in this region was Japan, all the other states being ruled by authoritarian or Communist regimes. Like North Korea, China remains, at least in political terms, a totalitarian regime. South Korea and Taiwan have moved in the direction of democracy since the late 1980s, while Mongolia and Russia are currently experiencing significant transitions toward democracy.

Several long-standing disputes are rampant in the region, involving both big and small powers. Yet these disputes *have not* escalated into war. The Japanese-Russian dispute over the Northern Territories (Kurile Islands), the vexed relationship between the two Chinas, the disagreement over Korean unification, and the territorial disputes between Japan and China and between Japan and South Korea have all remained peaceful (see Friedberg 1994, 18). A third of these conflicts involve disputes over maritime boundaries and offshore territorial claims (Ball 1994, 89). Only the Sino-Soviet territorial dispute escalated into a brief armed conflict in 1969. However, unlike South America and West Africa, this zone of negative peace is composed by pairs of status quo and revisionist states: Japan (revisionist) against Russia; North Korea (revisionist) against South Korea; China (revisionist) against Taiwan; China (revisionist) against Japan; and Japan (revisionist) against the Koreas. Moreover, the prevalence of authoritarian and totalitarian regimes, in addition to the dissatisfaction with the territorial status quo among at least half of the members of this region, have made East Asia a precarious and volatile zone of negative peace. Economic expansion and prosperity have raised the stakes of regional political conflict by providing the economic base for a considerable military buildup in the region (Wallace 1996, 1). In this case, it is neither the common satisfaction with the territorial status quo nor a normative consensus or a shared regional identity that has kept the peace, but rather a multipolar (regional) balance of power among the four regional powers—Russia, Japan, China, and the U.S. military presence in the Pacific area (see Friedberg 1994, 25; Simon 1992; Betts 1994, 46; and Inoguchi 1995, 125). This multipolar balance of power might become institutionalized as a "concert," granted that the major powers do share similar attitudes toward peace and war and concentrate their efforts upon "geoeconomics"—economic development and prosperity—rather than upon traditional geopolitics (see Job 1996).

Unlike that in South America, where the last wave of democratization has swept the entire region; and that in West Africa, in which authoritarian regimes are still predominant, the political scene in Northeast Asia is very complicated, including a series of interactions involving democratic and nondemocratic regimes. There has been a long and continuing tradition of authoritarianism, perhaps more salient in social, cultural, and religious fields than in politics (Palmer 1991, 24). According to the democratic peace theory, mixed dyadic relationships such as those in Northeast Asia should be inherently volatile. However, war has not taken place in the region and, despite rapid economic change, domestic politics has remained notably stable (see Inoguchi 1995, 130).

From an economic point of view East Asia, in comparison to the less-developed South American and West African regions, is underdeveloped in its economic integration and institutionalization. It has been basically reluctant to go ahead with regional integration. At the same time, it seems that all the East Asian states, with the exception of North Korea, have come to accept the norm of seeking prosperity through promotion of market economic activity (see Job 1996, 12).

Finally, from a normative perspective, there is an interesting debate among academics and practitioners alike whether East Asia has developed a sense of community and a normative consensus of its own. On the one hand, there is the view that East Asia possesses a distinctive (superior) diplomatic culture, with particular values such as war aversion and the primacy of economic objectives over military ones (see Wallace 1996, 5; Job 1996, 10; Haas 1989, 3; and Mahbubani 1995). On the other hand, there is a more pessimistic view that denies the existence of such a normative consensus or a sense of a community, since "trade, investment, and a Pacific coastline do not necessarily make for a broader sense of community" (Manning and Stern 1994, 91).

(2) The ASEAN countries (1967–)
Following a change of government in Indonesia in 1965 that ended the hostilities between that country and Malaysia, several states in the Southeast Asian region—Thailand, Malaysia, Singapore, Indonesia, and the Philippines—established in August 1967 the Association of Southeast Asian Nations (ASEAN), later joined by Brunei in January 1984, Vietnam in 1995, and most recently by Myanmar and Laos in 1997. The association was conceived initially in response to the perceived Communist threat emanating from China, North Vietnam, and Laos. The lack of war or even acute international conflicts among the ASEAN countries stands in sharp contrast to the long Vietnam War and the Vietnamese occupation of Cambodia from 1979 to 1989, and with the domestic violence widespread within some of these countries (especially in Indonesia [East Timor], and the Philippines). This regional peace has been preserved in spite of several territorial and maritime disputes involving most of the Southeast Asian countries, such as the possession of the Paracel and Spratly Islands in the South China Sea, contested by China, Vietnam, Brunei, Malaysia, Taiwan, and the Philippines.[1]

With the setting of mechanisms for regional cooperation in all areas of policy, ranging from international refugees to trade liberalization, the ASEAN countries have moved from a zone of negative peace to the establishment of stable peace among themselves. The volume of economic, military, political, intellectual, and social interaction among the ASEAN countries has grown tremendously since the late 1960s. The ASEAN states have managed to change their international milieu, leading to a security environment of cooperation and collaboration. The initial Vietnamese military threat has receded, being replaced in our day by economic threats from the major economic powers in the Asia-Pacific region—Japan and China.

It is possible to refer to ASEAN as a "nascent" pluralistic security community. For instance, a sense of community and common identity became enshrined in its Treaty on Amity and Cooperation (1976), which stipulated a code of conduct for regional relations and the use of institutional mechanisms for settling disputes peacefully. This sense of community is based upon a common colonial past, upon its regional history, and upon a strict adherence to an ideology of economic growth (Foong Khong 1994). In contrast to Northeast Asia and to West Africa, and like South America, the ASEAN countries sustain a clear sense of "we-ness," bolstered by a wide-ranging multilateral dialogue and by a dense network of international and transnational links in several issue-areas such as business, military exercises, academic exchanges, and chief executive visits. Dialogue is regarded as a means of building relationships rather than as a means of achieving formal agreements (Mack and Kerr 1995, 128–29). ASEAN may thus be viewed as an evolving security community, with a progressive trajectory of growth, deeper institutionalization, and stable peace (see Chalmers 1996, 3; and Deng 1996). It is not an alliance but rather a security regime with an institutional framework that embodies the concepts of "common" and "comprehensive" security. Comprehensive security deliberately plays down its military dimension, while emphasizing nonmilitary factors such as political dialogue, interdependence, economic cooperation, and good and efficient governance.[2]

As a nascent or emergent pluralistic security community, one could expect the ASEAN countries, like their South American counterparts, to have democratic political regimes. Yet what is most striking about this region is the fact that in terms of civil liberties its countries are rated even below Central Asia, North Africa, and the Middle East (Deng 1996, 15). Only Malaysia can be considered fully democratic, as opposed to "democratizing" (or partly free) Philippines, Singapore, and Thailand, and authoritarian Brunei, Indonesia, Laos, Myanmar, and Vietnam. This lack of common democratic values does not mean that the ASEAN countries do not share common values and norms. These common norms include noninterference in domestic affairs, consultation and consensual decision-making at the regional level, shared principles of amity (restraint, respect, and responsibility), and the primacy of growth and development, since economics is perceived as the crucial factor to reach national and regional resilience.

From an economic, rather than political, point of view, several factors have contributed to the maintenance and consolidation of regional peace among the ASEAN countries. Foremost among them is an amazing 6–9 percent GDP growth of their national economies, which today include four NICs—Singapore, Thailand, Malaysia, and Indonesia. The last few years have seen great progress in economic cooperation in the form of transnational "growth triangles." Moreover, the level of economic interdependence—estimated in 1989 as 20 percent for intra-ASEAN exports and 16 percent for imports—is increasing, with a tremendous growth in the volume of diplomatic, political, military, cultural, and social interactions (Foong Khong 1994, 3; see also Bobrow et al. 1995, 2–3). With the enlargement of ASEAN to include Cambodia, Laos, and Myanmar, the association might consist of ten members, with a combined population of 450 million and a formidable aggregate GNP exceeding $450 billion (Deng 1996, 6).

THEORETICAL RELEVANCE

Some basic comparisons among the four regions (i.e., South America, West Africa, East Asia, and Southeast Asia) are summarized in table 5.6. On the basis of this table, I assess how well the different hypotheses have fared regarding the maintenance of regional peace, examine possible links among the relevant variables, and refine the theoretical model.

How Well Did the Different Explanations Fare?

Nine different explanations for the maintenance of regional peace at different gradations (i.e., negative, stable, and security communities) were grouped in three categories: realist, liberal, and satisfaction hypotheses. The relevance of each explanation is examined below.

Table 5.6. Comparisons across Zones of Peace

Variable	South America	West Africa	Northeast Asia	ASEAN
Type of peace	stable	negative	negative	stable
Pluralistic security community?	yes (part)	no	no	yes (nascent)
Democracies	all	part	part	part
Type of states	strong and weak	weak	strong	mostly strong
Domestic peace	yes (mostly)	no	yes	yes (mostly)
War prospects	no	civil	yes	no
Economic development	varied	low	developed and NICs	NICs
Homogeneity	yes	no	no	no
Satisfaction with the territorial status quo	yes	yes	no	yes (mostly)
Hegemon	Brazil	Nigeria	no	Indonesia(?)
Balance of power (today)	no	no	yes	no

(1) Realist Hypotheses
They include: (a) regional hegemony; (b) regional balance of power; (c) relevance of third-party threats; and (d) irrelevance, impotence, and lack of means to fight external wars.

(a) Regional hegemony. The pacifying and conservative role of a regional hegemon in keeping the negative peace has been played out by both extraregional and regional powers. In the cases of South America and West Africa, that external role has been attributed to the United States (in Latin America as a whole) and to France (regarding the Francophone countries in West Africa and Equatorial Africa). Even more important has been the role played by local hegemons, either actual or potential, such as Brazil in South America, Nigeria in West Africa, and perhaps Indonesia in Southeast Asia. The fact that there has not been a clear extraregional or regional hegemon in Northeast Asia has exacerbated the volatility and fragility of the negative peace in that region.

(b) A Regional balance of power. It is clear that the key for understanding regional conflicts and regional peace among Third World states resides in the immediate regional environment within which these states operate (Wriggins 1992, 300). Yet, the formation and re-creation of regional balances of power (BOPs) do not seem to be widespread in the Third World, with the possible exceptions of the Middle Eastern and Southern Asian zones of conflict. In this respect, BOPs were important in keeping the peace only at specific periods of time in both South America (1883–1930 and the 1970s), and West Africa (1957–66). Moreover, in Southeast Asia, the intraregional configuration of a BOP among the ASEAN countries has been less evident, perhaps expressed through a balance of mutual influences among Indonesia, Thailand, Malaysia, and Singapore in the economic and military spheres.[3] By contrast, a delicate and complicated balance of power in Northeast Asia, which includes Russia, the United States, Japan, and China, has kept a negative and armed peace.

(c) Third-party threats. Third-party threats have been minor in the cases of South America and West Africa, unless we refer to the extraregional and/or local hegemons as the sources of that threat. In the case of ASEAN, that role has been filled by Vietnam and China in military and ideological terms, and later on by Japan and China in economic terms. In the Northeast Asian case, only if we consider the United States as an extraregional

power, then several of the states in the region might refer to it as a potential third-party threat.

(d) *Irrelevance, impotence, and lack of means.* Irrelevance (lack of intraregional interactions) has been crucial in explaining the long South American negative peace, at least until the 1960s. Similarly, impotence, in terms of lack of material and institutional means to fight across borders, has clearly explained the predilection of most of the West African states to focus their efforts upon their domestic problems, rather than embarking upon international wars. These factors have been less relevant in the Asia-Pacific region, because of economic prosperity and growing levels of interdependence involving the countries of both Northeast Asia and Southeast Asia.

(2) Liberal Hypotheses

They include: (a) democratic regimes; (b) economic development and prosperity; (c) economic integration and interdependence; and (d) normative consensus.

(a) *Democratic regimes.* Democratization has been very relevant in South America as a factor in the transition from negative peace to stable peace, and even more from stable peace to the formation of an incipient pluralistic security community in the Southern Cone, centered around the MERCO-SUR core of Brazil and Argentina. By contrast, in West Africa the partial democratization that has affected several of the countries has not had a significant effect upon the quality of their regional peace, partly because of the continuing military rule in Nigeria, still the pivotal regional actor. Furthermore, in Northeast Asia and in Southeast Asia, regional powers such as Indonesia and China are far away from democratizing. Interestingly, the ASEAN countries have managed to move along the continuum from negative peace all the way to the formation of an incipient pluralistic security community, in spite of the fact that most of them are not democracies.

(b) *Degree of economic development and prosperity.* This variable has been very relevant in the two Asian cases, which include NICs and highly developed economies, as a rationale for the maintenance of at least a negative peace. Moreover, the goal of economic development has been important for both South America and West Africa as a justification for their international, if not domestic, pacification. In the case of the LDCs in general, the goal of economic development has been usually linked to an external condition of dependence upon the developed countries, with a clear bias in favor of both domestic and international peace. In this sense, there is a clear relationship between peace and prosperity in which both bolster each other in a "virtuous circle" of political and economic stability (see Russett 1983).

(c) Degree of economic integration and interdependence. These two variables have been important in explaining the deepening or upgrading of regional peace in the direction of stable peace. As with economic prosperity, economic interdependence and economic liberalism in general are usually considered in conjunction with political liberalism (i.e., democratization) as a beneficial force for peace (see for instance Oneal et al. 1996, 12–13).[4] This has been most obvious in the cases of MERCOSUR and the Andean Pact in the South American context and in the case of ECOWAS in West Africa, at least at the rhetorical level. In the case of Southeast Asia, ASEAN as an economic and political integrative framework has institutionalized the regional movement from a zone of negative peace toward a pluralistic security community. In Northeast Asia, by contrast, an institutionalized regional forum of integration has not been developed, despite the growing economic interdependence among the countries of the region, and several attempts to enhance economic cooperation through political and economic fora such as APEC.

(d) Common "diplomatic culture" and normative consensus. A common cultural framework, and especially the emergence of a normative consensus related to the peaceful settlement of international disputes, has contributed to the maintenance of regional peace, notwithstanding the changing character of the political regimes. The development of a normative consensus has become evident in the long peace of South America and in the negative peace of West Africa. In both cases, their states have formally adopted the principle of *uti possidetis* in order to respect their inherited colonial borders. The emergence of a common diplomatic culture has recurred in the Asia-Pacific region as well, particularly among the ASEAN countries. The variance among the four regions resides, however, in the different degree of *institutionalization* of this common diplomatic culture and normative consensus: the Southern Cone of South America is the most developed in this sense, followed by ASEAN in Southeast Asia and ECOWAS in West Africa. At the bottom of the list we find Northeast Asia, which is characterized by low levels of regional institutionalization.

The South American countries, through a gradual historical and learning process, have managed in the last one hundred years to establish a unique Latin "diplomatic culture" that has helped their governments to resolve their international conflicts short of war. Based upon their common historical and cultural framework, they have built a strong normative consensus, including a normative and legal reluctance to engage in war against fellow South American nations. Their diplomatic system incorporated a culture of legalism imbued with formal norms, including a specifically Spanish American international law and diplomacy (Holsti 1996, 169–70). Their major norms and principles have included: (1) *uti possidetis* (recognition of the former colonial borders); (2) peaceful international coexistence (the principle of *convivencia*); (3) nonintervention and mutual respect of national sovereignties; and (4) peaceful settlement of international disputes, including the recourse to arbitration, mediation, and other similar juridical and diplomatic techniques.

The West African states have developed a normative consensus of their own in the form of a reciprocal respect for the norms of territorial integrity and *uti possidetis*. The norms of behavior sanctioned by the OAU in 1964 in favor of the freezing of the international borders were designed to keep the regional interstate peace and to delegitimize international wars as a mechanism to resolve international disputes. The policies of the vast majority of the states have indeed reflected their respect for their existing borders, with the exceptions of Somalia, Morocco, Ghana, and Togo in 1957–66 and, to a lesser extent, Senegal vis-à-vis Mauritania in 1989–90. The basic norms agreed upon included: (1) nonintervention in the domestic affairs of other African states; (2) nonrecourse to force in inter-African relations, so that interstate wars were not considered as legitimate policy alternatives; (3) belief in African solutions for African problems; and (4) respect for the territorial status quo, as established by the colonial powers.

(3) Satisfaction as a Linking Hypothesis
In chapter 2 I have suggested an additional hypothesis about the maintenance of regional peace that focuses upon the concept of satisfaction with the status quo. To avoid tautology, I have examined its domestic and international sources. Satisfaction with the status quo refers basically to the territorial dimension, although it is not exhausted by it. "Status quo" refers in general to the economic, military, and diplomatic rules that govern a sys-

tem at a certain point of time, so it is directly linked to the preservation and legitimacy of the regional order.

An active satisfaction with the territorial status quo has been widespread in the cases of South America and West Africa; there have been very few cases of dissatisfaction (Bolivia and Ecuador in South America; Ghana, Togo, and Burkina Faso in West Africa at certain periods of time). Satisfaction with the territorial status quo is nowadays current among the ASEAN countries, including Indonesia and Vietnam, in spite of some enduring maritime (territorial) disputes. In the Northeast Asian case, the situation is radically different, given the revisionist postures of China, Russia, North Korea, and even Japan.

The sources for this satisfaction with the territorial status quo have varied across regions and across time. West Africa epitomizes the case of weak states and nondemocratic regimes, which are also weak powers in international relations. Accordingly, most of its states have adopted conservative postures vis-à-vis their international borders as a rational survival strategy to cope with their domestic problems and to turn their "juridical" sovereignty into a more "empirical" form of statehood. By contrast, South America has included throughout its longer diplomatic history both weak and strong states, democracies and authoritarian regimes, and middle-range regional powers such as Brazil, Argentina, and Chile, along with other states that are very weak in terms of international relations. In this sense, many of the South American countries fall in a "middle range" in terms of state strength: they have been strong enough not to fall apart as in other postcolonial situations in the Third World (especially in Africa), but at the same time they have been weak enough that they find it hard to mobilize their societies for external war and conquest. In contrast to alternate cycles of political transitions from and to democratic regimes, the international relations of South America have been characterized in the last sixty years by a high level of conservatism and continuity, which is a reflection of the widespread satisfaction of most of its countries with the territorial status quo.

As we move from South America and West Africa to the Asia-Pacific region, we find stronger forms of state. In the Southeast Asian area the picture is even more complex than in South America: there are many strong states and a few weak ones, some authoritarian regimes (Indonesia, Laos, Vietnam, Brunei, Myanmar) and a few democratic states or democratizing ones (Malaysia, Philippines, and Thailand). In international terms, we can identify an emergent important position in the hierarchy of international power accompanied by a concomitant rise in status. Finally, in the case of Northeast Asia, we find many strong states, both democratic and non-democratic regimes, and among the most important powers in the international hierarchy in terms of economic and military power. Yet Northeast Asia is by far the most volatile region among all the zones of peace, since it includes both satisfied and revisionist states.

After reviewing the different explanations, we can summarize them in table 5.7.

A reading of table 5.7 suggests the following conclusions: First, there is no single explanation for the maintenance of regional peace, be it negative, stable, or a pluralistic security community. Second, while satisfaction with the territorial status quo by the majority of the states in a region might be a sufficient condition for reaching negative peace, it is not a necessary one (as in the case of Northeast Asia). Third, the realist explanations (i.e., regional hegemony, regional balance of power, third-party threats, irrelevance and impotence) are more useful for the analysis of negative peace than for understanding the more advanced stages of stable peace and pluralistic security communities. Fourth, the grouping of democratic states and prosperous economies in a contiguous geographic area tends to result in the development of stable peace and pluralistic security communities. Pluralistic security communities might emerge among mostly strong (but not democratic) states, granted they share a normative consensus of their own and develop a regional identity, as in the case of ASEAN in Southeast Asia. Finally, peace can be indeed maintained among nondemocratic states, though there seems to be a direct relationship between the quality of the regional peace and the type of political regime sustained by the countries in any given region.

Links among the Variables

In this section, I suggest several propositions that can be empirically tested in these four cases, as well as in other zones of peace and zones of conflict.[5] These propositions suggest logical and empirical links between types of political regimes and gradations of peace; types of states and gradations of peace; and among types of regime, types of state, degree of power and status, and regional outcomes of peace and war.

Table 5.7. Explanations for the Maintenance of Regional Peace

Independent Variables	South America	West Africa	Northeast Asia	ASEAN
Regional hegemon	yes	yes	no	yes (?)
Regional BOP	no	no	yes	no(?)
External threat	no	no	no	yes
Irrelevance	yes	no	no	no
Impotence	no	yes	no	no
Democracies	yes (1980s-)	no	no	no
Development	no yes (1980s-)	no	yes	yes
Integration	no yes (1980s-)	yes	no	yes
Normative consensus	yes	yes	no (?)	yes
Satisfaction with the territorial status quo	yes	yes	no	yes
Dependent Variables	South America	West Africa	Northeast Asia	ASEAN
Negative peace	yes	yes	yes	yes
Stable peace	yes	no	no	yes
Pluralistic security community	yes (emerging)	no	no	yes (emerging)

(1) Links between types of political regime and gradations of peace

1. Regions composed by clusters of authoritarian regimes tend to be zones of conflict or at best zones of negative peace (such as the militocracies of South America until the 1980s or in West Africa). Only if these authoritarian regimes are embedded within strong states can a zone of stable peace be established, as in the case of ASEAN.

2. Since there seems to be an inherent incompatibility between the internal and external uses of the armed forces, authoritarian regimes ruled directly by the military (militocracies) tend to be involved in domestic conflicts. At the same time, they tend to keep their regional peace, at least at the level of negative peace.

3. Regions composed by clusters of democratic regimes tend to be zones of stable peace and even evolve into pluralistic security communities, such as in the cases of Western Europe and North America, and more recently in the Southern Cone of South America (the MERCOSUR countries).

4. As the theory of democratic peace predicts, mixed clusters of authoritarian and democratic regimes tend to be zones of conflict (South Asia, Middle East). However, if authoritarian regimes are embedded within strong states, negative peace might be maintained within a framework of a regional balance of power, as in Northeast Asia.

(2) Links between types of state and gradations of peace

5. States vary not only with respect to their status as powers in international relations, but also regarding their weakness or strength as members of the category of states, vis-à-vis their own societies (see Buzan 1983, 66; Holsti 1996). The domestic strength or weakness of the member states in a given region, associated with their institutional capabilities, degree of legitimacy, and mobilization resources, seems to affect the overall quality of their regional peace (see Desch 1996; Job 1992; and Migdal 1974). Hence, there are important international consequences for different categories of states.

6. Regions composed of clusters of weak states tend to be zones of armed conflict (Central America until the late 1980s, Equatorial Africa), or at best zones of negative peace still affected by civil wars and domestic conflicts (West Africa). Paradoxically, the domestic weaknesses of these states can be explained partly by the absence of interstate war and serious external threats at the time of their postcolonial independence (see Desch 1996, 242).[6]

7. Regions composed of clusters of strong states fill the entire gamut of possibilities from violent interstate conflict through negative and stable peace, all the way up to pluralistic security communities. To predict the regional outcome of war or peace we have to link the strength of any specific state to its particular type of political regime or to other explanatory variables (such as regional normative consensus or dissent).

(3) Links among types of state, types of regime, and gradations of peace
8. Regions composed of strong *and* democratic states tend to be zones of stable peace and pluralistic security communities (as in the case of Western Europe and today's Southern Cone of South America).

9. Regions composed of a myriad of weak and strong states, and democratic and nondemocratic regimes, tend to be characterized by international and domestic conflicts (as in the cases of the Middle East or South Asia).

10. Pluralistic security communities seem to be a prerogative of clusters of strong states, which enjoy a high degree of domestic peace (i.e. integration), whether they are democratic regimes (in Western Europe) or authoritarian ones (in ASEAN).

11. Stable peace seems to be a prerogative of clusters of strong states, or at least weak states (and powers) with democratic regimes. By definition stable peace requires pacification both within and across the borders of states.

12. Negative peace seems to characterize clusters of strong states with "mixed" regimes (Northeast Asia, and to a lesser extent South America before the wave of democratization in the 1980s) and of weak and nondemocratic states, such as in West Africa.

(4) Links between civil and international wars, and between domestic and international peace
13. Civil wars tend to occur within weak and nondemocratic states (as in West Africa and in South America before the 1980s). Domestic conflicts can even worsen as a consequence of the persistence of international peace. Conversely, international wars tend to involve mixed types of regimes (democratic and nondemocratic), nondemocratic regimes, and mixed types of states (strong and weak).

14. Regarding clusters of weak and nondemocratic states, there seems

to be a negative relationship between the occurrence of civil and international wars, as the cases of negative peace in South America (until the 1980s) and West Africa illustrate. For clusters of strong states there is a similar negative correlation between the possibility of international wars and the lack of civil wars (as in the case of Northeast Asia).[7] These findings seem to contradict the tenets of the scapegoat or diversionary theory of war.

15. As a state advances in its level of bilateral/regional peace vis-à-vis other state(s), it has to reach a sufficient level of domestic peace. In other words, for stable peace and for pluralistic security communities to develop, domestic peace (i.e., lack of civil wars and other violent domestic conflicts) has to prevail.

Refining the Theoretical Model

The theoretical model presented in chapter 2 can now be refined and summarized, pinpointing the following arguments: (1) there are different conditions for the maintenance of distinct gradations of peace; (2) the liberal explanation of democratic peace should not be dismissed, but put in (regional) perspective; and (3) regional norms and the emergence of a normative consensus seem to be crucial for the movement from war to negative peace, and from negative peace to stable peace.

(1) There are different conditions for the maintenance of distinct gradations of peace
Back in 1991, Emanuel Adler explained the subtleties of a "peace trap" by referring to several "seasons of peace" that have taken place in the developed world. These seasons were differentiated and arranged according to the quality of peace (or absence of war), ranging from general stability, common security, and concert, all the way up to pluralistic security community and (perpetual?) peace (see Adler, 1991). In this book, I have simplified Adler's "seasons" by referring to three basic gradations of regional peace: negative peace, stable peace, and pluralistic security communities. One of the major theoretical goals of this book has been to offer a systematic list of pertinent explanations (or "conditions") for the persistence of regional peace at different gradations. What became evident from my empirical research, however, is the fact that there are separate but overlapping conditions for different gradations of peace. Hence, peace is probably

overdetermined: there are many reasons (or "conditions") for its maintenance, as follows:

(a) There are no necessary conditions to reach a state of negative peace. This means that it might be a by-product of one or several favorable conditions, such as democratization, economic prosperity, interdependence, economic integration, normative consensus, regional hegemony, regional balance of power, third-party threats, and/or geographical irrelevance or impotence. Negative peace can then be accidental or fortuitous, a result of terror (such as through nuclear deterrence), hegemony, equilibrium, impotence, or irrelevance. At the same time, if the majority of the states in a given region are satisfied with the territorial status quo, either actively or passively, that might be enough to get at least negative peace (that is, a simple absence of war), although it is insufficient to stabilize and deepen it.

(b) Since stable peace encompasses also a previous state of negative peace, it is clear that an active satisfaction with the territorial status quo by the majority of the states becomes a necessary condition to reach a more stable peace, along with a common normative framework that emphasizes the preference for peaceful change and peaceful settlement of international disputes. These two conditions do not have to be fulfilled only by democratic regimes. However, if all the countries of a given region are full-fledged democracies, that in itself will be sufficient (although not necessary) to reach regional stable peace. In turn, economic prosperity, interdependence, and economic integration might contribute to its achievement.

(c) Finally, to establish pluralistic security communities, one should add to the two necessary conditions mentioned above a third one related to high degrees of interdependence and economic integration among the states and peoples of the region, leading to the creation of a regional identity and a sense of "we-ness." If, and only if, these three conditions come together do they become sufficient. Moreover, pluralistic security communities might be assisted by economic prosperity, regional hegemony, and third-party threats.

(2) The liberal explanations should not be dismissed, but put in (regional) perspective
Negative peace has preceded chronologically and logically the evolution of a region into a zone of stable peace and a pluralistic security community. While liberal arguments such as democratization, economic interdependence, and normative consensus might explain the upgrading in the quality

of regional peace, they do not explain per se its origins and initial persistence. For instance, there is no possible way that more than one hundred years of regional peace in South America can be explained by the Kantian liberal "pacific union." There are too many years in which there were too few democracies, too little trade or interdependence, and too few shared liberal norms. Conversely, the Kantian argument appears to provide a persuasive explanation for the greatly enhanced cooperation in the last decade. Hence, the liberal explanations might be sufficient to understand *today* the maintenance of a zone of peace, but they are not necessary for its occurrence in the first place.

In an indirect way, my empirical research on South America and West Africa has criticized the tenets of the democratic peace theory by arguing that zones of negative peace are not a sole prerogative of democratic regimes. In other words, democracy is not a necessary condition for the peaceful resolution of serious militarized disputes involving nondemocratic or mixed dyads, especially if these dyads are embedded in a regional context that has developed over time a diplomatic culture that favors the maintenance of the territorial status quo over abrupt and violent changes. In South America, a unique Latin diplomatic culture has evolved that in many instances has facilitated the resolution of such conflicts short of war. At the same time, it is clear that democratization has been very relevant for understanding the evolution and upgrading of peaceful relations from mere negative peace to a stable, lasting peace, such as in the case of the Southern Cone of Latin America since the mid 1980s. Scholars from the Kantian school have been too wrapped up in explaining the negative peace among liberal states, when the logic of their approach suggests that democratic regimes are supposed to go well beyond merely avoiding war with one another. Thus, democratic regimes are destined to form zones of stable peace and pluralistic security communities, not just zones of negative peace.

(3) Regional norms and the emergence of a normative consensus seem to be crucial for the movement from war to regional negative peace, and especially from negative peace to stable peace
It is important to differentiate between the norms that stem directly from a democratic type of regime in favor of peaceful change and peaceful settlement of disputes and regional norms that might evolve independently from the changing or nondemocratic character of these regimes, leading to very

similar, if not identical, results. For instance, the norms of *uti possidetis* and peaceful settlement of disputes have been adopted by the South American and West African states independently of their oscillating political regimes. This suggests that nondemocratic regimes do not necessarily export their internal norms of political (mis)behavior.

Regional normative frameworks play a crucial role regarding peaceful management of international crises and conflicts. Normative structures do not merely influence the behavior of democracies—they can also impact upon the war and peace propensities of nondemocratic or mixed dyads as well. Thus, nondemocracies, as well as mixed pairs of states, can establish and maintain peaceful relations among themselves, even beyond the initial level of negative peace.[8]

POLICY-ORIENTED CONCLUSIONS

In addition to these theoretical and logical propositions, I suggest the following *policy-oriented conclusions*:

1. It is crucial to understand not only how peace is obtained or lost, but also how it is maintained over time. We have to discern its different necessary, sufficient, and favorable conditions. This presupposes a bias in favor of stability and the status quo, since obviously "peace reflects the interest of those who create it in that it distributes stakes and resolves issues to institutionalize a status quo that will be enforced by the dominant balance of forces . . ." (Vasquez 1993, 266).

2. It is equally important to grasp the regional perspective, as opposed to the systemic and dyadic levels of analysis. We have to focus our policy analysis upon the relationships within clusters of states that are linked together by geography, history, permeability of their frontiers, and high degrees of interdependence, interactions, and transactions. According to this view, the most important international relations that determine war, peace, and trade are the *intraregional* ones, rather than the bilateral or extraregional (systemic) ones.

3. Given the salience of satisfaction with the territorial status quo as a sufficient condition for the maintenance of negative regional peace, one has to address the important but elusive question of "how to get satisfaction"—in other words, how we should turn a zone of conflict into a zone

of negative peace. It is clear that there will always be some dissatisfaction in both the distribution of the world's territory and the status/prestige attributed to different states, due to historical, cultural, economic, political, ethnic, and military grievances (Wright 1964, 1341). Therefore, the puzzle of getting satisfaction implies the art of crafting political compromises and avoiding psychological misperceptions so that, after reaching a point of equilibrium in which the status quo becomes legitimate and apt, all the parties concerned will rationally prefer the existing order to any disruptive change of it. In turn, the explanation for their *motivations* and volitions is directly related to the old normative issues of finding a balance between order and justice, and between order and change.[9]

4. The issue of satisfaction with the status quo transcends the mere territorial dimension, which is considered nowadays less important in international relations (see Rosecrance 1996). Yet the distribution of satisfaction with the status quo may still shape the prospects for conflict or cooperation in the international system, though not necessarily through war and peace only (see Stoll and Champion 1985, 76). Therefore, the emphasis upon satisfaction leads us to examine more closely not only the capabilities of states, but also their willingness and volition, in order to grasp their attitudes toward change and continuity in international relations.

5. If we comprehend the different conditions for the distinctive gradations of regional peace as depicted above, that might help us to construct the building blocks for turning a zone of conflict into a zone of (initially) negative peace, with the teleological goal of reaching stable peace and a security community by the end of the process. The recent rhetoric of the "New Middle East," as suggested by the former Israeli prime minister Shimon Peres (1995), illustrates this point. His vision was somehow confused or convoluted since people in the region—scholars, practitioners, and many parts of the Israeli electorate as well—did not recognize the different gradations of regional peace to be experienced in the Middle East. When Peres wrote about the "New Middle East," he was already assuming the transition from war to negative peace (absence of war). He suggested a series of stages (binational and multinational cooperative projects, international consortia, and a regional community policy through a common market) in order to move the region ahead from a preexisting negative peace toward stable peace and even a security community (Peres 1995, 1-1-3). His rationale was essentially economic liberalism (prosperity, economic develop-

ment, increasing interdependence and economic integration). However, the Middle East is stuck at the very transition from being a zone of conflict into becoming a zone of negative peace; it is still far away from stable peace, despite the peaceful relations of Israel with both Egypt and Jordan, and the incipient peace process involving Israelis and Palestinians. Hence, it becomes crucial to differentiate among these three types of regional peace, as it is to be aware of the restricted scope of my concept of "zones of peace," dealing mainly with the absence of international wars.

After all, the phenomenon studied in this book, "zones of peace in the Third World," has been characterized mainly by regional negative peace, at most an imperfect reality that leaves intact the possibility of war within the borders of many states of today's world. These regions of negative peace still experience the virulent phenomena of civil wars, which is nowadays almost the only type of war known (Holsti 1996), as well as the persistence of serious international conflicts and crises below the threshold of conventional wars. In fact, even within the areas of the most developed and democratic countries in Western Europe and North America, the very realm of stable peace and of pluralistic security communities, we remain far from a state of "perpetual peace," still knowing crises, conflicts, disputes, and sporadic shows of violence below war. Immanuel Kant said sardonically, in the guise of quoting a Dutch innkeeper, that perpetual peace belongs only to the graveyard rather than to this world (Kant 1970, 93). Perhaps, then, we should content ourselves (be satisfied?) with the realizable and the feasible regarding our limited zones of peace. Indeed, we should try to expand and upgrade them in the progressive direction pointed out by liberals and Marxists alike. At the same time, as realists prudently warned us, we should not prematurely celebrate an impossible nirvana of perpetual peace, which seems to contradict human nature.

Appendices

1. *North America* (1917–)
   Canada, Mexico, United States
2. *Western Europe* (1945–)
   Austria, Belgium, Denmark, Finland, France, Germany, Great Britain, Greece, Iceland, Ireland, Italy, Luxembourg, Malta, Netherlands, Norway, Portugal, Spain, Sweden, Switzerland.
3. *Australasia/Oceania* (1945–)
   Australia, Fiji, Kiribati, Naru, New Zealand, Papua/New Guinea, Solomon Islands, Tonga, Tuvatu, Vanuatu, Western Samoa.
4. *Eastern Europe* (1945–89)
   Albania, Bulgaria, Czechoslovakia, East Germany, Hungary, Poland, Romania, Soviet Union, Yugoslavia.
5. *South America* (1883–)
   Argentina, Bolivia, Brazil, Chile, Colombia, Ecuador, Guyana, Paraguay, Peru, Suriname, Uruguay, Venezuela.
6. *West Africa* (1957–)
   Benin, Burkina Faso, Cape Verde, Gambia, Ghana, Guinea, Guinea Bissau, Ivory Coast, Liberia, Mali, Mauritania, Niger, Nigeria, Senegal, Sierra Leone, Togo.

7. *Northeast Asia* (1953–)
China, Japan, Mongolia, North Korea, Russia (former U.S.S.R.), South Korea, Taiwan.

8. *ASEAN* (1967–)
Brunei, Indonesia, Malaysia, Philippines, Singapore, Thailand, Vietnam (also since the beginning of 1997: Laos, Myanmar).

Appendix B. Contemporary Zones of Conflict in the International System

1. *Central America* (up to 1989)
Belize, Costa Rica, El Salvador, Guatemala, Honduras, Nicaragua, Panama.

2. *North Africa/Maghreb* (1945–)
Algeria, Chad, Morocco, Libya, Tunisia.

3. *East Africa/Horn of Africa* (1945–)
Burundi, Eritrea, Ethiopia, Kenya, Madagascar, Rwanda, Somalia, Sudan, Uganda, Tanzania.

4. *Central Africa/Equatorial Africa* (1960–)
Cameroon, Central African Republic, Congo, Equatorial Guinea, Gabon, Sao Tome, Zaire (Congo).

5. *Southern Africa* (until 1991)
Angola, Botswana, Lesotho, Malawi, Mozambique, Namibia, South Africa, Swaziland, Zambia, Zimbabwe.

6. *Middle East* (1945–)
Bahrain, Egypt, Iran, Iraq, Israel, Jordan, Kuwait, Lebanon, Oman, Qatar, Saudi Arabia, Syria, Turkey, United Arab Emirates, Yemen.

7. *South Asia* (1947–)
Bangladesh, Bhutan, Burma (Myanmar), India, Nepal, Pakistan, Sri Lanka.

8. *Central Asia* (since 1945, especially since 1991)
Afghanistan, Armenia, Azerbaijan, Georgia, Kazakhstan, Kyrgystan, Russia, Tajikistan, Turkmenistan, Uzbekistan.

Notes

Chapter 1. Zones of Peace in the International System

1. By contrast, for Singer and Wildavsky (1993, 3) the democratic zone of peace includes "Western Europe, the United States and Canada, Japan, and the Antipodes, which together have about 15 percent of the world's population." In their view, "an area becomes a zone of peace and democracy only when all the sizable countries in that area are democratic enough so that (1) they are confident they will not go to war with each other and (2) they believe that the strength of their military will not influence their negotiations with each other" (32).

2. The overlap holds in the cases of South America (Treaty of Tlatelolco for the entire Latin American region), Australasia (Treaty of Raratonga), and ASEAN.

3. This definition comes close to the concept of "unstable peace" as formulated by Boulding (1978, 13), and Alexander George's concepts of "precarious peace" and "conditional peace." According to Prof. George, precarious peace assumes the need for one or the two parties in the dyad to rely on active deterrence to discourage the resort to war. Similarly, under conditional peace, "one or both sides rely on general deterrence to discourage the other from thinking seriously of resorting to war as an instrument of power in their disputes" (personal correspondence with the author, 20 July 1993).

4. The concept of stable peace is based on Boulding (1978, 13). A zone of stable peace is similar to the concept of "peace system," as developed by Nazli Choucri (1972, 240). According to Choucri, a peace system is characterized by "the institutionalization of non-violent modes of international behavior and conflict resolution."

5. By "peaceful change" Deutsch et al. (1957, 5) mean the "resolution of social problems, normally by institutionalized procedures, without resort to large-scale physical force." For alternative definitions see Kacowicz (1994a, 5–7).

6. I thank Emanuel Adler for encouraging me to draw this important distinction in clear terms. Interestingly, Russett (1982, 173), Singer and Wildavsky (1993), and Boulding

211

(1991, 108) refer to zones of peace and to pluralistic security communities in almost identical terms. It should be also noticed that in its original formulation Deutsch et al. did not consider democracy as a necessary condition for the establishment of pluralistic security communities. For more recent formulations of pluralistic security communities, see Adler and Barnett (1996, forthcoming).

7. I thank Alexander George for his comments on this point.

8. One can easily reject the obvious arbitrariness of this characterization of zones of peace. For instance, Martin Wight strongly criticized Matthew Melko's similar definition of "peaceful societies" as follows: "It seems to me unreal to think of a nation [the United States] which is to a considerable extent organized for war, its economy dependent on the production of armaments, its politics dominated by the issues of extending or ending the war [the Vietnam War], its young men dominated by the expectation of being drafted—to say that such a nation is at peace simply because its citizens have not suffered foreign action on its own soil. Surely you are engaged in a marvelous piece of concealed imperialistic philosophizing? Have you concealed it from yourself? Great nations and empires which can do their fighting at a distance from the home country and not on their home soil, are in your system at peace. The little fellows who have the misfortune to be the battleground are the warlike ones" (quoted in Melko 1973, 81). At the same time, this differentiation is much more sensitive than the only democratic zone of peace offered by the liberals, or the indiscriminate characterization, by the realists, of the international system as a "state of war."

9. These definitions come close to the concept of "polyarchy," as developed by Robert Dahl (1971). According to Dahl, polyarchies are regimes that have been substantially popularized and liberalized; in other words, they are highly inclusive and extensively open to public contestation.

10. I am grateful to Moshe Abalo and to Andrew Hurrell for their comments on this point.

11. After a period of severe conflict, the Roman Republic was followed by a long period of Pax Romana (31 B.C.–161 A.D.), imposed by the Roman Empire over a large area of the world. Yet, this Pax Romana cannot be considered as an international zone of peace, since it included only *one* sovereign entity, the Roman Empire.

12. Finland was part of that zone of peace, though it was not an independent state until 1918.

13. The list of democracies is drawn from Doyle (1983a).

14. While Michael Doyle classifies Mexico as a liberal/democratic regime, the Freedom House still regards Mexico as a "partly free" regime, due to the paramountcy of the Institutional Revolutionary Party (PRI) since 1929. See McColm et al. (1993, 361–64). Following the last presidential elections, Mexico has moved further in the direction of consolidating its democratic regime.

15. There were two other violent sequels to the war of 1941: in 1981 and more recently in 1995. I am not considering the Falklands/Malvinas War of 1982, since it involved Argentina and an extraregional power, the United Kingdom.

16. I am not including the colonial war of Guinea Bissau against Portugal in 1965–74. The criterion for inclusion of sixteen states in this region is their membership in the

Economic Community of West African States (ECOWAS), consisting of Benin, Burkina Faso, Cape Verde, Côte d'Ivoire, Gambia, Ghana, Guinea, Guinea-Bissau, Liberia, Mali, Mauritania, Niger, Nigeria, Senegal, Sierra Leone, and Togo.

17. "Quasi-states" are defined by Robert Jackson (1987) as juridical artifacts that owe their creation more to the international community than to their own populations. These states lack many of the empirical characteristics of "real" states; state officers possess uncertain authority, government organizations are corrupt and ineffective, and the political community is atomized into several, segmented ethnic "publics." The characterization of "quasi-states" aptly describes the reality of several sub-Saharan African states.

Chapter 2. Explaining Zones of Peace in the International System

1. The fascination with war throughout human history has been linked to its tragic consequences. By comparison, peace is usually regarded as "dull" and uninteresting as a subject matter.

2. Similarly, George Blainey (1988, 3) argues that "the causes of war and peace, logically, should dovetail into one another. A weak explanation of why Europe was at peace will lead to a weak explanation of why Europe was at war. A valid diagnosis of war will be reflected in a valid diagnosis of peace."

3. On security regimes see Jervis 1983, 173–94; Stein 1985, 599–627; Nye 1987, 371–402; and Smith 1989, 227–44.

4. For instance, the European balance of power of the nineteenth century has been cited as a major cause of the long periods of peace in that continent up to World War I. On this issue see Polanyi 1944, 3; and Taylor 1971, xix.

5. For sophisticated statistical analyses see Maoz and Russett 1993. For cross-cultural tests see Ember et al. 1992; and Crawford 1994.

6. For recent analyses of the "normative" and "structural" causes of the democratic peace see Russett 1989, 1993; Maoz and Russett 1992, 1993; Siverson and Emmons 1991; Starr 1992; Gleditsch 1994; and Raymond 1994.

7. For critiques of the democratic peace argument see Mearsheimer 1990, 185–86; Cohen 1994; Mueller 1991, 58–59; Layne 1994; Spiro 1994; Farber and Gowa 1994; and Merritt and Zinnes 1991, 227.

8. I am not arguing here, as does Huntington (1993), that lack of normative consensus among different cultures (or "civilizations") will necessarily lead to an all-out violent conflict (or "clash") between different regions of the globe.

9. This argument, which is based on the premise that the territorial status quo preserves peace and avoids wars, is open to criticism. For instance, Bueno de Mesquita and Lalman (1992, 135) argue that mutual regard for the status quo is not sufficient to maintain peace, while mutual disdain for the status quo does not necessarily preclude cooperation. Similarly, a few theories on the causes of war, such as diversionary theories (or "linkage conflict" theories), seem to contradict my hypothesis. The contention here is that the argument holds for most, if not all, of the cases of territorial disputes, not for the entire universe of international wars. In this sense, satisfaction becomes almost tanta-

mount to territoriality, and almost exhausted by territorial issues. I thank Michael Barnett for his comments on this point.

10. At a more primary level of analysis, we could also point out the psychological sources of satisfaction, as emphasized by prospect theory. According to this theory, leaders are generally risk-averse with respect to gains, and risk-acceptant with respect to losses. Thus, people have a tendency to remain at the status quo. Since states are reifications of human activity, we can then infer that states are also likely to share a status quo bias (see Levy 1992a; 1992b, 284–85).

11. Kalevi Holsti claims that strong states are a necessary condition for peace, and that weak states are a primary location of war (Holsti 1993, 1; 1996). In this book, I argue that the presence of strong and democratic states is a sufficient condition for negative and stable peace. Conversely, I maintain that weak states are a primary location of civil, though not necessarily international, wars.

12. Katzenstein (1978) argues that the United States belongs to this category. His argument is forcefully opposed by Krasner (1978), who demonstrates the paramountcy of the U.S. state in order to explain its foreign policy.

13. The norm of *uti possidetis* implies that the new postcolonial states accepted the boundaries of the colonial empires they had replaced. See Prescott 1965, 11, 117.

14. Weakness and strength are relative and subjective attributes of international relations. Thus, it is plausible that a weak state could also "feel strong" towards a neighboring country, due to misperceptions and other cognitive failures. I thank Moshe Abalo for his comments on this point.

15. The former Soviet Union and its relations with the East European countries in 1945–89 is a case in point.

16. I am thankful to Bruce Russett for his comments on this point.

17. Similarly, Emanuel Adler refers to five international security arrangements, or "seasons of peace," in terms of the quality of that peace. In ascending order these are "general stability" (negative peace), "common security," "concert" (stable peace), "pluralistic security communities," and (perpetual) "peace." See Adler, 1991, 134–39.

18. Scholars disagree on this point. For instance, Emanuel Adler (1992, 294) defines a pluralistic security community as "a group of democratic sovereign states that, agreeing on the unbearable destructiveness of modern war and on political, economic, social, and moral values consistent with democracy, the rule of law, and economic freedom, have transferred their domestic practices to the international arena and allowed their civil societies as well as their institutions to become integrated to the point that the idea of using force loses any practical meaning and even becomes unthinkable." By contrast, Michael Barnett (1993) does not include the democratic regime as a requirement for the development of pluralistic security communities.

19. I thank Miriam F. Elman for her suggestions on this important point.

Chapter 3. The South American Zone of Peace, 1883–1996

1. Ecuador is sometimes classified as belonging to the Northern Tier.
2. In still another categorization, Myers (1991b, 231) includes only four nations—

Argentina, Uruguay, Chile, and Paraguay—in the Southern Cone subregion. Six nations—Peru, Ecuador, Colombia, Venezuela, Guyana, and Suriname—comprise the
Northern Tier. Bolivia belongs to both subregions, while Brazil stands on its own as a
separate South American subregion.

3. The most important territorial conflicts and disputes in South America have
involved Argentina and Chile; Argentina and Brazil; Peru and Ecuador; Colombia and
Venezuela; Chile and Bolivia; Chile, Bolivia, and Peru; Colombia and Venezuela; Venezuela and Guyana; and Guyana and Suriname. For a detailed list of territorial conflicts
see Ireland 1938. See also Gonzalez and Lira 1992; Little 1987; and Escudé 1988.

4. According to Grabendorff (1982, 271), in Latin America as a whole twenty-
three civil wars and other violent domestic conflicts took place between 1945 and 1976
alone. Thus, we should be cautious to conclude that the region is inherently peaceful in
domestic terms.

5. Quoted from the Comisión Sudamericana de Paz, La Seguridad Regional y la
Democracia, in *Documentos de la Primera Plenaria*, 2–24 April 1987, Santiago de Chile; my
translation from Spanish.

6. For instance, Philippe Schmitter wrote a seminal article (1991, 89–127) about
the effects of regime change in the Southern Cone upon progress and peace in international relations. More recently, Michael Barletta (1994) examined how the Argentine
and Brazilian transitions to democracy had an impact upon the quality of their bilateral
peace.

7. For further details of the Pactos de Mayo see Meneses 1991, 346–47; Ruiz Moreno
1961, 229–44; Burr 1965, 245–52; and Scenna 1981, 124–29.

8. On the Chaco War see Goldstein 1992, 199–200; Barclay 1971, 43–55; Calvert
1969, 97–107; Finan 1977, 191–98; Windass 1970, 68–75; and Ireland 1938, 66–76.

9. On the Peruvian-Ecuadorean War of 1941 see Goldstein 1992, 200–201; Finan
1977, 215–17; St.John 1992, 182–83; Maier 1969; Ireland 1938, 219–30; and Wood
1978.

10. On the Leticia dispute see Bushnell 1975, 408–9; Finan 1977, 216–17; Ireland
1938, 196–206; Hudson 1933; López 1936, 19–24; and Kacowicz 1997.

11. On the diplomacy of "national security" in the 1970s see: Grabendorff 1982,
268–77; Ronfeldt and Einaudi 1980, 195; Child 1984, 22; Gorman 1981, 122–24; Selcher
1984, 110–11; Goldblat and Millán 1982, 404–12; Hirst and Rico 1992, 26–32; and
Varas 1985, 54–56.

12. It should be noticed, however, that the rapprochement between Argentina and
Brazil dated from 1979 with their resolution of the Itaipú dispute, well before the transitions to democracy in Argentina (1983) and Brazil (1985). Similarly, Argentina finally
resolved the Beagle dispute with Chile in 1984, while the military regime of Pinochet
was still in power.

13. On the uncertain future of democracies in the region, see Sunkel 1995 and Fitch
1992.

14. On the Argentine-Brazilian economic integration and MERCOSUR, see
Manzetti 1990, 1992; Hirst and Bocco 1992; Bouzas 1995; Klaveren 1993; Guadagni
1992; and Peña 1995.

15. This quotation is from Brooke 1994. For further details on the Argentine-Bra-zilian bilateral relations, and their transition from negative to stable peace, see especially Barletta 1994. See also Finan 1975, 265; Selcher 1985, 1990; Justo 1983; Hirst and Bocco 1992; Tulchin 1983; Redick et al. 1995; Milenky 1978, 183–84; and Russell 1988, 73–74.

16. On the U.S. pacifying role in South America see Poitras 1990; Pastor 1992; Einaudi 1972, 148; Ronfeldt and Einaudi 1980, 186–90; Parkinson 1990; Bailey 1967, 65–66; Kurth 1973; Lowenthal 1979, 1987; Whitehead 1991; Black 1986; and Schoultz 1987.

17. On the role of Brazil vis-à-vis its neighbors see Kelly 1989; Rodrigues 1969; Turner 1991; and Myers 1991b.

18. There are two exceptions to this statement. First, there was some German influ-ence in South America, especially after World War I. Second, Argentina identified (or better, perceived) a permanent external threat in the United Kingdom, following the British occupation of the Falkland/Malvinas Islands in 1833.

19. This point has been clearly demonstrated by the poor performance of the Argen-tine army in the Falklands/Malvinas War, the first armed international conflict the Ar-gentine military was involved in since the end of the Paraguayan War in 1870. Only a few years before, it had waged the "Dirty War" (1976–80) against its own citizens.

20. I thank Michael Barletta, Moshe Abalo, and Rut Diamint for their suggestions on this point.

21. I am grateful to Roberto Russell and to Carlos Moneta for their comments and suggestions on this point.

22. Helio Jaguaribe, personal correspondence with the author, 2 January 1996.

23. See Redick 1981, 111; Somavía 1992, 17; and Lyon 1973, 34. On the distinc-tive culture and politics of the region, and their link to foreign policy, see Smith 1985, 155 and especially Ebel et al. 1991.

24. For a discussion of these principles see Quintanilla 1957, 175–81; Rippy 1932, 513–14; Claude 1968, 8; and Davis 1977, 11–12.

25. On Pan-Americanism and these legal instruments see Claude 1968; Aguilar 1968; Faundez-Ledezma 1988; Inter-American Institute 1966; Bailey 1967, 69–77; and Puig 1983.

26. The complete list includes: Yaguarón (1851) between Brazil and Uruguay; Amazonas (1859) between Venezuela and Brazil; Atacama (1866) between Bolivia and Chile; Acre (1867 and 1903) between Bolivia and Brazil; Misiones (1895) between Brazil and Argentina; Venezuela and British Guiana (the United Kingdom), in 1899; Amapá (1900), between Brazil and French Guiana (France); Patagonia/Los Andes (1902), be-tween Chile and Argentina; the Iza region (1904) between Ecuador and Brazil; Pirará (1904), between Brazil and British Guiana (the United Kingdom); Apaporis (1907) be-tween Colombia and Brazil; Acre/Madre de Dios (1909) between Bolivia and Peru; Arauca/Yavita (1922) between Colombia and Venezuela; and Tacna/Arica (1929), be-tween Chile and Peru. The list is drawn from Kacowicz 1994a (appendix B).

27. The references are to the Rio de Janeiro Convention of 27 August 1828, which concluded the First Argentine-Brazilian War and created Uruguay; the Treaty of Ancón,

signed on 20 October 1883, which ended the War of the Pacific; the Treaty of Buenos Aires, concluded on 21 July 1938, after the Chaco War; and the Protocol of Rio de Janeiro, signed on 29 January 1942, by which Ecuador recognized Peruvian sovereignty over their disputed territory.

28. On the definition and role of the state in Latin America in general, see Cardoso 1979; Wiarda and Kline 1990, 81; Knight 1992, 19–20; and Smith 1992.

29. I thank Andrew Hurrell for suggesting to me this characterization.

30. On the South American hierarchy of power see Child 1985, 7; Burr 1967, 79–80; Burr 1970, 102; and Mace et al., 1993.

31. I am grateful to Michael Barletta and Andrew Hurrell for their comments on this point. On Brazil as a "geopolitically satisfied" country see Kelly 1989; Meira Penna 1988; Hormazabal 1980, 124; Pinto 1969, 237–39; Rodrigues 1969, 205; Roett 1975; Bailey and Schneider 1974; Barros 1984, 30; and Quadros 1969, 256.

32. On the Argentine position see Escudé 1988; Milenky 1978; Tulchin 1983, 46–47; Barclay 1971; and Manwaring 1983, 170.

33. On the Peruvian foreign policy and its changing postures, see St.John 1992; Jaworski 1984, 200–201; and Lowenthal 1983, 422.

34. On the linkage between domestic and foreign policy in the Venezuelan case see Levine 1989; Hazelton 1984; Matthews 1984; Barros 1975, 148; and Martz 1991.

35. On the foreign policy of Uruguay and its relatively high status, see Fitzgibbon 1966, 245–54; Atkins 1975; and Abente 1991, 527–28.

36. On the foreign policy of Chile and the linkage between its strong state and its conservative policy in foreign relations, see Valenzuela and Valenzuela 1991; Valenzuela 1990; Varas 1984; Mulhenbrock 1995; Pittman 1988, 175; Cope 1975; Fortin 1975; and Burr 1965.

37. On the Bolivian diplomacy of the *salida al mar* see Glassner 1988; Holland 1975; and Shumavon 1981, 180.

38. On the Ecuadorean foreign policy and its continuing dispute with Peru see Yopo 1985; M. Martz, 1975; J. Martz 1990; Maier 1969; St.John 1977; Aravena 1995; Child 1985, 93–97; Dodd 1975; and Carrión Mena 1989.

39. On the Paraguayan "pendulum diplomacy" see Roett and Sacks 1991; Abente 1988; and Hoyer 1975.

40. On the Colombian foreign policy and its link to domestic politics see Hazelton 1984; Bagley and Totkatlian 1985; Bushnell 1975; Kline 1990; and Hartlyn 1989.

Chapter 4. West Africa, 1957–1966

1. It is interesting to contrast Smith and Bull's "relatively benign" view of wars in precolonial West Africa with Ada Bozeman's cultural analysis, which emphasizes the paramountcy of war in the conduct of inter-African affairs (see Bozeman 1976).

2. On the processes of peaceful decolonization in West Africa see Hargreaves 1976; Welch 1966; Yansané 1984, 372; Crowder 1970; and Aluko 1987.

3. This was reflected in the resolution adopted by the OAU at Kinshasa, on 11–14 September 1967. See the resolution in Brownlie 1970, 364–65.

4. On the Mali-Burkina War of 1985 see Agyeman-Duah 1990, 563–64; Asiwaju 1993, 82; Copson 1994, 27; Johnson 1986, 295–97; French 1986a, 28–29; Goldstein 1992, 183–84; and Malley 1986, 10.

5. On the Senegalese-Mauritanian dispute see Parker 1991; Doyle 1989; Soudan 1990, 34–37; Bluwey 1994; Pazzanita 1992; Chowdry and Beeman 1994, 165; Gellar 1982, 72–73; Asiwaju 1993; and Kacowicz 1997.

6. This periodicization is based on Burguess 1995 and Mortimer 1996, 149–61.

7. I thank Crawford Young for his suggestions on the different motivations for interstate conflicts in West Africa.

8. On the linkage between domestic conflict and international peace, see Matthews 1970a, 356–57; Bienen 1980, 171; Kapil 1966, 670; Zartman 1965; Jackson 1991, 88–90; and Wright 1992, 359.

9. On the emergence of civil society in Africa and its impact upon the process of democratization, see Chabal 1992, 142; Shaw and Okolo 1994, 2; Hawthorn 1993; Harbeson 1994; Bratton 1994; Blaney and Pasha 1993; and Rothchild and Lawson 1994.

10. For a complete list see Abangwu 1975. On the formation of the CEAO and other integration schemes see Yansané 1984; Thompson 1972; and French 1986b.

11. My argument here directly contradicts Michael Walzer's. Walzer eloquently argues that "borders, and the movement of individuals and groups across borders, are bitterly disputed as soon as imperial rule recedes and nations begin the process of liberation" (Walzer 1983, 44). And yet, Walzer justifies from both an ethical and practical point of view the triumph of the territorial state, "specifying the rights of its inhabitants and recognizing the collective right of admission and refusal." I thank Jeffrey Herbst for drawing this interesting quotation to my attention.

12. On Guinea Bissau and Cape Verde see Dunn 1978, 5–7; Decraene 1988; Davidson 1981; Cahen 1991; and Murphy 1994.

13. On Senegal see Hawthorn 1993; Kane and Villalon 1995; and Coulon 1988.

14. On the Ivory Coast see Sandbrook 1985, 28–29; Segal 1962, 238–48; Crook 1990, 24–28; and Campbell 1978.

15. On Ghana see Matthews 1970a, 340; Boyd 1979, 3; Azarya and Chazan 1987; Agyeman-Duah and Daddieh 1994, 35–36; Crook 1990; Chazan 1988, 1992; Rothchild 1995; and Gyimah-Boadi 1994.

16. For instance, in 1986 the Nigerian foreign minister, Prof. Akinyemi, declared a doctrine of reciprocity, saying, "[W]e [Nigerians] have responsibilities for Africa . . . just as Africa has responsibilities to Nigeria . . ." (quoted in Akindele and Ate 1986, 18). See also Akinyemi 1987; Kraus 1994; Pedder 1993; Johnson 1986; Ihonvbere 1987, 1991; Diamond 1993, 217–28; Nweke 1985; Ogunbambi 1985; and Shaw 1987.

17. On Ivory Coast see Pedler 1979; Thompson 1972, xvii–xxiii; Shaw 1978, 241–42; and French 1986b, 9.

18. On Guinea see Whiteman 1971; Clapp 1994; Pedler 1979, 144–56; Hippolyte 1972; and Suret-Canale 1974.

19. On Ghana see Kraus 1994; Pedler 1979; Aluko 1976; Mazrui 1967, 59–68; and Thompson 1972.

20. On Senegal see Pedler 1979, 171–72; Parker 1991; Hughes 1992, 205–8; Coulon 1988, 171–72; and Gellar 1982.

21. I thank Oded Levenhaim for his comments on this point. Interestingly, this conclusion both overlaps and contradicts that reached recently by Kalevi Holsti (1996). According to Holsti, strong states are a necessary condition for peace, while weak states are sites of war. I concur with him that weak states are sites of *civil* wars, although weak states and weak powers can also maintain external (negative) peace among themselves, as in the case of West Africa.

Chapter 5. Zones of Peace in a Comparative Perspective

1. Other disputes include those between Malaysia and Singapore over the island of Pulau Batu Putih in the Straits of Johnore and between Malaysia and Indonesia over the islands of Sipadan and Ligitan in the Celebes Sea. See Ball 1994, 89.

2. On the security aspects of ASEAN see Wriggins 1992, 290; and Acharya 1991, 1992.

3. I thank James Ferguson for his comments on this point.

4. It should be emphasized, however, that there is no overall consensus about the pacifying effects of interdependence. For a more subtle argument about the links between interdependence and peace (or conflict), see Barbieri 1996.

5. For a succinct list of zones of peace and zones of conflict, see appendices A and B.

6. Conversely, Third World states that had faced a hostile environment—Israel, South Korea, Cuba, and Taiwan—emerged as stronger states.

7. In 1994, thirty-one major armed conflicts were waged in twenty-seven locations around the world, all of them within the borders of independent states ("civil wars"). As Kalevi Holsti convincingly argues (1993, 1996), most of these civil wars involved weak states in the developing world (see a complete list in Sollenberg and Wallensteen 1995).

8. I thank Miriam F. Elman for her suggestions on this point.

9. This discussion brings us back to the issue of peaceful change, as I discussed in my previous book (see Kacowicz 1994a).

Bibliography

Abangwu, George C. 1975. "Systems Approach to Regional Integration in West Africa." *Journal of Common Market Studies* 13 (January–February): 116–33.

Abente, Diego. 1988. "Constraints and Opportunities: Prospects for Democratization in Paraguay." *Journal of Interamerican Studies* 30 (February): 73–104.

———. 1991. "Uruguay and Paraguay." In *Latin America: Its Problems and Its Promise*, edited by Jan Knippers Black, pp. 525–45. Boulder, Colo.: Westview.

Acharya, Amitav. 1991. "The Association of Southeast Asian Nations: 'Security Community' or 'Defense Community'?" *Pacific Affairs* 64 (summer): 159–77.

———. 1992. "Regional Military-Security Cooperation in the Third World: A Conceptual Analysis of the Relevance and Limitations of ASEAN." *Journal of Peace Research* 29 (February): 7–22.

Adedeji, Adebayo. 1970. "Prospects of Regional Economic Cooperation in West Africa." *Journal of Modern African Studies* 8 (July): 213–31.

———. 1993. "Africa in a World in Transition: Laying the Foundation for Security, Stability, Structural Transformation and Cooperation." In *Africa: Rise to Challenge*, edited by Olusegun Obasanjo and Felix G. N. Mosha, pp. 1–11. New York: Africa Leadership Forum.

Adibe, Clement. 1994. "Hegemony, Security, and West African Integration." Summary Report for SSRC Program. Watson Institute, Brown University, typescript.

Adler, Emanuel. 1991. "Seasons of Peace: Progress in Postwar International Security." In *Progress in Postwar International Relations*, edited by Emanuel Adler and Beverly Crawford, pp. 128–73. New York: Columbia University Press.

————. 1992. "Europe's New Security Order: A Pluralistic Security Community." In *The Future of European Security*, edited by Beverly Crawford, pp. 287–326. Berkeley: University of California, International and Area Studies.

Adler, Emanuel, and Michael N. Barnett. 1996. "Governing Anarchy: A Research Agenda for the Study of Security Communities." *Ethics and International Affairs* 10:63–98.

————. Forthcoming. *Security Communities*. Cambridge: Cambridge University Press.

Agor, Weston H. 1972. "Latin American Inter-State Politics: Patterns of Cooperation and Conflict." *Inter-American Economic Affairs* 26 (autumn): 19–33.

Agor, Weston H., and Andres Suárez. 1972. "The Emerging Latin American Political Subsystem." *Proceedings of the Academy of Political Science* 30 (August): 153–66.

Aguilar, Alonso. 1968. *Pan Americanism, From Monroe to the Present: A View from the Other Side*. New York: Monthly Review Press.

Agyeman-Duah, Baffour. 1990. "Military Coups, Regime Change, and Interstate Conflicts in West Africa." *Armed Forces and Society* 16 (summer): 547–70.

Agyeman-Duah, Baffour, and Cyril K. Daddieh. 1994. "Ghana." In *The Political Economy of Foreign Policy in ECOWAS*, edited by Timothy M. Shaw and Julius Emeka Okolo, pp. 32–46. London: Macmillan.

Agyeman-Duah, Baffour, and Olatunde J. B. Ojo. 1991. "Interstate Conflicts in West Africa: The Reference Group Theory Perspective." *Comparative Political Studies* 24 (October): 299–318.

Ake, Claude. 1993. "Rethinking African Democracy." In Larry Diamond and Marc F. Plattner, eds., *The Global Resurgency of Democracy*, pp. 70–82. Baltimore: Johns Hopkins University Press.

Akindele, R. A. 1973. "The Conduct of Nigeria's Foreign Relations." *International Problems* 12 (October): 46–65.

Akindele, R. A., and Bassey E. Ate. 1986. "Nigeria's Foreign Policy, 1986–2000 A.D.: Background to and Reflections on the Views from Kuru." *Nigerian Journal of International Affairs* 12 (1–2): 12–22.

Akinrinade, Olusola. 1992. "From Hostility to Accommodation: Nigeria's Policy in West Africa, 1984–1990." *Nigerian Journal of International Affairs* 18 (1): 47–77.

Akinterinwa, Bola A. 1990. "The Role of France in Nigeria's Relations with its Neighbors." *Jerusalem Journal of International Relations* 12 (January): 112–47.

Akinyemi, A. B. 1987. "Reciprocity in Nigerian Foreign Policy (The Akinyemi Doctrine)." *Nigerian Forum* 7 (May–June): 151–56.

Alfonsín, Raúl. 1992. "America del Sur: Zona de Paz en un Nuevo Orden Internacional." In *America del Sur Hacia el 2,000*, edited by Carlos Conteras Quina, pp. 25–38. Caracas: Nueva Sociedad.

Allen, Chris K. 1992. "Democratic Renewal in Africa: Two Essays on Benin." Centre of African Studies, University of Edinburgh, Occasional Papers 40, pp. 25–49.

Aluko, Olajide. 1976. *Ghana and Nigeria, 1957–1970: A Study in Inter-African Discord.* London: Rex Collings.

———. 1987. "Politics of Decolonization in British West Africa, 1945–1960." In vol. 2 of *History of West Africa*, edited by J. F. A. Ajaki and Michael Crowder, pp. 622–63. 3d ed. London: Longman.

Andersen, Robert B. 1993. "Democratic Crises, Regional Responses: The OAS and Democracy since 1991." Paper presented at the APSA Annual Meeting, Washington, D.C., 2–5 September.

Anderson, Charles W. 1967. *Politics and Economic Change in Latin America: The Governing of Restless Nations.* New York: Van Nostrand Reinhold.

Andreski, Stanislav. 1992. *Wars, Revolutions, and Dictatorships.* London: Frank Cass.

Aravena, Francisco R. 1995. "Conflicto Internacional Ecuador-Perú: Un Desafío a la Seguridad Hemisférica." *La Época* (Chile), 6 February, 4–5.

Aribisala, Femi. 1985. "The ECOWAS: A Progress Report." *Nigerian Journal of International Affairs* 11 (1): 74–91.

Aron, Raymond. 1966. *Peace and War: A Theory of International Relations.* New York: Doubleday.

Asiwaju, A. I. 1993. "West Africa." In *Workshop on the Role of Border Problems in African Peace and Security*, by the UN Regional Centre for Peace and Disarmament in Africa, pp. 72–99. . New York: United Nations.

Astiz, Carlos A. 1969. "The Latin American Countries in the International System." In *Latin American International Politics: Ambitions, Capabilities, and the National Interests of Mexico, Brazil, and Argentina*, ed. Carlos A. Astiz, pp. 3–17. South Bend, Ind: Notre Dame University Press.

Atkins, G. Pope. 1975. "Uruguay." In *Latin American Foreign Policies: An Analysis*, ed. Harold E. Davus abd Karn C. Wilson, pp. 273–93. Baltimore: Johns Hopkins University Press.

———. 1989. *Latin America in the International Political System.* 2d ed. Boulder, Colo.: Westview.

Austin, Dennis. 1984. "Things Fall Apart." In *Africa in the Post-Decolonization Era*, ed. Richard E. Bissell and Michael S. Radu, pp. 205–27. New Brunswick, N.J.: Transaction Books.

Ayoob, Mohammed. 1989. "The Third World in the System of States: Acute Schizophrenia or Growing Pains?" *International Studies Quarterly* 33 (March): 67–79.

———. 1991. "The Security Problematic of the Third World." *World Politics* 43 (January): 257–83.

————. 1995. *The Third World Security Predicament: State Making, Regional Conflict, and the International System.* Boulder, Colo.: Lynne Rienner.

Azarya, Víctor. 1988. "Reordering State-Society Relations: Incorporation and Disengagement." In *The Precarious Balance: State and Society in Africa,* ed. Donald Rotchild and Naomi Chazan, pp. 3–21. Boulder, Colo.: Westview.

Azarya, Víctor, and Naomi Chazan. 1987. "Disengagement from the State in Africa: Reflections on the Experience of Ghana and Guinea." *Comparative Studies in Society and History* 29 (January): 106–31.

Babangida, Ibrahim B. 1991. "Nigeria, Africa, and the Rest of the World." *Nigerian Forum* 11 (January–February): 6–15.

Bach, Daniel. 1983. "The Politics of West African Economic Cooperation: CEAO and ECOWAS." *Journal of Modern African Studies* 21 (autumn): 605–23.

————. 1995. "Frontiers versus Boundary Lines: Changing Patterns of State-Society Interactions in Sub-Saharan Africa." Paper presented at the APSA Annual Meeting, 31 August–3 September, Chicago.

Bagley, Bruce M., and Juan G. Totkatlian. 1985. "Colombian Foreign Policy in the 1980s: The Search for Leverage." *Journal of Interamerican Studies* 27 (fall): 27–62.

Bailey, Norman A. 1967. *Latin America in World Politics.* New York: Walker.

Bailey, Norman A., and Ronald Schneider. 1974. "Brazil's Foreign Policy: A Case-Study in Upward Mobility." *Inter-American Economic Affairs* 27 (spring): 3–25.

Balewa, Tafawa, Alhaji Abubakar Sir. 1964. *Nigeria Speaks: Speeches made between 1957 and 1964.* London: Longman of Nigeria.

Ball, Desmond. 1994. "Arms and Affluence: Military Acquisitions in the Asia-Pacific Region." *International Security* 18 (winter): 78–112.

Baranyi, Stephen. 1995. "Central America: A Fine and Lasting Peace?" In *SIPRI Yearbook, 1995: Armaments, Disarmament and International Security,* pp. 147–70. Oxford: Oxford University Press.

Barbieri, Katherine. 1996. "Economic Interdependence: A Path to Peace or a Source of Interstate Conflict?" *Journal of Peace Research* 33 (February): 29–49.

Barclay, Glen St.John. 1971. *Struggle for a Continent: The Diplomatic History of South America, 1917–1945.* London: Sidgwick and Jackson.

Barletta, Michael. 1994. "Democratic States and the Prospects for International Peace: The Argentine and Brazilian Transitions to Democracy." Paper presented at the Thirty-fifth International Studies Association Meeting, Washington, D.C., 28 March–1 April.

Barnett, Michael N. 1993. "Institutions, Roles, and Disorder: The Case of the Arab States System." *International Studies Quarterly* 37 (September): 271–96.

Barros, Alexandre S. C. 1975. "The Diplomacy of National Security: South American International Relations in a Defrosting World." In *Latin America: The Search for a New International Role*, edited by Ronald G. Hellman and H. Jon Rosenbaum, pp. 131–50. New York: John Wiley.

———. 1984. "The Formulation and Implementation of Brazilian Foreign Policy: Itamaraty and the New Actors." In *Latin American Nations in World Politics*, edited by Heraldo Muñoz and Joseph S. Tulchin, pp. 30–44. Boulder, Colo.: Westview.

Bawa, Vasant Kumar. 1980. *Latin American Integration*. Atlantic Highlands, N.J.: Humanities Press.

Berton, Peter. 1969. "International Subsystems." *International Studies Quarterly* 13 (December): 329–34.

Best, Kenneth. 1991. "The Continuing Quagmire." *African Report* 36 (April): 39–41.

Bethel, Leslie. 1989. *Latin America: Economy and Society, 1870–1930*. Cambridge: Cambridge University Press.

Betts, Richard K. 1994. "Wealth, Power, and Instability: East Asia and the United States after the Cold War." *International Security* 18 (winter): 34–77.

Bienen, Henry. 1980. "African Militaries as Foreign Policy Actors." *International Security* 5 (fall): 168–86.

———. 1985. "Populist Military Regimes in West Africa." *Armed Forces and Society* 11 (spring): 357–78.

Black, Jan Knippers. 1986. *Sentinels of Empire: The United States and Latin American Militarism*. New York: Greenwood.

Blainey, Geoffrey. 1988. *The Causes of War*. 3d ed. London: Macmillan.

Blaney, David L., and Mustapha Kamal Pasha. 1993. "Civil Society and Democracy in the Third World: Ambiguities and Historical Possibilities." *Studies in Comparative International Development* 28 (spring): 3–24.

Bluwey, Gilbert K. 1994. "Mauritania." In *The Political Economy of Foreign Policy in ECOWAS*, edited by Timothy M. Shaw and Julius E. Okolo, pp. 86–102. London: Macmillan.

Bobrow, David B., Steve Chan, and Simon Reich. 1995. "Southeast Asia Prospects and Realities: Beyond Regional Simplification." Paper presented at the ISA Meeting, Chicago, 22–25 February.

Bolin, William H. 1992. "The Transformation of South America's Borderlands." In *Changing Boundaries in the Americas: New Perspectives on the U.S.-Mexican, Central American, and South American Borders*, edited by Lawrence A. Herzog, pp. 169–83. San Diego: University of California at San Diego.

Boulding, Elise. 1992. "The Zone of Peace Concept in Current Practice: Review and Evaluation." In *Prospects for Peace: Changes in the Indian Ocean Region*, edited by Robert H. Bruce, pp. 75–104. Perth, Australia: Indian Ocean Centre for Peace Studies.

Boulding, Kenneth E. 1977. "Twelve Friendly Quarrels with Johan Galtung." *Journal of Peace Research* 14 (February): 75–86.

———. 1978. *Stable Peace*. Austin: University of Texas Press.

———. 1989. "Peace Theory." In *A Reader in Peace Studies*, edited by Paul Smoker, pp. 3–8. Oxford: Pergamon Press.

———. 1991. "Stable Peace among Nations: A Learning Process." In *Peace Culture and Society*, edited by Elise Boulding et al., pp. 108–14. Boulder, Colo.: Westview.

Bouzas, Roberto. 1995. "Mercosur and Preferential Trade Liberalisation in South America: Record, Issues, and Prospects." Serie de Documentos e Informes de Investigación, no. 176. FLACSO (Buenos Aires).

Boyd, J. Barron. 1979. "African Boundary Conflict: An Empirical Study." *The African Studies Review* 22 (December): 1–15.

Bozeman, Adda B. 1976. *Conflict in Africa: Concepts and Realities*. Princeton: Princeton University Press.

Bratton, Michael. 1994. "Civil Society and Political Transitions in Africa." In *Civil Society and the State in Africa*, edited by John W. Harbeson, Donald Rothchild, and Naomi Chazan, pp. 51–81. Boulder, Colo.: Lynne Rienner.

Bratton, Michael, and Nicolas van de Walle. 1994. "Neopatrimonial Regimes and Political Transitions in Africa." *World Politics* 36 (July): 453–89.

Bremer, Stuart A. 1992. "Dangerous Dyads: Conditions Affecting the Likelihood of Interstate War, 1816–1965." *Journal of Conflict Resolution* 36 (June): 309–41.

———. 1993. "Democracy and Militarized Interstate Conflict, 1816–1965." *International Interactions* 18 (February): 231–49.

Brogan, Patrick. 1990. *The Fighting Never Stopped: A Comprehensive Guide to World Conflict since 1945*. New York: Random House.

Brooke, James. 1994. "The New South Americans: Friends or Partners?" *New York Times*, 8 April.

Brownlie, Ian, ed. 1970. *Basic Documents on African Affairs*. Oxford: Clarendon Press.

Brydon, Lynne. 1985. "Ghanaian Responses to the Nigerian Expulsion of 1983." *African Affairs* 83 (337): 561–85.

Bueno de Mesquita, Bruce. 1981. *The War Trap*. New Haven: Yale University Press.

Bueno de Mesquita, Bruce, and David Lalman. 1992. *War and Reason: Domestic and International Imperatives*. New Haven: Yale University Press.

Bull, Hedley. 1977. *The Anarchical Society: A Study of Order in World Politics*. London: Macmillan.

————. 1984. "European States and African Political Communities." In *The Expansion of the International Society*, edited by Hedley Bull and Adam Watson, pp. 99–114. Oxford: Clarendon Press.

Burguess, Stephen F. 1995. "Multilateral Security Maintenance in Africa: Problems and Prospects." Paper Presented at the Annual Meeting of the International Studies Association, Chicago, 21–25 February.

Burns, E. Bradford. 1969. "Tradition and Variation in Brazilian Foreign Policy." In *Latin American International Politics*, Carlos Astiz, ed., pp. 175–95. Notre Dame, Ind.: University of Notre Dame Press.

Burr, Robert N. 1955. "The Balance of Power in Nineteenth-Century South America: An Exploratory Essay." *Hispanic American Historical Review* 35 (February): 37–60.

————. 1965. *By Reason or Force: Chile and the Balancing of Power in South America*. Berkeley, Calif.: University of California Press.

————. 1967. *Our Troubled Hemisphere: Perspectives on United States–Latin American Politics*. Washington, D.C.: Brookings Institution.

————. 1970. "International Interests of Latin American Nations." In *The International Politics of Regions: A Comparative Approach*, edited by Louis J. Cantori and Steven L. Spiegel, pp. 99–108. Englewood Cliffs, N.J.: Prentice-Hall.

Bushnell, David. 1975. "Colombia." In *Latin American Foreign Policies: An Analysis*, edited by Harold E. Davis and Larman C. Wilson, pp. 401–18. Baltimore: Johns Hopkins University Press.

Bushnell, David, and Neil Macaulay. 1994. *The Emergence of Latin America in the Nineteenth Century*. 2d ed. New York: Oxford University Press.

Buzan, Barry. 1983. *People, States, and Fear: The National Security Problem in International Relations*. Chapel Hill: University of North Carolina Press.

————. 1991. "Third World Regional Security in Structural and Historical Perspective." In *The Insecurity Dilemma*, edited by Brian L. Job, pp. 167–89. Boulder, Colo.: Lynne Rienner.

Cahen, Michel. 1991. "Vent des Iles: La Victorie de l'Opposition aux Iles du Cap-Vert et Sao Tomé e Principe." *Politique Africaine* 43 (October): 63–78.

Callaghy, Thomas M. 1995. "Africa and the World Political Economy: Still Caught Between a Rock and a Hard Place." In *Africa in World Politics: Post–Cold War Challenges*, edited by John W. Harbeson and Donald Rothchild, pp. 41–68. Boulder, Colo.: Westview.

Calvert, Peter. 1969. *Latin America: Internal Conflict and International Peace*. New York: St. Martin's Press.

Campbell, Bonnie. 1978. "The Ivory Coast." In *West African States: Failure and Promise,* edited by John Dunn, pp. 66–116. Cambridge: Cambridge University Press.

Cantori, Louis J., and Steven L. Spiegel, eds. 1970. *The International Politics of Regions: A Comparative Approach.* Englewood Cliffs, N.J.: Prentice-Hall.

Cardoso, Fernando H. 1979. "On the Characterization of Authoritarian Regimes in Latin America." In *The New Authoritarianism in Latin America,* edited by David Collier, pp. 33–57. Princeton: Princeton University Press.

Carr, Edward H. 1964. *The Twenty Years' Crisis, 1919–1939: An Introduction to the Study of International Relations.* 3d ed. New York: Harper and Row.

Carrión Mena, Francisco. 1989. *Política Exterior del Ecuador: Evolución, Teoría, y Práctica.* Quito: Editorial Universitaria.

Castañeda, Jorge G. 1994. "Latin America and the End of the Cold War: An Essay in Frustration." In *Latin America in a New World,* edited by Abraham F. Lowenthal and Gregory F. Treverton, pp. 28–52. Boulder, Colo.: Westview, 1994.

Chabal, Patrick. 1992. *Power in Africa: An Essay in Political Interpretation.* New York: St. Martin's Press.

Chalmers, Malcolm. 1996. "Transparency and Security in South-East Asia: The Debate on a Regional Arms Register." Paper presented at the ISA Annual Meeting, San Diego, April.

Charlton, Roger. 1983. "Predicting African Military Coups." *Futures* (August): 281–91.

Chazan, Naomi. 1988. "Patterns of State-Society Incorporation and Disengagement in Africa." In *The Precarious Balance: State and Society in Africa,* edited by Donald Rothchild and Naomi Chazan, pp. 121–48. Boulder, Colo.: Westview.

———. 1992. "Liberalization, Governance, and Political Space in Ghana." In *Governance and Politics in Africa,* edited by Goran Hyden and Michael Bratton, pp. 121–41. Boulder, Colo.: Lynne Rienner.

Chazan, Naomi, Robert Mortimer, John Ravenhill, and Donald Rothchild. 1992. *Politics and Society in Contemporary Africa.* Boulder, Colo.: Lynne Rienner.

Child, Jack. 1984. "Inter-State Conflict in Latin America in the 1980s." In *The Dynamics of Latin American Foreign Policies,* edited by Jennifer K. Lincoln and Elizabeth G. Ferris, pp. 21–45. Boulder, Colo.: Westview.

———. 1985. *Geopolitics and Conflict within South America: Quarrels among Neighbors.* New York: Praeger.

Choucri, Nazli, and Robert C. North. 1972. "In Search of Peace Systems: Scandinavia and the Netherlands; 1870–1970." In *Peace, War, and Numbers,* edited by Bruce M. Russett, pp. 239–74. Beverly Hills, Calif.: Sage.

Chowdry, Geeta, and Mark Beeman. 1994. "Senegal." In *The Political Economy of*

Foreign Policy in ECOWAS, edited by Timothy M. Shaw and Julius E. Okolo, pp. 147–72. London: Macmillan.

Clapham, Christopher. 1991. "The African State." In *Africa: Thirty Years On*, edited by Douglas Rimmer, pp. 91–104. London.

———. 1994. "Liberia." In *The Political Economy of Foreign Policy in ECOWAS*, edited by Timothy M. Shaw and Julius E. Okolo, pp. 66–85. London: Macmillan.

Clapp, Jennifer A. 1994. "Guinea." In *The Political Economy of Foreign Policy in ECOWAS*, edited by Timothy M. Shaw and Julius E. Okolo, pp. 47–65. London: Macmillan.

Clark, Ian. 1989. *The Hierarchy of States: Reform and Resistance in the International Order*. Cambridge: Cambridge University Press.

Claude, Inis L. 1968. "The OAS, the UN and the United States." In *International Regionalism*, edited by Joseph Nye, pp. 3–21. Boston: Little, Brown.

Clissold, Stephan, and Alistair Hennesy. 1968. "Territorial Disputes." In *Latin America and the Caribbean*, edited by Claudio Veliz, pp. 403–12. New York: Praeger.

Cohen, Raymond. 1994. "Pacific Unions: A Reappraisal of the Theory that 'Democracies Do Not Go to War with Each Other'" *Review of International Studies* 20 (April): 207–33.

Cohen, Herman J. 1995. "Political and Military Security." In *Africa in World Politics: Post–Cold War Challenges*, edited by John W. Harbeson and Donald Rothchild, pp. 278–94. Boulder, Colo.: Westview.

Comisión Sudamericana de Paz. 1987. *Documentos de la Primera Plenaria*. Santiago de Chile: Comisión Sudamericana de Paz.

Cope, Orville G. 1975. "Chile." In *Latin American Foreign Policies: An Analysis*, edited by Harold E. Davis and Larman C. Wilson, pp. 309–37. Baltimore: Johns Hopkins University Press.

Copson, Raymond W. 1994. *Africa's Wars and Prospects for Peace*. Armonk, N.Y.: Sharpe.

Coulon, Christian. 1988. "Senegal: The Development and Fragility of Semidemocracy." In *Democracy in Developing Countries: Africa*, edited by Larry Diamond et al., pp. 141–78. Boulder, Colo.: Lynne Rienner.

Craig, Gordon A., and Alexander L. George. 1990. *Force and Statecraft: Diplomatic Problems of Our Time*. 2d ed. New York: Oxford University Press.

Crawford, Neta C. 1994. "A Security Regime among Democracies: Cooperation among Iroquois Nations." *International Organization* 48 (summer): 345–85.

Crook, Richard C. 1990. "State, Society, and Political Institutions in Côte d'Ivoire and Ghana." *IDS Bulletin* 21 (April): 24–34.

Crowder, Michael. 1970. "Colonial Rule in West Africa: Factor for Division or

Unity." In *Governing in Black Africa: Perspectives on New States*, edited by Marion E. Doro and Newell M. Stultz, pp. 299–310. Englewood Cliffs, N.J.: Prentice-Hall.

Curtin, Philip D. 1966. "Nationalism in Africa, 1945–1965." *Review of Politics* 28 (April): 143–53.

Da Costa, Peter. 1993. "Talking Tough to Taylor." *African Report* 38 (January): 18–21.

Dahl, Robert. 1971. *Polyarchy: Participation and Opposition*. New Haven: Yale University Press.

Davidson, Basil. 1981. *No Fist is Big Enough to Hide the Sky: The Liberation of Guinea and Cape Verde, Aspects of an African Revolution*. London: Zed Press.

Davis, Harold E. 1977. "The Origins and Nature of Latin American Foreign Policies." In *Latin American Diplomatic History: An Introduction*, edited by Harold E. Davis, John J. Finan, and F. Taylor Peck, pp. 1–22. Baton Rouge: Louisiana State University Press.

Decraene, Philippe. 1988. "La Guinee-Bissau, République Populaire en Voie de Liberalisation." *L'Afrique et l'Asie Modernes* 158 (autumn): 54–62.

Dedring, Juergen. 1976. *Recent Advances in Peace and Conflict Research: A Critical Survey*. Beverly Hills, Calif.: Sage.

Deng, Yong. 1996. "Minor Countries at the Center: ASEAN in Asia-Pacific Regime Formation." Paper presented at the ISA Meeting, San Diego, 16–20 April.

Desch, Michael C. 1996. "War and Strong States, Peace and Weak States?" *International Organization* 50 (spring): 237–68.

Deutsch, Karl W., and Dieter Senghaas. 1971. "A Framework for a Theory of War and Peace." In *The Search for World Order*, edited by Albert Lepawsky, Edward H. Buehring, and Harold D. Lasswell, pp. 23–46. New York: Appleton-Century-Crofts.

Deutsch, Karl W., et al. 1957. *Political Community and the North Atlantic Area*. Princeton: Princeton University Press.

Diamond, Larry. 1988. "Nigeria: Pluralism, Statism, and the Struggle for Democracy." In *Democracy in Developing Countries: Africa*, edited by Larry Diamond, Juan J. Linz, and Seymour M. Lipset, pp. 33–91. Boulder, Colo.: Lynne Rienner.

———. 1989. "Beyond Authoritarianism and Totalitarianism: Strategies for Democratization." *The Washington Quarterly* 12 (winter): 141–63.

———. 1993. "Nigeria's Perennial Struggle." In *The Global Resurgence of Democracy*, edited by Larry Diamond and Marc F. Plattner, pp. 217–29. Baltimore: Johns Hopkins University Press.

Diamond, Larry, and Juan J. Linz. 1989. "Introduction: Politics, Society, and Democracy in Latin America." In *Democracy in Developing Countries: Latin America*, edited by Larry Diamond et al., pp. 1–58. Boulder, Colo.: Lynne Rienner.

Diamond, Larry, and Seymour M. Lipset. 1990. "Introduction: Comparing Experiences with Democracy." In *Politics in Developing Countries: Comparing Experiences with Democracy*, edited by Larry Diamond et al., pp. 1–37. Boulder, Colo.: Lynne Rienner.

Dodd, Thomas J. 1975. "Peru." In *Latin American Foreign Policies: An Analysis*, edited by Harold E. Davis and Larman C. Wilson, pp. 360–80. Baltimore: Johns Hopkins University Press.

Doyle, Mark. 1989. "Blood Brothers." *Africa Report* 34 (July/August): 13–16.

Doyle, Michael W. 1983a. "Kant, Liberal Legacies, and Foreign Affairs, Part I." *Philosophy and Public Affairs* 12 (summer): 205–33.

———. 1983b. "Kant, Liberal Legacies, and Foreign Affairs, Part II." *Philosophy and Public Affairs* 12 (fall): 323–53.

———. 1986. "Liberalism and World Politics." *American Political Science Review* 80 (December): 1151–65.

Dunn, John. 1978. "Comparing West African States." In *West African States—Failure and Promise: A Study in Comparative Politics*, edited by John Dunn, pp. 1–21. Cambridge: Cambridge University Press.

Ebel, Ronald H., Raymond Taras, and James D. Cochrane. 1991. *Political Culture and Foreign Policy in Latin America: Case Studies from the Circum-Caribbean*. Albany, N.Y.: State University of New York Press.

Einaudi, Luigi R. 1972. "Conflict and Cooperation among Latin American States." In *Latin America in the 1970s*, edited by Luigi R. Einaudi, pp. 148–57. Santa Monica, Calif.: Rand Corporation.

Elrod, Richard B. 1976. "The Concert of Europe." *World Politics* 28 (January): 159–74.

Ember, Carol R., Melvin Ember, and Bruce Russett. 1992. "Peace between Participatory Polities: A Cross-Cultural Test of the 'Democracies Rarely Fight Each Other' Hypothesis." *World Politics* 44 (July): 573–99.

Emerson, Rupert. 1962. "Pan-Africanism." *International Organization* 16 (spring): 275–90.

Ero, Comfort. 1995. "Subregional Peacekeeping and Conflict Management: The Ecowas Intervention in Liberia." Paper presented at the Second Pan-European Conference in International Relations, Paris, 13–16 September.

Escudé, Carlos. 1988. "Argentine Territorial Nationalism." *Journal of Latin American Studies* 20 (May): 139–65.

Ezenwe, Uka. 1983. *ECOWAS and the Economic Integration of West Africa*. New York: St. Martin's Press.

Farber, Henry S., and Joanne Gowa. 1994. "Polities and Peace." *International Security* 20 (fall): 123–46.

Fáundez-Ledezma, Hector. 1988. "The Inter-American System: Its Framework for Conflict Resolution." In *Latin America: Peace, Democratization and Economic Crisis*, edited by Jose Silva-Michelena, pp. 168–86. London: Zed.

Feit, Edward. 1968. "Military Coups and Political Development: Some Lessons from Ghana and Nigeria." *World Politics* 21 (January): 179–93.

Finan, John H. 1975. "Argentina." In *Latin American Foreign Policies: An Analysis*, edited by Harold E. Davis and Larman C. Wilson, pp. 261–72. Baltimore: Johns Hopkins University Press.

Finan, John H. 1977. "Foreign Relations in the 1930s: Effects of the Great Depression." In *Latin American Diplomatic History: An Introduction*, edited by Harold E. Davis, John J. Finan, and F. Taylor Peck, pp. 191–221. Baton Rouge: Louisiana State University Press.

Fitch, J. Samuel. 1992. "Democracy, Human Rights, and the Armed Forces in Latin America." In *The United States and Latin America in the 1990s*, edited by Jonathan Hartyln et al., pp. 181–213. Chapel Hill: University of North Carolina Press.

Fitzgibbon, Russell. 1966. *Uruguay: Portrait of a Democracy*. New York: Russell and Russell.

Foong Khong, Yuen. 1994. "ASEAN and the Idea of a Security Community." Paper presented at the APSA Annual Meeting, New York, 1–4 September.

Fortin, Carlos. 1975. "Principled Pragmatism in the Face of External Pressure: The Foreign Policy of the Allende Government." In *Latin America*, edited by Ronald G. Hellman and H. Jon Rosenbaum, pp. 217–45. New York: John Wiley.

French, Howard. 1986a. "Burkina Faso at the Eye of a West African Storm." *Africa Report* 31 (January/February): 28–30.

———. 1986b. "Houphouet's Region." *Africa Report* 31 (November/December): 9–13.

Friedberg, Aaron. 1994. "Ripe for Rivalry: Prospects for Peace in a Multipolar Asia." *International Security* 18 (winter): 5–33.

Gaddis, John L. 1986. "The Long Peace: Elements of Stability in the Postwar International System." *International Security* 10 (spring): 99–142.

———. 1991. "Great Illusions, the Long Peace, and the Future of the International System." In *The Long Postwar Peace*, edited by Charles W. Kegley, pp. 25–55. New York: Harper Collins.

———. "International Relations Theory and the End of the Cold War." *International Security* 17 (winter): 5–58.

Galtung, Johan. 1964. "Editorial." *Journal of Peace Research* 1 (February): 1–4.

————. 1975. *Essays in Peace Research.* Vol. 1. Copenhagen: Christian Ejlers.

Gambari, Ibrahim A. 1975. "Nigeria and the World: A Growing Internal Stability, Wealth, and External Influence." *Journal of International Affairs* 29 (fall): 155–69.

Gellar, Sheldon. 1982. *Senegal: An African Nation between Islam and the West.* Boulder, Colo.: Westview.

George, Alexander L. 1979. "Case Studies and Theory Development: The Method of Structured Focused Comparison." In *Diplomacy: New Approaches in History, Theory, and Policy,* edited by Paul G. Lauren, pp. 43–68. New York: Free Press.

Gilpin, Robert. 1981. *War and Change in World Politics.* Cambridge: Cambridge University Press.

Glassner, Martin Ira. 1988. "Bolivia's Orientation: Toward the Atlantic or the Pacific?" In *Geopolitics of the Southern Cone and Antarctica,* edited by Philip Kelly and Jack Child, pp. 154–69. Boulder, Colo.: Lynne Rienner.

Gleditsch, Nils P. 1993. "Geography, Democracy, and Peace." Paper presented at the ISA Annual Meeting, Acapulco, March.

————. 1994. "Peace and Democracy: Three Levels of Analysis." Paper presented at the Sixteenth World Congress of Political Science, Berlin, 21–25 August.

Glick, Edward B. 1965. "The Feasibility of Arms Control and Disarmament in Latin America." *Orbis* 9 (fall): 743–59.

Goldblat, Jozef, and Victor Millán. 1982. "Militarization and Arms Control in Latin America." In *World Armaments and Disarmaments, SIPRI Yearbook,* pp. 391–425. London: Taylor and Francis.

Goldstein, Erik. 1992. *Wars and Peace Treaties, 1816–1991.* London: Routledge.

González, Daniel V., and Pedro Lira B. 1992. "Los Muros de America del Sur: Dos Siglos de Controversias Fronterizas." In *America del Sur Hacia el 2,000,* edited by Carlos Contreras Quina, pp. 39–52. Caracas: Nueva Sociedad.

Good, Robert C. 1964. "Changing Patterns of African International Relations." *American Political Science Review* 58 (September): 632–41.

Gorman, Stephen M. 1981. "Peruvian Foreign Policy since 1975: External Political and Economic Initiatives." In *Latin American Foreign Policies: Global and Regional Dimensions,* edited by Elizabeth G. Ferris and Jennifer K. Lincoln, pp. 115–29. Boulder, Colo.: Westview.

Grabendorff, Wolf. 1982. "Interstate Conflict Behavior and Regional Potential for Conflict in Latin America." *Journal of Inter-American Studies and World Affairs* 24 (August): 267–94.

Griffiths, Ieuan. 1994. *The Atlas of African Affairs.* 2d ed. London: Routledge.

Grundy, Kenneth W. 1985. "The Impact of Region on Contemporary African Politics." In *African Independence: The First Twenty-Five Years,* edited by Gwendden

M. Carter and Patrick O'Meara, pp. 97–125. Bloomington: Indiana University Press.

Guadagni, Alieto A. 1992. "Mercosur: Una Herramienta de Desarrollo." In *El Mercado Común del Sur*, edited by Ministerio de Relaciones Exteriores, pp. 17–34. Buenos Aires: Ministerio de Relaciones Exteriores.

Guglialmelli, Juan E. 1979. *Geopolítica del Cono Sur*. Buenos Aires: El Cid Editor.

Gurr, Ted R. 1993. *Minorities at Risk: A Global View of Ethnopolitical Conflict*. Washington, D.C.: United States Institute of Peace.

Gyimah-Boadi, E. 1994. "Associational Life, Civil Society, and Democratization in Ghana." In *Civil Society and the State in Africa*, edited by John W. Harbeson et al., pp. 125–48. Boulder, Colo.: Lynne Rienner.

Haas, Ernst. 1971. "The Study of Regional Integration: Reflections on the Joy and Anguish of Pretheorizing." In *Regional Integration: Theory and Research*, edited by Leon N. Lindberg and Stuart A. Scheingold, pp. 3–42. Cambridge: Harvard University Press.

Haas, Michael. 1970. "International Subsystems." *American Political Science Review* 64 (March): 98–123.

———. 1989. *The Asian Way to Peace: A Story of Regional Cooperation*. New York: Praeger.

Hagan, Joe D. 1994. "Domestic Political Systems and War Proneness." *Mershon International Studies Review* 38 (October): 183–207.

Haggard, Stephan. 1994. "Thinking about Regionalism: The Politics of Minilateralism in Asia and the Americas." Paper presented at the APSA Meeting, New York, 1–4 September.

Hagopian, Frances. 1994. "State Retreat and the Reformulation of Political Representation in Latin America." Paper presented at the APSA Meeting, New York, 1–4 September.

Halperín Dongui, Tulio. 1993. *The Contemporary History of Latin America*. Durham, N.C.: Duke University Press.

Harbeson, John W. 1994. "Civil Society and Political Renaissance in Africa." In *Civil Society and the State in Africa*, edited by John W. Harbeson et al., pp. 1–29. Boulder, Colo.: Lynne Rienner.

———. 1995. "Africa in World Politics: Amid Renewal, Deepening Crisis." In *Africa in World Politics: Post–Cold War Challenges*, edited by John W. Harbeson and Donald Rothchild, pp. 3–20. Boulder, Colo.: Westview.

Hargreaves, John D. 1976. *The End of Colonial Rule in West Africa*. London: The Historical Association.

Hartlyn, Jonathan. 1989. "Colombia: The Politics of Violence and Accommodation." In *Democracy in Developing Countries: Latin America*, edited by Larry Diamond et al., pp. 291–334. Boulder, Colo.: Lynne Rienner.

Hawthorn, Geoffrey. 1993. "Sub-Saharan Africa." In *Prospects for Democracy: North, South, East, West*, edited by David Held, pp. 330–54. Stanford, Calif.: Stanford University Press.

Hazelton, William A. 1981. "Will There Always Be a Uruguay? Interdependence and Independence in the Inter-American System." In *Latin American Foreign Policies: Global and Regional Dimensions*, edited by Elizabeth G. Ferris and Jennifer K. Lincoln, pp. 61–78. Boulder, Colo.: Westview.

———. 1984. "The Foreign Policies of Venezuela and Colombia: Collaboration, Competition, and Conflict." In *The Dynamics of Latin American Foreign Policies*, edited by Jennifer K. Lincoln and Elizabeth G. Ferris, pp. 151–70. Boulder, Colo.: Westview.

Herbst, Jeffrey. 1989. "The Creation and Maintenance of National Boundaries in Africa." *International Organization* 43 (autumn): 673–92.

———. 1990. "War and the State in Africa." *International Security* 14 (spring): 117–39.

Hippolyte, Manigat M. 1972. "Guinea's Foreign Policy." *Africa Quarterly* 11 (January–March): 302–6.

Hirst, Mónica. 1994. "Las Relaciones Internacionales de America Latina a Mediados de los '90s: Nuevos Desafíos y Viejos Dilemas." *America Latina/Internacional* 1 (autumn): 65–84.

Hirst, Mónica, and Carlos Rico. 1992. "Regional Security Perceptions in Latin America." Documentos e Informes de Investigación, no. 120. FLACSO (Buenos Aires).

Hirst, Mónica, and Hector E. Bocco. 1992. "Nuclear Cooperation in the Context of the Programme for Argentine-Brazilian Integration and Cooperation." In *Averting a Latin American Nuclear Arms Race*, edited by Paul Leventhal and Sharon Tanzer, pp. 214–29. London: Macmillan.

Hoffmann, Stanley. 1987. *Janus and Minerva: Essays in the Theory and Practice of International Politics*. Boulder, Colo.: Westview.

Hoge, James F. 1995. "A Conversation with President Cardoso." *Foreign Affairs* 74 (July/August): 62–75.

Holland, James. 1975. "Bolivia." In *Latin American Foreign Policies: An Analysis*, edited by Harold E. Davis and Larman C. Wilson, pp. 338–59. Baltimore: Johns Hopkins University Press.

Holsti, Kalevi J. 1991. *Peace and War: Armed Conflict and International Order, 1648–1989*. Cambridge: Cambridge University Press.

———. 1993. "Armed Conflict in the Third World: Assesing Analytical Approaches and Anomalies." Paper presented at the ISA Annual Meeting, Acapulco, Mexico, March.

———. 1996. *The State, War, and the State of War.* Cambridge: Cambridge University Press.

Hoyer, Hans J. 1975. "Paraguay." In *Latin American Foreign Policies: An Analysis,* edited by Harold E. Davis and Larman C. Wilson, pp. 294–305. Baltimore: Johns Hopkins University Press.

Hudson, Manley O. 1933. *The Verdict of the League: Colombia and Peru at Leticia.* Boston: World Peace Foundation.

Hughes, Arnold. 1992. "The Collapse of the Senegambian Confederation." *Journal of Commonwealth and Comparative Politics* 30 (July): 200–222.

Huntington, Samuel P. 1968. *Political Order in Changing Societies.* New Haven: Yale University Press.

———. 1993. "The Clash of Civilizations?" *Foreign Affairs* 72 (Summer): 22–49.

Hurrell, Andrew. 1994a. "Regionalism in the Americas." In *Latin America in a New World,* edited by Abraham F. Lowenthal and Gregory F. Treverton, pp. 167–90. Boulder, Colo.: Westview.

———. 1994b. "An Emerging Security Community in South America?" Paper Presented at the APSA Annual Meeting, New York, 1–4 September.

Huxtable, Philip A., and Trisha C. Hobson. 1994. "The Institutionalization of Cooperation in Non-First World States: ECOWAS and the CIS." Paper presented at the ISA Annual Meeting, Washington, D.C., 28 March–1 April 1994.

Ihonvbere, Julius O. 1987. "Economic Contraction and Foreign Policy in the Periphery: A Study of Nigeria's Foreign Policy Towards Africa in the Second Republic (1979–1983)." *Afrika Spectrum* 22 (3): 267–84.

———. 1991. "Nigeria as Africa's Great Power: Constraints and Prospects for the 1990's." *International Journal* 46 (summer): 510–35.

Ikenberry, G. John, and Charles A. Kupchan. 1990. "Socialization and Hegemonic Power." *International Organization* 44 (summer): 283–315.

Inegbedion, E. John. 1994. "Ecomog in Comparative Perspective." In *The Political Economy of Foreign Policy in ECOWAS,* edited by Timothy M. Shaw and Julius E. Okolo, pp. 218–44. London: Macmillan.

Inoguchi, Takashi. 1995. "Dialectics of World Order: A View from Pacific Asia." In *Whose World Order? Uneven Globalization and the End of the Cold War,* edited by Hans-Henrik Hom and Georg Sorensen, pp. 119–36. Boulder, Colo.: Westview.

Inotai, András. 1994. "The New Regionalism and Latin America." In *The New Regionalism,* edited by Bjorn Hettne and András Inotai, pp. 51–79. Helsinki: UNU/WIDER.

Interamerican Institute of International Legal Studies. 1966. *The Inter-American System: Its Development and Strengthening.* Dobbs Ferry, N.Y.: Oceana.

Ireland, Gordon. 1938. *Boundaries, Possessions, and Conflicts in South America.* Cambridge: Harvard University Press.

Jackson, Robert H. 1987. "Quasi-states, Dual Regimes, and Neoclassical Theory: International Jurisprudence and the Third World." *International Organization* 41 (autumn): 519–49.

———. 1991. "The Security Dilemma in Africa." In *The Insecurity Dilemma*, edited by Brian L. Job, pp. 81–94. Boulder, Colo.: Lynne Rienner.

———. 1993. "Continuity and Change in the State System." In *States in a Changing World: A Contemporary Analysis*, edited by Robert H. Jackson and Alan James, pp. 346–67. Oxford: Clarendon Press.

Jackson, Robert H., and Carl G. Rosberg. 1982. "Why Africa's Weak States Persist: The Empirical and Juridical in Statehood." *World Politics* 35 (October): 1–24.

———. 1985. "Democracy in Tropical Africa: Democracy versus Autocracy in African Politics." *Journal of International Affairs* 38 (winter): 293–305.

Jaworski, Helan C. 1984. "Presente y Futuro de la Política Exterior Peruana." In *America Latina: Políticas Exteriores Comparadas*, edited by Juan C. Puig, pp. 529–35. Buenos Aires: GEL.

Jervis, Robert. 1976. *Perception and Misperception in International Politics.* Princeton: Princeton University Press.

———. 1978. "Cooperation Under the Security Dilemma." *World Politics* 30 (January): 167–214.

———. 1983. "Security Regimes." In *International Regimes*, edited by Stephen D. Krasner, pp. 173–94. Ithaca, N.Y.: Cornell University Press.

———. 1985. "From Balance to Concert: A Study of International Security Cooperation." *World Politics* 38 (October): 58–79.

———. 1991. "The Future of World Politics: Will It Resemble the Past?" *International Security* 16 (winter): 39–73.

Job, Brian L. 1991. "The Insecurity Dilemma: National, Regime, and State Securities in the Third World." In *The Insecurity Dilemma: National Security of Third World States*, edited by Brian L. Job, pp. 11–35. Boulder, Colo.: Lynne Rienner.

———. 1996. " A Matter of 'Delicate Diplomacy': The Prospects of a Concert of Powers in the Asia Pacific?" Paper presented at the ISA Annual Meeting, San Diego, 16–20 April.

Johnson, L. Gunnar. 1976. *Conflicting Concepts of Peace in Contemporary Peace Studies.* Beverly Hills, Calif.: Sage.

Johnson, James T. 1991. "International Norms and the Regulation of War." In *The*

Long Postwar Peace, edited by Charles W. Kegley, pp. 290–303. New York: Harper Collins.

Johnson, Segun. 1986. "Burkina-Mali War: Is Nigeria Still a Regional Power?" *India Quarterly* (July–September): 294–308.

Jones, Dorothy V. 1991. *Code of Peace: Ethics and Security in the World of the Warlord States.* Chicago: University of Chicago Press.

Justo, Liborio. 1983. *Argentina y Brasil en la Integración Continental.* Buenos Aires: Centro Editor de America Latina.

Kacowicz, Arie M. 1994a. *Peaceful Territorial Change.* Columbia: University of South Carolina Press.

———. 1994b. "Pluralistic Security Communities and 'Negative' Peace in the Third World." Working Paper Series on Regional Security , no. 2 (June). University of Wisconsin, Madison: Global Studies Research Program.

———. 1997. "Peru vs. Colombia and Senegal vs. Mauritania: Mixed Dyads and 'Negative' Peace." In *Paths to Peace: Is Democracy the Answer?*, edited by Miriam Fendius Elman, pp. 335–69. Cambridge: MIT Press.

Kaiser, Karl. 1968. "The Interaction of Regional Subsystems." *World Politics* 21 (October): 84–107.

Kane, Ousmane, and Leonardo Villalón. 1995. "Islam and Democracy in Senegal: The Crisis of Legitimacy and the Emergence of a Muslim Opposition Movement." Paper presented at the ISA Annual Meeting, 22–25 February Chicago.

Kant, Immanuel. 1970. *Perpetual Peace.* 1795. Reprinted in *Kant's Political Writings*, edited by Hans Reiss, pp. 93–130. Cambridge: Cambridge University Press.

Kapil, Ravi L. 1966. "On the Conflict Potential of Inherited Boundaries in Africa." *World Politics* 18 (July): 656–73.

Kaplan, Robert D. 1994. "The Coming Anarchy." *Atlantic Monthly,* February, 44–76.

Katzenstein, Peter J. 1978. "Introduction: Domestic and International Forces and Strategies of Foreign Economic Policy." In *Between Power and Plenty: Foreign Economic Policies of Advanced Industrial States*, edited by Peter J. Katzenstein, pp. 3–22. Madison: University of Wisconsin Press.

Kaufman, Edy. 1976. *The Superpowers and Their Spheres of Influence: The United States and the Soviet Union in Eastern Europe and Latin America.* London: Croom Helm.

Kegley, Charles W., and Gregory A. Raymond. 1986. "Normative Constraints on the Use of Force Short of War." *Journal of Peace Research* 23 (September): 213–26.

Keller, Edmond J. 1996. "Introduction: Toward a New African Political Order." In *Africa in the New International Order: Rethinking State Sovereignty and Regional Security*, edited by Edmond J. Keller and Donald Rothchild, pp. 1–14. Boulder, Colo.: Lynne Rienner.

Kelly, Philip. 1989. "Geopolitical Tension Areas in South America: The Question of Brazilian Territorial Expansion." In *Inter-American Relations: The Latin American Perspective*, edited by Robert Biles, pp. 190–209. Boulder, Colo.: Lynne Rienner.

Kelman, Herbert C. 1981. "Reflections on the History and Status of Peace Research." *Conflict Management and Peace Science* 5 (spring): 95–110.

Kemp, Geoffrey. 1973. "The Prospects for Arms Control in Latin America: The Strategic Dimensions." In *Military Rule in Latin America: Function, Consequences and Perspectives*, edited by Philippe C. Schmitter, pp. 189–243. Beverly Hills, Calif.: Sage.

Keohane, Robert O., and Joseph S. Nye. 1971. *Transnational Relations and World Politics*. Cambridge: Harvard University Press.

Klaveren, Alberto van. 1984. "The Analysis of Latin American Foreign Policies: Theoretical Perspectives." In *Latin American Nations in World Politics*, edited by Heraldo Muñoz and Joseph S. Tulchin, pp. 1–21. Boulder, Colo.: Westview.

———. 1993. "Why Integration Now? Options for Latin America." In *Challenges of Integration: Europe and the Americas*, edited by Peter H. Smith, pp. 115–45. New Brunswick, N.J.: Transaction.

Kline, Harvey F. 1990. "Colombia: The Struggle between Traditional 'Stability' and New Visions." In *Latin American Politics and Development*, edited by Howard J. Wiarda and Harvey F. Kline, pp. 231–57. Boulder, Colo.: Westview.

Knight, Franklin W. 1992. "The State of Sovereignty and the Sovereignty of States." In *Americas: New Interpretative Essays*, edited by Alfred Stepan, pp. 11–29. New York: Oxford University Press.

Kornfeld, Phoebe. 1990. "Togo." In *The Political Economy of Foreign Policy in ECOWAS*, edited by Timothy M. Shaw and Julius E. Okolo, pp. 173–86. London: Macmillan.

Krasner, Stephen D. 1978. *Defending the National Interest: Raw Materials Investments and U.S. Foreign Policy*. Princeton: Princeton University Press.

Kraus, Jon. 1994. "The Political Economy of African Foreign Policies: Marginality and Dependency, Realism and Choice." In *The Political Economy of Foreign Policy in ECOWAS*, edited by Timothy M. Shaw and Julius E. Okolo, pp. 245–83. London: Macmillan.

Kumar, Ashok, and Eghoas Osagie. 1978. "Problems of the Economic Community of West African States." In *Nigeria and the World: Readings in Nigerian Foreign Policy*, edited by Bolaji Akinyemi, pp. 45–55. Ibadan: Oxford University Press.

Kurth, James R. 1973. "United States Foreign Policy and Latin American Military Rule." In *Military Rule in Latin America: Functions, Consequences, and Perspectives*, edited by Philippe C. Schmitter, pp. 244–322. Beverly Hills, Calif.: Sage.

Lake, David A. 1992. "Powerful Pacifists: Democratic Statse and War." *American Political Science Review* 86 (March): 24–37.

Lamouse-Smith, Willie B. 1992. "Towards Stability in Africa." In *Africa: Rise to Challenge*, edited by Olusegun Obasanjo and Felix G. N. Mosha, pp. 69–73. New York: ALF.

Lancaster, Carol. 1995. "The Lagos Three: Economic Regionalism in Sub-Saharan Africa." In *Africa in World Politics: Post–Cold War Challenges*, edited by John W. Harbeson and Donald Rothchild, pp. 189–206. Boulder, Colo.: Westview.

Lascano, Víctor. 1938. *America y la Política Argentina.* Buenos Aires: Ediciones Perrott.

Lauren, Paul G. 1983. "Crisis Prevention in Nineteenth Century Diplomacy." In *Managing U.S.-Soviet Rivalry: Problems of Crisis Prevention*, edited by Alexander L. George, pp. 31–58. Boulder, Colo.: Westview.

Lawler, James J. 1976. "Conflict-Avoidance in Africa." *Peace Research Review* 7 (June): 1–163.

Layne, Christopher. 1994. "Kant or Cant: The Myth of the Democratic Peace." *International Security* 19 (fall): 5–49.

Lebow, Richard N. 1981. *Between Peace and War: The Nature of International Crises.* Baltimore: Johns Hopkins University Press.

Legum, Colin. 1990. "The Coming of Africa's Second Independence." *The Washington Quarterly* 13 (winter): 129–40.

Lemke, Douglas, and Suzanne Werner. 1996. "Power Parity, Commitment to Change, and War." *International Studies Quarterly* 40 (June): 235–60.

Lenin, Vladimir I. 1939. *Imperialism: The Highest Stage of Capitalism.* New York: International.

Levine, Daniel H. 1989. "Venezuela: The Nature, Sources, and Future Prospects of Democracy." In *Democracy in Developing Countries: Latin America*, edited by Larry Diamond et al., pp. 247–89. Boulder, Colo.: Lynne Rienner.

Levy, Jack S. 1989a. "Domestic Politics and War." In *The Origin and Prevention of Major Wars*, edited by Robert I. Rotberg and Theodore K. Rabb, pp. 79–99. Cambridge: Cambridge University Press.

———. 1989b. "The Diversionary Theory of War: A Critique." In *Handbook of War Studies*, edited by Manus I. Midlarsky, pp. 259–88. Boston: Unwin Hyman.

———. 1992a. "An Introduction to Prospect Theory." *Political Psychology* 13 (June): 171–86.

———. 1992b. "Prospect Theory and International Relations: Theoretical Applications and Analytical Problems." *Political Psychology* 13 (June): 283–310.

Little, Walter. 1987. "International Conflict in Latin America." *International Affairs* 63 (autumn): 589–602.

López, Alfonso. 1936. *La Política Internacional.* Bogotá: Imprenta Nacional.

Lowenthal, Abraham F. 1979. "The United States and Latin America: Ending the Hegemonic Presumption." *Foreign Affairs* 55 (fall): 199–213.

———. 1983. "The Peruvian Experiment Reconsidered." In *The Peruvian Experiment Reconsidered,* edited by Cynthia McClintock and Abraham F. Lowenthal, pp. 415–30. Princeton: Princeton University Press.

———. 1987. *Partners in Conflict: The United States and Latin America.* Baltimore: Johns Hopkins University Press.

———. 1994. "Latin America and the United States in a New World: Prospects for Partnership." In *Latin America in a New World,* edited by Abraham F. Lowenthal and George Treventon, pp. 237–46. Boulder, Colo.: Westview.

Lyon, Peter. 1973. "New States and International Order." In *The Bases of International Order: Essays in Honour of C. A. W. Manning,* edited by Alan James, pp. 24–59. Oxford: Oxford University Press.

Mace, Gordon, Louis Belanger, and Jean Philippe Therien. 1993. "Regionalism in the Americas and the Hierarchy of Power." *Journal of Interamerican Studies and World Affairs* 35 (summer): 115–57.

Mack, Andrew, and Pauline Kerr. 1995. "The Evolving Security Discourse in the Asia-Pacific." *The Washington Quarterly* 18 (winter): 123–40.

Mahbubani, Kishore. 1995. "The Pacific Way." *Foreign Affairs* 74 (January/February): 100–111.

Maier, Georg. 1969. "Ecuadorian-Peruvian Boundary Dispute." *American Journal of International Law* 63 (January): 28–46.

Malley, Simon. 1986. "Burkina-Mali: Au Dela des Frontières . . ." *Afrique-Asie* 365 (January): 10–19.

Manning, Robert A., and Paula Stern. 1994. "The Myth of the Pacific Community." *Foreign Affairs* 73 (December): 79–93.

Manwaring, Max G. 1983. "Monitoring Latin American Arms Control Agreements." In *Controlling Latin American Conflicts: Ten Approaches,* edited by Michael A. Morris and Victor Millán, pp. 163–84. Boulder, Colo.: Westview.

Manzetti, Luigi. 1990. "Argentine-Brazilian Economic Integration: An Early Appraisal." *Latin American Research Review* 25 (December): 109–40.

———. 1992. "Economic Integration in the Southern Cone." *North-South Focus,* December, 1–6.

Maoz, Zeev. 1994. "Domestic Political Change and Strategic Response: The Impact of Domestic Conflict on State Behavior, 1816–1986." Paper presented at the ISA Annual Meeting, Washington, D.C., March.

Maoz, Zeev, and Ben D. Mor. 1995. "Satisfaction, Capabilities, and the Evolution of Enduring Rivalries, 1816–1990: A Statistical Analysis of a Game-Theoretical Model." Paper presented at the APSA Annual Meeting, Chicago, 31 August–3 September.

Maoz, Zeev, and Bruce Russett. 1992. "Alliances, Contiguity, Wealth and Political Stability: Is the Lack of Conflict among Democracies a Statistical Artifact?" *International Interactions* 17 (February): 245–67.

———. 1993. "Normative and Structural Causes of Democratic Peace, 1946–86." *American Political Science Review* 87 (September): 624–38.

Martin, Guy. 1995. "Francophone Africa in the Context of Franco-African Relations." In *Africa in World Politics*, edited by John W. Harbeson and Donald Rothchild, pp. 163–88. Boulder, Colo.: Westview.

Martz, John D. 1990. "Ecuador: Fragility of Dependent Democracy." In *Latin American Politics and Development*, edited by Howard Wiarda and Harvey F. Kline, pp. 378–92. Boulder, Colo.: Westview.

———. 1991. "Venezuela, Colombia, and Ecuador." In *Latin America: Its Problems and Its Promise*, edited by Jan Knippers Black, pp. 427–47. Boulder, Colo.: Westview.

Martz, Mary J. R. 1975. "Ecuador." In *Latin American Foreign Policies: An Analysis*, edited by Harold E. Davis and Larman C. Wilson, pp. 383–400. Baltimore: Johns Hopkins University Press.

Matthews, Robert O. 1970a. "Interstate Conflicts in Africa: A Review." *International Organization* 24 (spring): 335–60.

———. 1970b. "Domestic and Interstate Conflict in Africa." *International Journal* 25 (summer): 459–85.

Matthews, Robert P. 1984. "Oil in Troubled Waters." *NACLA* 18 (July/August): 21–51.

Mazrui, Ali A. 1967. *Towards a Pax Africana: A Study of Ideology and Ambition*. Chicago: University of Chicago Press.

———. 1993. "The Bondage of Boundaries." *The Economist*, 11 September, pp. 34–38.

McColm, R. Bruce. 1993. *Freedom in the World: The Annual Survey of Political Rights and Civil Liberties, 1992–1993*. New York: Freedom House.

McIntyre, David. 1993. "'La Paz Larga': Why Are There So Few Interstate Wars in South America?" Department of Political Science, University of Chicago, typescript.

Mearsheimer, John J. 1990. "Back to the Future: Instability in Europe after the Cold War." *International Security* 15 (summer): 5–56.

Meira Penna, Jose Osvaldo de. 1988. "Brazilian Geopolitics and Foreign Policy." In

Geopolitics of the Southern Cone and Antarctica, edited by Philip Kelly and Jack Child, pp. 100–110. Boulder, Colo.: Lynne Rienner.

Melko, Matthew. 1973. *Fifty-two Peaceful Societies*. Toronto: Canadian Peace Research Institute Press.

Melko, Matthew, and John Hord. 1984. *Peace in the Western World*. Jefferson, N.C.: McFarland.

Melko, Matthew, and Richard D. Weigel. 1981. *Peace in the Ancient World*. Jefferson, N.C.: McFarland.

Meneses, Emilio C. 1991. "Maintaining a Regional Navy with Very Limited Resources: The Chilean Case, 1900–1990." *Defense Analysis* 7 (4): 345–62.

Merritt, Richard, and Dinna A. Zinnes. 1991. "Democracies and War." In *On Measuring Democracy*, edited by Alex Inkeles, pp. 207–34. New Brunswick, N.J.: Transaction.

Migdal, Joel S. 1974. "Internal Structure and External Behaviour: Explaining Foreign Policies of Third World States." *International Relations* 4 (May): 510–25.

———. 1988. *Strong Societies and Weak States: State-Society Relations and State Capabilities in the Third World*. Princeton: Princeton University Press.

Milenky, Edward S. 1978. *Argentina's Foreign Policies*. Boulder, Colo.: Westview.

Miller, Lynn H. 1985. *Global Order: Values and Power in International Politics*. Boulder, Colo.: Westview.

Mitrany, David. 1966. *A Working Peace System*. Chicago: Quadrangle.

Modelski, George. 1961. "International Relations and Area Studies." *International Relations* 2 (April): 143–55.

Morgenthau, Hans J., and Kenneth W. Thompson. 1985. *Politics among Nations: The Struggle for Power and Peace*. 6th ed. New York: Alfred A. Knopf.

Morris, Michael A., and Victor Millán. 1983. Introduction to *Controlling Latin American Conflicts: Ten Approaches*, edited by Michael A. Morris and Victor Millán, pp. 1–10. Boulder, Colo.: Westview.

Mortimer, Robert A. 1996. "ECOMOG, Liberia, and Regional Security in West Africa." In *Africa in the New International Order: Rethinking State Sovereignty and Regional Security*, edited by Edmond J. Keller and Donald Rothchild, pp. 149–64. Boulder, Colo.: Lynne Rienner.

Moyosore, Toyin. 1990. "Nigeria's Historic Mission in Africa: Is She Still Relevant in African Affairs?" *Nigerian Forum* 10 (January–February): 33–40.

Mueller, John. 1989. *Retreat from Doomsday: The Obsolescence of Major War*. New York: Basic.

———. 1991. "Is War Still Becoming Obsolete?" University of Rochester, Department of Political Science, 5 August, typescript.

Mulhenbrock, Gisela von. 1995. "Reconciliation in Chile: Politics and Policies." Paper presented at the ISA Annual Meeting, Chicago, 21–25 February.

Murphy, Craig N. 1994. "Cape Verde." In *The Political Economy of Foreign Policy in ECOWAS*, edited by Timothy M. Shaw and Julius E. Okolo, pp. 17–31. London: Macmillan.

Myers, David J. 1991a. "Threat Perception and Strategic Response of the Regional Hegemons: A Conceptual Overview." In *Regional Hegemons: Threat Perception and Strategic Response*, edited by David J. Myers, pp. 1–29. Boulder, Colo.: Westview.

——. 1991b. "Brazil: The Quest for South American Leadership." In *Regional Hegemons: Threat Perception and Strategic Response*, edited by David J. Myers, pp. 225–68. Boulder, Colo.: Westview.

Naím, Moises. 1995. "Latin America: The Morning After." *Foreign Affairs* 74 (July/August): 45–61.

Neff, Jorge, and Remonda Bensabat. 1992. "'Governability' and the Receiver State in Latin America: Analysis and Prospects." In *Latin America to the Year 2,000*, edited by Archibald R. M. Ritter et al., pp. 161–76. New York: Praeger.

Nelson, Daniel N. 1994. "Great Powers and World Peace." In *World Security: Challenges for a New Century*, edited by Michael T. Klare and Daniel C. Thomas, pp. 27–42. New York: St. Martin's Press.

Neuberger, Benyamin. 1991. "Irredentism and Politics in Africa." In *Irredentism in International Politics*, edited by Naomi Chazan, pp. 97–109. Boulder, Colo.: Lynne Rienner.

Nordlinger, Eric. 1981. *On the Autonomy of the Democratic State*. Cambridge: Cambridge University Press.

Novicki, Margaret A. 1990. "Obed Asomoah: A New Role for ECOWAS." *Africa Report* 35 (May): 17–20.

Nweke, G. Aforka. 1985. "Nigeria's National Interest and Foreign Policy." *Nigerian Journal of International Affairs* 11 (1): 3–32.

Nwokedi, Emeka. 1985. "Strands and Strains of 'Good Neighbourness': The Case of Nigeria and its Francophone Neighbors." *Genève-Afrique* 23 (January): 39–60.

——. 1992. "Regional Integration and Regional Security: Ecomog, Nigeria, and the Liberian Crisis." *Centre d'Etude d'Afrique Noire, Université de Bourdeaux I, Travaux et Documents* 35.

Nye, Joseph S. 1968. *International Regionalism*. Boston: Little, Brown.

——. 1971. *Peace in Parts: Integration and Conflict in Regional Organizations*. Boston: Little, Brown.

——. 1987. "Nuclear Learning and U.S.-Soviet Security Regimes." *International Organization* 41 (summer): 371–402.

Nzongola-Ntalaya, Georges. 1987. "The National Question and the Crisis of Instability in Africa." In *Africa: Perspectives on Peace and Development*, edited by Emmanuel Hansen, pp. 55–86. London: Zed.

O'Donnell, Guillermo A. 1976. "Modernization and Military Coups: Theory, Comparisons, and the Argentine Case." In *Armies and Politics in Latin America*, edited by Abraham F. Lowenthal, pp. 197–243. New York: Holmes and Meier.

————. 1986. "Toward an Alternative Conceptualization of South American Politics." In *Promise of Development: Theories of Change in Latin America*, edited by Peter F. Klaren and Thomas J. Bossert, pp. 239–74. Boulder, Colo.: Westview.

————. 1988. "State and Alliances in Argentina, 1956–1976." In *Toward a Political Economy of Development: A Rational Choice Perspective*, edited by Robert H. Bates, pp. 176–205. Berkeley, Calif.: University of California Press.

Ofoegbu, Mazi R. 1971. "Functional Cooperation in West Africa." *Odu: A Journal of West African Studies* 6 (October): 21–53.

Ogunbambi, Rafiq O. 1985. "The Dilemma of Nigeria's African Policy." *Journal of African Studies* 12 (spring): 10–13.

Ojo, Olatunde. 1980. "Nigeria and the Formation of ECOWAS." *International Organization* 34 (autumn): 571–604.

Okolo, Julius E. 1985. "Integrative and Cooperative Regionalism: The Economic Community of West African States." *International Organization* 39 (winter): 121–53.

Okwechime, Mike. 1988. "Economic Integration in West Africa: Reality or Farce?" *Nigerian Forum* 8 (April–May): 100–110.

Olaniyan, R. Omotayo. 1986. "Nigeria and West Africa: Problems and Prospects in Future Relations." *Nigerian Journal of International Affairs* 12 (1–2): 135–49.

Oliver, Roland. 1992. *The African Experience*. New York: Harper and Collins.

Omede, Adedoyin J. 1995. "Nigeria's Military-Security Role in Liberia." *African Journal of International Affairs and Development* 1 (1): 46–55.

Oneal, John R., Frances H. Oneal, Zeev Maoz, and Bruce Russett. "The Liberal Peace: Interdependence, Democracy, and International Conflict, 1950–1985." *Journal of Peace Research* 33 (February): 11–28.

Organski, Abraham F. K. 1968. *World Politics*. 2d ed. New York: Alfred A. Knopf.

Oxford Analytica. 1991. *Latin America in Perspective*. Boston: Houghton Mifflin.

Palmer, Norman D. 1991. *The New Regionalism in Asia and the Pacific*. Lexington, Mass.: Lexington Books.

Parker, Ron. 1991. "The Senegal-Mauritania Conflict of 1989: A Fragile Equilibrium." *Journal of Modern African Studies* 29 (January): 155–71.

Parker, Paulette. 1994. " A Separate Peace? The Pacific Relations between Democracies." Paper presented at the ISA Annual Meeting, Washington, D.C., March.

Parkinson, Fred. 1990. "South America, the Great Powers and the Global System." In *Great Power Relations in Argentina, Chile, and Antarctica*, edited by Michael A. Morris, pp. 176–96. London: Macmillan.

———. 1993. "Latin America." In *States in a Changing World: A Contemporary Analysis*, edited by Robert H. Jackson and Alan James, pp. 240–61. Oxford: Clarendon Press.

Pastor, Robert A. 1992. *Whirlpool: U.S. Foreign Policy toward Latin America and the Caribbean*. Princeton: Princeton University Press.

Payne, Douglas W. 1994. "Giving Democracy a Bad Name." *Freedom Review* 25 (January–February): 26–37.

Pazzanita, Anthony G. 1992. "Mauritania's Foreign Policy: The Search for Protection." *Journal of Modern African Studies* 30 (June): 281–304.

Pedder, Sophie. 1993. "Nigeria: Let Down Again." *The Economist*, August 21st, special supplement.

Pedler, Frederick. 1979. *Main Currents of West African History, 1940–1978*. New York: Barnes and Noble.

Peña, Felix. 1995. "New Approaches to Economic Integration in the Southern Cone." *Washington Quarterly* 18 (summer): 113–22.

Perera, Srilal. 1985. "The OAS and the Interamerican System: History, Law, and Diplomacy." In *The Falklands War: Lessons for Strategy, Diplomacy, and International Law*, edited by Alberto R. Coll and Anthony C. Arend, pp. 132–55. Boston: George Allen and Unwin.

Peres, Shimon. 1995. "The New Middle East/East Mediterranean: Towards a New Era." In *Development Options for Cooperation: The Middle East, 1996*, edited by Joseph Vardi and Rafi Benvenisti, pp. 1–4. Jerusalem: Ministry of Foreign Affairs.

Pinto, Luis Bastian. 1969. "Brazil's Foreign Policy toward Latin America." In *Latin American International Politics*, edited by Carlos Astiz, pp. 234–47. South Bend, Ind.: University of Notre Dame Press.

Pittman, Howard T. 1988. "Harmony and Discord: The Impact of Democratization on Geopolitics and Conflict in the Southern Cone." In *Geopolitics of the Southern Cone and Antarctica*, edited by Philippe Kelly and Jack Child, pp. 30–51. Boulder, Colo.: Lynne Rienner.

Poitras, Guy. 1990. *The Ordeal of Hegemony: The United States and Latin America*. Boulder, Colo.: Westview.

Polanyi, Karl. 1944. *The Great Transformation: The Political and Economic Origins of Our Time*. Boston: Beacon Press.

Post, Kenneth W. J. 1968. *The New States of West Africa*. Harmondsworth: Penguin.

Prescott, J. R. V. 1965. *The Geography of Frontiers and Boundaries*. Chicago: Aldine.

Puig, Juan Carlos. 1983. "Controlling Latin American Conflicts: Current Juridical Trends and Perspectives for the Future." In *Controlling Latin American Conflicts*, edited by Michael A. Morris and Victor Millán, pp. 11–39. Boulder, Colo.: Westview.

Quadros, Janio. 1969. "Brazil's New Foreign Policy." In *Latin American International Politics*, edited by Carlos Astiz, pp. 248–58. South Bend, Ind.: Notre Dame University Press.

Quintanilla, Luis. 1957. "Latin America." In *Control of Foreign Relations in Modern Nations*, edited by Philip W. Buck and Martin B. Travis, pp. 167–233. New York: W. W. Norton.

Rapoport, Anatol. 1992. *Peace: An Idea Whose Time Has Come*. Ann Arbor: University of Michigan Press.

Ravenhill, John. 1988. "Redrawing the Map of Africa?" In *The Precarious Balance: State and Society in Africa*, edited by Donald Rothchild and Naomi Chazan, pp. 282–306. Boulder, Colo.: Westview.

Ray, James L. 1991. "The Future of International War." Paper presented at the Annual Meeting of the American Political Science Association, Washington, D.C., September.

———. 1993. "Wars between Democracies: Rare, or Nonexistent?" *International Interactions* 18 (February): 251–76.

Raymond, Gregory A. 1994. "Democracies, Disputes, and Third-Party Intermediaries." *Journal of Conflict Resolution* 38 (March): 24–42.

Raynal, Jean-Jacques. 1991. "Le Renouveau Démocratique Beninois: Modèle ou Mirage?" *Afrique Contemporaine* 160:3–25.

Redick, John R. 1981. "The Tlatelolco Regime and Nonproliferation in Latin America." *International Organization* 35 (winter): 103–34.

Redick, John R., Julio C. Carasales, and Paulo S. Wrobel. 1995. "Nuclear Rapprochement: Argentina, Brazil, and the Non-Proliferation Regime." *Washington Quarterly* 18 (winter): 107–22.

Rippy, J. Fred. 1932. *Historical Evolution of Hispanic America*. New York: F. S. Crofts.

Rock, Stephen R. 1989. *Why Peace Breaks Out: Great Power Rapprochement in Historical Perspective*. Chapel Hill: University of North Carolina Press.

Rodrígues, Jose H. 1969. "The Foundations of Brazil's Foreign Policy." In *Latin American International Politics*, edited by Carlos Astiz, pp. 196–215. South Bend, Ind.: Notre Dame University Press.

Roett, Riordan. 1975. "Brazil Ascendant: International Relations and Geopolitics in the Late Twentieth Century." *Journal of International Affairs* 29 (spring/summer): 139–54.

————. 1984. *Brazil: Politics in a Patrimonial Society.* 3d ed. New York: Praeger.

Roett, Riordan, and Richard Scott Sacks. 1991. *Paraguay: The Personalist Legacy.* Boulder, Colo.: Westview.

Ronfeldt, David F., and Luigi R. Einaudi. 1980. "Conflict and Cooperation among Latin American States." In *Beyond Cuba: Latin America Takes Charge of Its Future,* edited by Luigi R. Einaudi, pp. 185–200. New York: Crane Russak.

Rosecrance, Richard. 1989. "War, Trade, and Interdependence." In *Interdependence and Conflict in World Politics,* edited by James N. Rosenau and Hylke Tromp, pp. 48–57. Aldershot, U.K.: Averbury.

————. 1996. "The Rise of the Virtual State." *Foreign Affairs* 75 (July/August): 45–61.

Rothchild, Donald. 1995. "Rawlings and the Engineering of Legitimacy in Ghana." In *Collapsed States: The Disintegration and Restoration of Legitimate Authority,* edited by I. William Zartman, pp. 49–65. Boulder, Colo.: Lynne Rienner.

Rothchild, Donald, and Letitia Lawson. 1994. "The Interactions between State and Civil Society in Africa: From Deadlock to New Routines." In *Civil Society and the State in Africa,* edited by John W. Harbeson et al., pp. 255–81. Boulder, Colo.: Lynne Rienner.

Rothchild, Donald, and Michael Foley. 1983. "The Implications of Scarcity for Governance in Africa." *International Political Science Review* 4 (July): 311–26.

Rothstein, Robert L. 1992. "Weak Democracy and the Prospect for Peace and Prosperity in the Third World." In *Resolving Third World Conflict: Challenges for a New Era,* edited by Sheryl J. Brown and Kimber M. Schraub, pp. 16–50. Washington, D.C.: U.S. Institute of Peace.

Rouquié, Alan. 1973. "Military Revolutions and National Independence in Latin America, 1968–1971." In *Military Rule in Latin America,* edited by Philippe C. Schmitter, pp. 2–56. Beverly Hills, Calif.: Sage.

Rousseau, Jean-Jacques. 1953. *Constitutional Project for Corsica.* In *Rousseau: Political Writings,* edited by F. Watkins, pp. 277–330. New York: Nelson.

Rubin, Leslie, and Brian Weinstein. 1974. *Introduction to African Politics: A Continental Approach.* New York: Praeger.

Ruiz Moreno, Isidoro J. 1961. *Historia de las Relaciones Exteriores Argentinas: 1810–1955.* Buenos Aires: Editorial Perrot.

Rummel, R. J. 1981. *Understanding Conflict and War.* Beverly Hills, Calif.: Sage.

Russell, Roberto. 1988. "Argentina: Ten Years of Foreign Policy Toward the Southern Cone." In *Geopolitics of the Southern Cone and Antarctica,* edited by Philip Kelly and Jack Child, pp. 67–82. Boulder, Colo.: Lynne Rienner.

————. 1994. "Los Ejes Estructurantes de la Política Exterior Argentina." *America Latina/Internacional* (otoño/invierno): 5–26.

Russett, Bruce. 1967. *International Regions and the International System: A Study in Political Ecology.* Chicago: Rand McNally.

————. 1982. "Causes of Peace." In *Alternative Methods for International Security,* edited by Carolyn M. Stephenson, pp. 171–94. Lanham, Md.: University Press of America.

————. 1983. "Prosperity and Peace." *International Studies Quarterly* 27 (December): 381–87.

————. 1989. "Democracy and Peace." In *Choices in World Politics: Sovereignty and Interdependence,* edited by Bruce Russett, Harvey Starr, and Richard J. Stoll, pp. 245–60. New York: W. H. Freeman.

————. 1993. *Grasping the Democratic Peace: Principles for a Post–Cold War World.* Princeton: Princeton University Press.

Russett, Bruce, and Harvey Starr. 1989. *World Politics: The Menu for Choice.* 3d ed. New York: W. H. Freeman.

Sandbrook, Richard. 1985. *The Politics of Africa's Economic Stagnation.* Cambridge: Cambridge University Press.

————. 1993. *The Politics of Africa's Economic Recovery.* Cambridge: Cambridge University Press.

Scenna, Miguel A. 1981. *Argentina-Chile: Una Frontera Caliente.* Buenos Aires: Editorial de Belgrano.

Schahzenski, Jeffrey J. 1991. "Explaining Relative Peace: Major Power Order, 1816–1976." *Journal of Peace Research* 28 (August): 295–309.

Schmitter, Philippe. 1991. "Change in Regime Type and Progress in International Relations." In *Progress in Postwar International Relations,* edited by Emanuel Adler and Beverly Crawford, pp. 89–127. New York: Columbia University Press.

Schmitter, Philippe, and Terry Lynn Karl. 1993. "What Democracy Is . . . and Is Not." In *The Global Resurgence of Democracy,* edited by Larry Diamond and Marc F. Plattner, pp. 39–52. Baltimore: Johns Hopkins University Press.

Schoultz, Lars. 1987. *National Security and United States Policy toward Latin America.* Princeton: Princeton University Press.

Schumpeter, Joseph A. 1950. *Capitalism, Socialism and Democracy.* 3d ed. New York: Harper and Row.

Segal, Ronald. 1962. *African Profiles.* Harmondsworth: Penguin.

Selcher, Wayne. 1984. "Recent Strategic Developments in South America's Southern Cone." In *Latin American Nations in World Politics,* edited by Heraldo Muñoz and Joseph S. Tulchin, pp. 101–18. Boulder, Colo.: Westview.

————. 1985. "Recent Strategic Developments in South America's Southern Cone."

In *Latin American Nations in World Politics*, edited by Heraldo Muñoz and Joseph S. Tulchin, pp. 101–18. Boulder, Colo.: Westview.

———. 1990. "Brazil and the Southern Cone Subsystem." In *South America into the 1990s*, edited by G. Pope Atkins, pp. 87–120. Boulder, Colo.: Westview.

Sesay, Amadu, Olusola Ojo, and Orobola Fasehun. 1984. *The OAU after Twenty Years*. Boulder, Colo.: Westview.

Shafter, Robert Jones. 1978. *A History of Latin America*. Lexington, Mass.: D. C. Heath.

Shaw, Timothy M. 1978. "Inequalities and Interdependence in Africa and Latin America." *Cultures et Development* 10:231–63.

———. 1987. "Nigeria Restrained: Foreign Policy under Changing Political and Petroleum Regimes." *Annals of the American Academy of Political and Social Science* 489 (January): 40–51.

Shaw, Timothy M., and Julius E. Okolo. 1994. "African Political Economy and Foreign Policy in the 1990s: Towards a Revisionist Framework for ECOWAS States." In *The Political Economy of Foreign Policy in ECOWAS*, edited by Timothy M. Shaw and Julius E. Okolo, pp. 1–16. London: Macmillan.

Simmons, André. 1972. "Economic Cooperation in West Africa." *Western Political Quarterly* 25 (June): 295–304.

Singer, Max, and Aaron Wildavsky, 1993. *The Real World Order: Zones of Peace/ Zones of Turmoil*. Chatham, N.J.: Chatham House.

Siverson, Randolph M., and Juliann Emmons. 1991. "Birds of a Feather: Democratic Political Systems and Alliance Choices in the Twentieth Century." *Journal of Conflict Resolution* 35 (June): 285–306.

Shumavon, Douglas H. 1981. "Bolivia: Salida al Mar." In *Latin American Foreign Policies*, edited by Elizabeth G. Ferris and Jennifer K. Lincoln, pp. 179–90. Boulder, Colo.: Westview.

Skidmore, Thomas E., and Peter H. Smith. 1992. *Modern Latin America*. 3d ed. New York: Oxford University Press.

Small, Melvin, and J. David Singer. 1976. "The War Proneness of Democratic Regimes." *The Jerusalem Journal of International Relations* 1 (fall): 50–69.

Smith, Peter H. 1985. "Political Legitimacy in Spanish America." In *Readings in Latin American History, Volume II*, edited by John J. Johnson and Peter J. Bakewell, pp. 153–75. Durham, N.C.: Duke University Press.

———. 1992. "The State and Development in Historical Perspective." In *Americas: New Interpretative Essays*, edited by Alfred Stepan, pp. 30–56. New York: Oxford University Press.

Smith, Robert S. 1976. *Warfare and Diplomacy in Pre-Colonial West Africa*. London: Methuen.

Smith, Roger K. 1989. "Institutionalization as a Measure of Regime Stability: Insights for International Regime Analysis from the Study of Domestic Politics." *Millennium* 18 (summer): 227–44.

Smock, David R. 1991. "Conflict Resolution in Africa: The Mediation of Africa's Wars." Paper presented at the 1991 APSA Meeting, Washington, D.C., summer.

Smoker, Paul. 1981. "Small Peace." *Journal of Peace Research* 18 (May): 149–57.

Sollenberg, Margareta, and Peter Wallensteen. 1995. "Major Armed Conflicts." In *SIPRI Yearbook 1995: Armaments, Disarmament and International Security*, pp. 21–35. New York: Oxford University Press.

Somavía, Juan. 1992. "America del Sur: Conciencia Expectante." In *America del Sur Hacia el 2,000*, edited by Carlos Contreras Quina, pp. 17–24. Caracas: Nueva Sociedad.

Soudan, François. 1990. "Interview: Maaouya Ould Taya: 'Le Senegal Nous Veut Du Mal.'" *Jeune Afrique* 1513 (January 1): 34–37.

Spiro, David E. 1994. "The Insignificance of the Liberal Peace." *International Security* 19 (fall): 50–86.

Starr, Harvey. 1992. "Why Don't Democracies Fight One Another? Evaluating the Theory-Findings Feedback Loop." *The Jerusalem Journal of International Relations* 14 (December): 41–59.

Stein, Arthur A. 1993. "Disequilibrium and Equilibrium Theory: Explaining War in a Theory of Peace, Explaining Alliances in a Theory of Autonomy." Paper presented at the APSA Annual Meeting, Washington, D.C., September.

Stein, Janice Gross. 1985. "Detection and Defection: Security 'Regimes' and the Management of International Conflict." *International Journal* 40 (autumn): 599–627.

Stephenson, Carolyn M. 1989. "The Evolution of Peace Studies." In *Peace and World Order Studies: A Curriculum Guide*, edited by Daniel C. Thomas and Michael T. Klare, pp. 9–19. 5th ed. Boulder, Colo.: Westview.

St.John, Ronald B. 1977. "The Boundary Dispute between Peru and Ecuador." *American Journal of International Law* 71 (April): 322–30.

———. 1992. *The Foreign Policy of Peru*. Boulder, Colo.: Lynne Rienner.

Stoll, Richard J., and Michael Champion. 1985. "Capability Concentration, Alliance Bonding, and Conflict among the Major Powers." In *Polarity and War: The Changing Structure of International Conflict*, edited by Alan N. Sabrosky, pp. 67–94. Boulder, Colo.: Westview.

Stremlau, John. 1977. *The International Politics of the Nigerian Civil War*. Princeton: Princeton University Press.

Sunkel, Osvaldo. 1995. "Uneven Globalization, Economic Reform, and Democracy:

A View from Latin America." In *Whose World Order? Uneven Globalization and the End of the Cold War*, edited by Hans-Henrik Holm and Georg Sorensen, pp. 43–67. Boulder, Colo.: Westview.

Suret-Canale, Jean. 1974. "Les Relations Internationales de la République de Guinée." In *Foreign Relations of African States*, edited by Kenneth Ingham, pp. 259–74. London: Butterworths.

Taylor, A. J. P. 1971. *The Struggle for Mastery in Europe, 1848–1918*. 2d ed. Oxford: Oxford University Press.

Thomas, Darryl C., and Ali A. Mazrui. 1992. "Africa's Post–Cold War Demilitarization: Domestic and Global Causes." *Journal of International Affairs* 46 (summer): 157–74.

Thompson, Virginia Mclean. 1972. *West Africa's Council of the Entente*. Ithaca, N.Y.: Cornell University Press.

Thompson, W. Scott. 1991. "The Antinomies of Peace: State-Oriented and Holistic Views." In *Approaches to Peace: An Intellectual Map*, edited by W. Scott Thompson and Kenneth M. Jensen, pp. 336–45. Washington, D.C.: United States Institute of Peace.

Timothy, Bankole. 1981. *Kwame Nkrumah: From Cradle to Grave*. Dorchester, U.K.: The Gavin Press.

Touval, Saadia. 1967. "The Organization of African Unity and African Borders." *International Organization* 21 (winter): 102–27.

———. 1972. *The Boundary Politics of Independent Africa*. Cambridge: Harvard University Press.

Tulchin, Joseph S. 1983. "La Relación Argentino-Brasileña: El Punto de Vista Argentino." In *Geopolítica y Política del Poder en el Atlántico Sur*, edited by Carlos J. Moneta, pp. 43–57. Buenos Aires: Pleamar.

———. 1994. "Inter-American Relations." In *Problems in Modern Latin American History: A Reader*, edited by John Charles Chasteen and Joseph S. Tulchin, p. 287–94. Wilmington, Del: Scholarly Resources.

Turner, Frederick C. 1991. "Regional Hegemony and the Case of Brazil." *International Journal* 46 (summer): 475–509.

Valenzuela, Arthuro. 1990. "Chile: Origins, Consolidation, and Breakdown of a Democratic Regime." In *Politics in Developing Countries*, edited by Larry Diamond et al., pp. 39–86. Boulder, Colo.: Lynne Rienner.

Valenzuela, J. Samuel, and Arthuro Valenzuela. 1991. "Chile: The Development, Breakdown, and Recovery of Democracy." In *Latin America: Its Problems and Its Promise*, edited by Jan Knippers Black, pp. 471–508. Boulder, Colo.: Westview.

Varas, Augusto. 1983. "Controlling Conflict in South America: National Approaches."

In *Controlling Latin American Conflicts: Ten Approaches*, edited by Michael A. Morris and Victor Millán, pp. 71–85. Boulder, Colo.: Westview.

———. 1984. "Política Exterior y Democracia en Chile." In *America Latina: Políticas Exteriores Comparadas*, edited by Juan C. Puig, pp. 392–402. Buenos Aires: GEL.

———. 1985. *Militarization and the International Arms Race in Latin America*. Boulder, Colo.: Westview.

Vasquez, John A. 1992. "A Territorial Explanation of War." Paper presented at the Annual Meeting of the International Studies Association, Atlanta, April 1992.

———. 1993. *The War Puzzle*. Cambridge: Cambridge University Press.

———. 1994. "Building Peace in the Post–Cold War Era." In *From Rivalry to Cooperation: Russian and American Perspectives on the Post–Cold War Era*, edited by Manus I. Midlarsky et al., pp. 207–18. New York: Harper and Collins.

Villagrán de León, Francisco. 1993. *The OAS and Regional Security*. Washington, D.C.: United States Institute of Peace.

Wagner, Robert Harrison. 1993. "The Causes of Peace." In *Stopping the Killing: How Civil Wars End*, edited by Roy Licklider, pp. 235–68. New York: New York University Press.

Wallace, Michael D. 1996. "Enduring and Emerging Rivalries in the Asia-Pacific Region: New Powers, Old Patterns?" Paper presented at the ISA Meeting, San Diego, 16–20 April.

Wallensteen, Peter. 1984. "Universalism vs. Particularism: On the Limits of Major Power Order." *Journal of Peace Research* 21 (August): 243–57.

Walt, Stephen. 1987. *The Origins of Alliances*. Ithaca, N.Y.: Cornell University Press.

———. 1991. "The Renaissance of Security Studies." *International Studies Quarterly* 35 (June): 211–39.

Waltz, Kenneth N. 1959. *Man, The State, and War: A Theoretical Analysis*. New York: Columbia University Press.

———. 1979. *Theory of International Politics*. Reading, Mass.: Addison-Wesley.

Walzer, Michael. 1983. *Spheres of Justice: A Defense of Pluralism and Equality*. New York: Basic Books.

———. 1986. "The Reform of the International System." In *Studies of War and Peace*, edited by Olyvind Osterud, pp. 227–50. Oslo: Norwegian University Press.

Welch, Claude E. 1966. *Dream of Unity: Pan-Africanism and Political Integration in West Africa*. Ithaca, N.Y.: Cornell University Press.

Whitehead, Laurence. 1991. "The Imposition of Democracy." In *Exporting Democracy: The United States and Latin America*, edited by Abraham F. Lowenthal, pp. 216–42. Baltimore: Johns Hopkins University Press.

Whiteman, Kaye. 1971. "Guinea in West African Politics." *World Today* 27 (August): 350–58.

Wiarda, Howard J., and Harvey F. Kline. 1990. "The Latin American Tradition and Process of Development." In *Latin American Politics and Development*, edited by Howard J. Wiarda and Harvey F. Kline, pp. 3–125. Boulder, Colo.: Westview.

Williams, David. 1961. "How Deep the Split in West Africa?" *Foreign Affairs* 40 (October): 118–27.

Williams, Gavin, and Terisa Turner. 1978. "Nigeria." In *West African States: Failure and Promise*, edited by John Dunn, pp. 132–72. Cambridge: Cambridge University Press.

Windass, Stan. 1970. "The League and Territorial Disputes." In *The International Regulation of Frontier Disputes*, edited by Evan Luard, pp. 31–85. New York: Praeger.

Wiseman, John A. 1990. *Democracy in Black Africa: Survival and Revival.* New York: Paragon House.

Wolfers, Arnold. 1961. *Discord and Collaboration: Essays on International Politics.* Baltimore: Johns Hopkins University Press.

Wood, Bryce. 1978. *The United States and Latin American Wars, 1932–1942.* New York: Columbia University Press.

Wriggins, Howard W. 1992. *Dynamics of Regional Politics: Four Systems on the Indian Ocean Rim.* New York: Columbia University Press.

Wright, Freeman J. 1992. "National Borders and Foreign Policy: The Case of Argentina." In *Changing Boundaries in the Americas*, edited by Lawrence A. Herzog, pp. 229–45. San Diego: University of California at San Diego.

Wright, Quincy. 1964. *A Study of War.* Abridged ed. Chicago: University of Chicago Press.

Yansané, Aguibou Y. 1984. *Decolonization in West African States with French Colonial Legacy.* Cambridge, Mass.: Schenkman.

Yopo, H., Mladen. 1985. "Bolivia: Democracia, Inestabilidad Interna y Política Exterior." In *Las Políticas Exteriores Latinoamericanas frente a la Crisis*, edited by Heraldo Muñoz, pp. 179–94. Buenos Aires: GEL.

Young, Crawford. 1988. "The African Colonial State and Its Political Legacy." In *The Precarious Balance*, edited by Donald Rotchild and Naomi Chazan, pp. 25–66. Boulder, Colo.: Westview.

———. 1991. "Self-Determination, Territorial Integrity, and the African State System." In *Conflict Resolution in Africa*, edited by Francis M. Deng and I. William Zartman, pp. 320–46. Washington, D.C.: Brookings.

———. 1995. "The Heritage of Colonialism." In *Africa in World Politics*, edited by John W. Harbeson and Donald Rothchild, pp. 23–40. Boulder, Colo.: Westview.

Zartman, I. William. 1965. "The Politics of Boundaries in North and West Africa." *The Journal of Modern African Studies* 3 (August): 155–73.

———. 1966. *International Relations in the New Africa*. Englewood Cliffs, N.J.: Prentice-Hall.

———. 1967. "Africa as a Subordinate State System in International Relations." *International Organization* 21 (summer): 545–64.

———. 1970. "Alliances and Regional Unity in West Africa." In *The International Politics of Regions: A Comparative Approach*, edited by Louis J. Cantori and Steven L. Spiegel, pp. 116–31. Englewood Cliffs, N.J.: Prentice-Hall.

———. 1984. "Africa and the West: The French Connection." In *African Security Issues*, edited by Bruce E. Arlinghau, pp. 39–58. Boulder, Colo.: Westview.

———. 1995. "Inter-African Negotiation." In *Africa in World Politics*, edited by John Harbeson and Donald Rothchild, pp. 234–49. Boulder, Colo.: Westview.

Zolberg, Aristide R. 1968. "The Structure of Political Conflict in the New States of Tropical Africa." *American Political Science Review* 62 (March): 70–87.

Index

A

Abacha, Sani, 142. *See also* Nigeria

Africa, 14, 17, 40, 107, 121, 179, 183, 184–87, 197. *See also* Equatorial Africa; North Africa; South Africa; West Africa

Agacher Strip. *See* Mali–Burkina Faso War

alliances, 33, 35, 37–38, 47, 57, 190; in South America, 72, 74, 92–94; in West Africa, 128, 130–32, 149–51

Amazon Cooperation Treaty (Amazon Pact), 79, 82

anarchy, 5, 32, 70, 165, 175. *See also* international system; realism; state of war

Andean Pact (ANCOM), 79, 81, 82, 101, 114, 117, 120, 195

arbitration, 102, 103, 104, 105, 196

Argentina, 13, 67, 71, 79, 80, 86, 91, 100, 102, 197; and balance of power, 68, 72, 73, 74, 89, 92, 94, 96; and Brazil, 69, 75, 76, 80, 81, 82, 83, 84–85, 87, 89, 90–91, 92, 94, 96, 98, 99, 101, 102, 111, 113, 117, 118, 119, 121; and Chile, 20, 73–74, 75, 80, 81, 82, 84–85, 87, 94, 95, 101, 102, 105, 111, 117, 121; civil war in, 73, 182; and democratization, 82, 109, 112, 114–15, 117; and hierarchy of power, 109, 110, 111, 113, 115; in MERCOSUR, 81,
118, 121, 194; military regime of, 21, 78, 107; and Paraguay, 76, 117, 118; and United Kingdom, 81, 105, 111; as a weak state, 107, 108. *See also* Falklands/Malvinas War; MERCOSUR

Argentine-Brazilian Economic Integration Program (ABEIP), 82, 83, 85. *See also* MERCOSUR

ASEAN (Association of Southeast Asian Nations), 4, 15, 24, 25, 40, 177, 178, 187, 189–91, 191–202

Asia, 17, 22, 121. *See also* ASEAN; East Asia; Northeast Asia; South Asia; Southeast Asia

Asia-Pacific Region. *See* ASEAN; East Asia; Northeast Asia; Southeast Asia

Australasia, 15, 23–24, 38

authoritarian regime, 19, 54, 59, 200; in ASEAN, 191, 197; in Australasia, 23; in Northeast Asia, 22, 40, 187–88; in South America, 77–78, 80, 94, 98, 106, 107, 108, 197; in West Africa, 126, 133, 142, 152, 153, 164, 165, 173, 188. *See also* bureaucratic-authoritarian regime; military regime

B

Babanguida, Ibrahim, 140, 149, 152. *See also* Nigeria

257